Published by
British Deaf History Society Publications
288 Bedfont Lane
Feltham
Middlesex
TW14 9NU
ENGLAND

A branch of
British Deaf History Society
49 Whitton Close
Doncaster
DN4 7RB
ENGLAND

British Library Cataloguing Publication Data

ISBN 1-902427-18-1

Printed in England by:

Palladian Press, Unit E, Chandlers Row, Port Lane, Colchester, Essex. CO1 2HG

A Beginner's Introduction
to
Deaf History

Raymond Lee

Editor

Editor's Note

The purpose of this book is twofold. Firstly, it is created to introduce anyone with an interest in the Deaf to their language, their community and their history. Secondly, this work has been created to form the basis for Deaf History courses and examinations as a part of the growth in Deaf Studies and British Sign Language courses.

The history described in this book is of a "rolling history" nature in which the reader and the students are gently introduced to the main issues and events in Deaf history without being thrusted into a "heavily in-depth and overbearing" version of history. This book can be taken as a complete source of reference for the planned CACDP Stage Two Deaf History and Culture course and examinations. Provisions have been made to incorporate further works that would stand in good stead to cover higher Deaf History courses and examinations that are currently under discussion both within the British Deaf History Society (BDHS) and among a good number of universities where Deaf Studies courses are being run.

The present work will always be continually edited, revised, corrected and updated as and when required. This will be due to the fact that history never ends and new discoveries are always being made from time to time. It is anticipated that the contents of this book will be revised every two to three years by the BDHS in consultation with the teaching and examination bodies.

Raymond Lee
Feltham
August 2004

A Beginner's Introduction
to
Deaf History

Genesis

Deaf people have always existed alongside hearing people since time immemorial. They are mentioned very early in the Old Testament book of Exodus, 4:11:

Who hath made man's mouth? Or who maketh the dumb,
or deaf, or the seeing, or the blind? Have not I the Lord?

There are other books in the Bible, both in the Old Testament and the New Testament, that mention the deaf, to name a few -

Leviticus	19:14	1 Samuel	10:27	Proverbs	31:8
Deuteronomy	27:18	Isaiah	29:18	Micah	7:10
Deuteronomy	28:28	Mark	7:33-37	Matthew	11:5

The Hebrew *Talmud* refers to Deaf families using sign language. This body of Jewish civil and religious law reveals that Deaf people could marry and divorce using gesture and sign language. Even so, speech was still held to be a superior form of communication in ceremonies and legal use, therefore Deaf people who were not able to recite orally any legal or religious formulae were not allowed to participate in these ceremonies. (*Yevamot* 110-112).

The deaf and dumb are also mentioned in the Islamic *Koran*.

Ancient Greeks and Romans, amongst those of other ancient civilisations, mention Deaf people as follows -

Herodotus (c.480-c.425 BC) wrote of the dumb son of King Croesus of Lydia in his work, *The Histories*. This son never spoke and was looked upon with disdain by his father the king, who favoured his hearing son. However, the hearing son was killed in a battle. During a war with the Persians, Croesus was cornered and was being attacked. A Persian raised his sword and was about to strike the king when the king's dumb son yelled out for the first time, begging the enemy to spare his father's life. He somehow saved his father's life, but the kingdom was lost. This story was supposed to have occurred some one hundred years before Herodotus wrote about it and therefore the tale became entwined with myths. What is clear, however, is that the dumb son was not deaf.

Socrates (469-399 BC) mentioned (in *Cratylus,* 422 BC) the existence of sign language when he enquired, "If we have no voice or tongue and wished to make things clear to one another, should we not try as the dumb actually do to make signs with our hands, head and person generally?" This appears to be an acknowledgement that the Deaf can communicate in an intelligent form, and it can be seen that the manner of communicating through signs used by deaf people around Socrates' time was no different to that of the present day as many Deaf people still make signs using their hands, head and person generally (for example, body/facial language and movements).

Hippocrates of Cos (c.460-c.359 BC) in his *Peri Sarkōn* (*About the Flesh*) contributed a passage in chapter 18:

Articulation is caused by the appules of the tongue; it renders the words distinct by intercepting them in the throat, and striking against the palate and the teeth. If the tongue did not articulate every time by striking, man would not speak distinctly; and he would only utter each of the single natural sounds. A proof of this is the case of deaf mutes from birth, who not knowing how to speak, utter only simple sounds.

Plato (427-347 BC), a pupil of Socrates and teacher of Aristotle, wrote on his philosophy of innate intelligence. According to him, all intelligence was present at birth and all people were born with perfect abstracts, ideas and language in their minds and required only time to demonstrate their intelligence. Without speech, Plato reasoned, there was no outward sign of intelligence; so deaf people must not be capable of ideas or language.

Aristotle (384-322 BC) in his *Hist. Anim.*, lib. IV, ch. 9, wrote that "those who are born deaf

all become speechless; they have a voice but are destitute of speech." Aristotle's use of the word, ἐνεοί, in this passage was rather unfortunate as it not only means 'rendered speechless', but may also mean 'senseless' and 'destitute of reason', so that if the latter meaning was adopted, the Deaf were classed with idiots and those suffering from incapacity and therefore received the same treatment in the form of public disdain. Aristotle's influence was taken up by many and reinforced by St. Augustine of Hippo and this was to deprive the Deaf of an education, equal rights and participation in society for over 2,000 years.

Pliny the Elder (23-79 AD), the Roman historian who perished in Pompeii the Mount Vesuvius eruption, wrote in his *Natural History* (35.7) of a deaf painter named Quintus

Pedius, who was a nephew of the Roman emperor, Augustus. Quintus Pedius was probably the first named deaf person to be recorded in history. He died very young at no more than 13 years of age and he was a person of very little renown, apart from the fact that he was taught painting and displayed artistic promise that was cut short by his early demise. Another passage in Pliny's same work refers to hearing people's misleading concepts of deafness around his time, the most serious being the statement that *when one is first of all denied hearing, he is also robbed of the power of talking, and there are no persons born deaf who are not also dumb* (X. 192-4).

St. Augustine (354-430 AD) [also known as St. Augustine of Hippo] followed Aristotle's dictum that the deaf are senseless. He summed up in his *Contra Julianum Pelagianum* (111.10):

Quo merito tanto innocentia nonnunquam caeca, nonnunquam surda nascatur. Quod vitium etiam ipsam impedit fidem, Apostolo testante qui dicit: igitur fides ex auditu?

(Translation - For what great fault is innocence sometimes born blind, sometimes born deaf, which blemish indeed hinders faith, as witness the Apostle who says: "Faith comes by hearing?")

St. Augustine also wrote in his *De quantitate anima* of a young man who was deaf and "consequently dumb," and who understood others only by their gestures, "nor otherwise does he express what he wants to say." It is therefore not surprising that St. Augustine shared Aristotle's ideas about the nature of dumbness and this Augustinian influence caused the deaf to be deprived of education and religious instruction for at least the next 1,300 years.

The Status of the Deaf throughout early History

It is of great importance to record here people's attitude towards the Deaf throughout history because the attitudes of various people of all races and creeds in various countries contributed enormously to the inhuman treatment of the Deaf. Inhuman in that the Deaf were denied legal and human rights. They were also denied education and equal participation in all levels of society throughout history.

One of the earliest sources of evidence is the *Talmud*, in which there is a mention in the book *Hagigah* of laws to legislate for the protection of the deaf. Under one of these laws, the deaf and dumb are classed with "a fool and a child," as not being responsible for their actions and were exempt from the ordinances of the Law. The *Talmud* was also exceptional in its early discrimination between the deaf and dumb and those who were deaf only (*Illem*) or dumb only (*Cheresh*). Only those who were deaf and dumb were completely free from obligation under the Law (*Hagigah 2b*), and it was accepted that they could not be taught. This implication that the Deaf were not able to be educated is linked in the *Hagigah* with the verse in *Deuteronomy 31.12*, which makes learning dependent on hearing. As for those who were deaf only or dumb only, they were treated as capable persons and not wholly exempt from legal obligations.

The wider meaning of the Hebraic law with regard to the deaf and dumb is that, being children at law, they were incapable of holding property, and therefore articles found in their possession might be recovered from them. However, (*Gittim 59b*) for the sake of peace they were allowed at times to retain a small amount of property and the community would compensate the owner for his loss. This attitude implies a degree of tolerance.

In the *Koran*, treatment of deaf people and the Islamic attitude towards the Deaf can be seen from the passage in 8:22-23:

> [22]*Verily, the worst of beasts in God's sight are the deaf, the dumb who do not understand.* [23]*Had God known any good in them, He would have made them hear; but had He made them hear, they would have turned back and swerved aside.*

The Jewish discrimination between grades of deafness was taken up in Roman law. The Roman emperor Justinian (c.482-565 AD) developed the Jewish classification on deafness and expanded it into five classes:

1. Congenitally deaf and dumb
2. Deaf and dumb from causes arising since birth.
3. Congenitally deaf but not dumb.
4. Deaf only from causes arising since birth.
5. Dumb only, whether congenital or from causes arising since birth.

Under Justinian law, only those who were congenitally deaf and dumb (1) were completely without rights and obligations and they were required to have legal guardians. The rest of the classes (2-5) were given limited freedom in that they could enter into contracts, including marriage, make a will and give evidence. They were not required to have legal guardians.

Records exist to indicate that the Deaf were victims of infanticidal practices in early communities such as in Rome and Sparta. According to Plutarch (c.46-c.120 AD) the Elders in Sparta approved the rearing of a child if it seemed well-built and vigorous, and ordered its death by exposure at the Apothetæ only if the child seemed degenerate and physically disabled (*Lyc., XVI*). It is unclear how the Elders could detect if a baby was deaf or not, for many deaf babies were well built and vigorous, making as much noise as hearing babies. This story that deafness was a reason for death by exposure immediately after birth is difficult to understand and to accept.

Dionysius of Halicarnassus (1st century BC) wrote in his *Antituitates Romanæ* (II, 15) of the early Roman practice of getting rid of children with visible physical deformities by murdering them when they were around three years of age. Such children were considered a liability to the State. According to Dionysius, the legendary founder of Rome, Romulus, forbade people from killing children under the age of three unless they were deformed from birth, and such might be exposed to the elements soon after birth provided that five neighbours had seen the child and approved of the parents' intention. Again, it is quite difficult to see how such crude eugenic practices involve deaf babies unless they had additional visual physical deformities.

As the years passed and countries slowly began to remove their own barbaric practices, there still remained the tendency to regard the Deaf and disabled as outcasts by both the family and society. Due to the persistent adherence to the Aristotelian dictum that decreed, however wrongly, that the Deaf be classed with idiots, the Deaf suffered hardship in their lives. They could not understand both the ill treatment and the abuse they received, but such were their lot. The early Christian Church was also averse to the capacity of the Deaf for instruction. Interestingly, the Deaf were not banned from marrying by signs, as the ceremony itself was a mere form. The Church's attitude to deafness was based almost wholly on *Romans X.17*, wherein it is said that "faith cometh by hearing." Fortified by the Holy Writ, the Church was content that the Deaf should be excluded from worshipping the Lord, who, according to *Exodus 4.11*, was responsible for their condition.

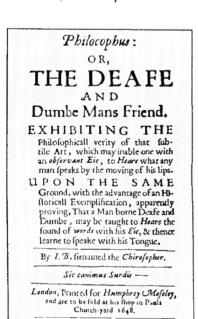

John Bulwer mentions in his *Philocophus: Or, The Deafe and Dumbe Mans Friend* (1648) in Observation VI, (pages 102 – 109) the status of the deaf under Roman law as outlined by Plato, and Bulwer further wrote in the next section of his famous book (Observation VII, page 176) that a *Deafe and Dumbe man cannot be appointed a Tutor*.

The Deaf's existence was in the main full of misery indeed, save for few exceptions where they were born into the wealthy classes. One such example is Quintus Pedius, a nephew of Octavian in Roman times and another is that of Princess Katherine, the daughter of Henry III of England in mediaeval times. The only way for the lives and future of many Deaf people to improve rested with a few pioneering individuals, some benevolent and some rebellious. Of these individuals, two names stand out – the Venerable Bede and Girolamo Cardano.

The Venerable Bede (c.673-735) was born near Monkwearmouth, Durham. At the age of seven, he was placed in the care of Abbot Benedict at the monastery of Wearmouth, and in 682 moved to the monastery at Jarrow where he was ordained priest in 703. Bede remained a monk for the rest of his life, studying and teaching. Bede's studies gained him knowledge in Hebrew, Latin and classical Greek as well as in patristic literature. He studied medicine and astronomy and wrote on the lives of saints and abbots, besides composing hymns, epigrams and commentaries on the Old and New Testaments. Bede translated the Gospel of St. John from Latin into Anglo-Saxon before his death.

Bede is known as the father of English history because of his famous work *Historia ecclesiastica gentis anglorum* (Ecclesiastical History of the English People), which he completed in 731. This work is the single and most valuable source for early English history and was later translated into Anglo-Saxon by King Alfred the Great (849-899).

In the annals of Deaf history, the contribution of the Venerable Bede was his creation of a method of counting and calculating using the hand and he wrote his famous *De temporum ratione*, describing the method in the chapter entitled *De computo vel loquela digitorum* (Of counting or speaking with the fingers), which is fully outlined in the next section. Although this work was primarily mathematical, Bede suggested that letters of the alphabet could replace numbers, and this gave birth to the single-handed manual alphabet. Bede also wrote on St. John of Beverley curing a dumb man and enabling him to speak.

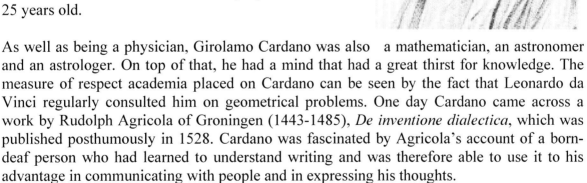

Girolamo Cardano (1501-1576), an illegitimate son of Fazio Cardano, a jurist, was born on 24 September 1501 in Pavia, Italy, after his mother's failed attempts to induce an abortion. As a child, he was very sickly, often tortured and abused by his father who gave him very little loving treatment, and he received no formal education until he was 21 years old when he was entered at the University of Pavia to escape his family. At the university, Cardano made such progress that he went on to become a Doctor of Medicine and rector of the university by the time he was 25 years old.

As well as being a physician, Girolamo Cardano was also a mathematician, an astronomer and an astrologer. On top of that, he had a mind that had a great thirst for knowledge. The measure of respect academia placed on Cardano can be seen by the fact that Leonardo da Vinci regularly consulted him on geometrical problems. One day Cardano came across a work by Rudolph Agricola of Groningen (1443-1485), *De inventione dialectica*, which was published posthumously in 1528. Cardano was fascinated by Agricola's account of a born-deaf person who had learned to understand writing and was therefore able to use it to his advantage in communicating with people and in expressing his thoughts.

In *Paralipomenon* (published posthumously in Basle,1622) Cardano discussed the subject of deafness with special reference to Agricola and his deaf pupil who had learned to read and write. Cardano declared that it was possible to place a deaf and dumb person in a position to hear by reading and to speak by writing. Cardano reasoned that "the Deaf person's memory would lead him to understand, by reflection, that bread, as written, signifies the thing which is eaten. He thus reads, by the light of his reason, as it were in a picture; for by this means, though nothing is referred to by sounds, not only objects, but also actions and results are made known. And just as after seeing a picture, we may draw another picture; guided simply by a conception of the objects represented, such is also the case with letters. For as different sounds are conventionally used to signify different things, so also may the various figures of objects and words."

"The significance of this passage cannot be overestimated," wrote the renowned deaf commentator on Deaf history Abraham Farrar (1861-1944), "for it shattered once for all the long established notion that the hearing of sounds is a necessary condition of the association of words with the ideas or things signified, and established the theoretical principle on which the possibility of teaching the Deaf is founded."

Cardano's insistence that the Deaf could be educated in some way brought him enemies who hung on to the traditional dictum of Aristotle and St. Augustine that the Deaf cannot be educated. Although Cardano never taught any deaf person, his insight that the Deaf could be educated and that they possessed intelligence gained him respect as the man who first saw the true relationship of the senses – and rolled away the rock that blocked the way to the education of the Deaf.

Early Development of Signs

<u>Origins of the Manual Alphabet</u>

The one handed manual alphabet has its origins in mathematics where the hand and fingers were used for counting purposes. There is for the Venerable Bede as the first known person to suggest that fingers could be used for both counting and spelling out words. This gave birth to the one handed manual system of spelling, or fingerspelling. Arthur F. Dimmock's translation of the Latin text of Bede's *De temporum ratione* that deals with finger counting, *De computo vel loquela digitorum*, is outlined here:

<u>Of Counting or Speaking with the Fingers</u>
(De computo vel loquela digitorum)

Turning now to a method of counting; we think we should, with the Lord's help, first explain briefly the very useful and rapid method of bending the fingers so that having once achieved a greater fluency in calculating, we may then come to an easier method of reading these quantities once they have been calculated.

We should respect and retain a system which almost all writers on the Sacred Scriptures, and other literary figures besides, are known to have adopted. So, among others, St. Jerome, that great interpreter of Sacred Scriptures, in whose 'Tractate on the Gospels', has no qualms in mentioning this useful system:

The fruit produced a hundredfold, sixtyfold, thirtyfold; although springing from one common patch of ground, nevertheless differs greatly in quantity. Thirtyfold signifies marriage; for that bringing together of the fingers, touching each other like a gentle kiss, signifies husband and wife. Sixtyfold signifies widows, for they are in sorrow and tribulation. for just as the end of the fingers is curved down, so the greater the difficulty for one who has experienced pleasure to refrain from it, and yet how much greater the prize.

Hundredfold, where the right hand takes over from the left (using the same finger but not the same hand): just as in the left hand the meaning is 'married women and widows', so by bringing the two fingers together to form a circle the meaning is 'the crown of virginity'.

[Note: St. Jerome is commenting here on the parable of the seeds in Matthew 13. His very fanciful interpretation (not untypical of its time) depends on imaginative symbolism arising from the sign language for numbers - as will be shown below. Among other things, Jerome's scale of values (married couples are 30, widows are 60 - because they have to cope with the lost outlet for sexual urges, while virgins are 100) is typical of the ultra-ascetic and anti-sexual mode of some of our Christian forebears which has caused no little harm in the presentation of the Gospel…]

For 1, bend the little finger of the left hand in to the middle joint of the palm. For 2, do likewise with the second finger. For 3, likewise with the middle finger. For 4, raise your little finger slightly. For 5, the same but with the second finger. For 6, do not raise the middle finger, but just place the middle finger (known as the 'medicus') right in the middle of the palm of the hand. For 7, place the little finger against the base of the palm while raising the other fingers slightly. for 8, do likewise but with the middle finger. For 9, with the index finger. For 10, place the nail of the index finger in the middle joint of the thumb. For 20, place the tip of the thumb between the middle joints of the index and middle fingers. For 30, bring the nails of the index finger and thumb lightly together. For 40, lift the thumb and index finger slightly and lay the thumb over the side of the index finger. For 50, bend the thumb at a right angle (like a capital Gamma in the Greek alphabet Γ) and hold towards the palm. For 60, bend the thumb as above and place it firmly over the top of the crooked index finger. For 70, bend the index finger and place over the bent thumb with just the nail of the thumb touching the bottom of the middle joint of the index finger. for 80, again keep the thumb straight and place the crooked index finger over the end of the thumb so that the nail of the thumb just touches the middle joint of the index finger. For 90, place the crooked index finger against the base of the nail of the thumb, while keeping the thumb quite straight.

All these are done with the left hand. For 100, do in the right hand as 10 in the left; for 200 as for 20 in the left; for 300 as for 30 in the left, and so on up to 900. For 1000, do it in the right hand as for 1 in the left. For 2000, in the right hand as for 2 in the left. For 3000, in the right hand as for 3 in the left, and so on up to 9000.

For 10000 place the left hand in the middle of the chest with the fingers pointing up towards one's neck.
For 20000 place the left hand broadside on across the chest.
For 30000 place the thumb vertically but face down over the centre of the chest.
For 40000 place the thumb vertically but face up but over the navel.
For 50000 place the thumb vertically but face down over the navel.
For 60000 grasp the left thigh with the fingers facing down.
For 70000 place the thumb face up over the thigh.
For 80000 place the thumb face down over the thigh.
For 90000 place the hand on the hip with the thumb pointing in towards the groin.
For 100000 to 900000 do as for 10000 to 90000 but with the right hand instead of the left.
For 1000000 clasp the fingers of both hands together.

There is another way of calculating using the fingers, which, since it applies especially to the method of calculating Easter, will be more appropriately explained when we come to that point in order. From this method of calculating one can devise a way of calculating on the hands using letters - an ingenious system and elegant to use. By this method, words are expressed through the individual letters which comprise them, and can be conveyed in a concealed manner, incomprehensible to those who lack the skill of interpretation. This way this code of letters works: when we want to say 'A', we sign '1', 'B' sign '2', 'C' sign '3' and so on. So if for example you want to say to a friend who is surrounded by spies "Watch out!" you can sign 3, 1, 20, 19, 5; 1, 7, 5 [= *Caute age!* Be careful!] It can also be written down in this way if there is the need for some secrecy. Greeks can more easily learn and apply this method than Romans for they usually write their numbers by the equivalent letter of the alphabet. Setting out the whole of their alphabet alongside numbers (and using special signs for the three numbers which remain over and above) we can render the alphabet by numbers in an almost complete sequence, viz:

A	I	H	VIII	Ξ	LX	Υ	CCCC
B	II	θ	IX	O	LXX	ö	D
Γ	III	I	X	π	LXXX	X	DC
Δ	IV	K	XX	Ч	XC	Ψ	DCC
E	V	Λ	XXX	P	C	ω	DCCC
Ϛ	VI	M	XL	C	CC	↑	DCCCC
Z	VII	N	L	T	CCC		

[Translator's note: The Greek alphabet has only 24 letters, so three numbers are supplied with alphabet symbols which are not actually letters of the alphabet, but special numerical signs: these are 6 (VI), 90 (XC) and 900 (DCCCC).]

So anyone who knows how to sign numerals will have no difficulty in signing letters in the same way as indicated above. Now with the help of the Lord, who is the maker and governor of all quantities, we will come onto quantities.

The spread of Bede's system in Europe

As the years went by, the Venerable Bede's finger counting and alphabet, known as Bede's alphanumerics, began to be used in many European countries, in particular Germany and Italy. A number of publications on the subject came out in academical circles and Bede's system was mainly used in mathematics. However, the hand/finger positions remained unchanged for centuries and the sample of published works mentioned here trace the passage and development of the single-handed manual alphabet system from Bede's time. His system was widely adopted among the Deaf in European countries.

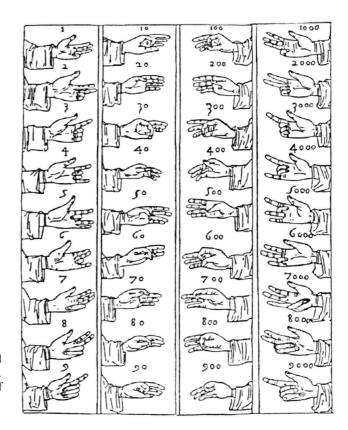

Visual representation of Bede's textual descriptions in *De temporum ratione*. This chart is also the correct version of Pacioli's erroneous descriptions.

11

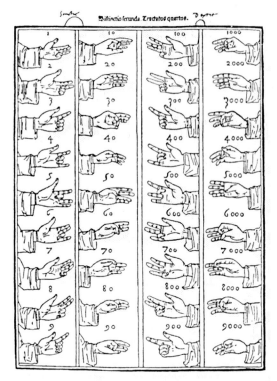

left hand   right hand

This chart was printed in Luca Pacioli's *Summa de arithmetica* (Venice, 1494). Note the errors of the positions on the right hand. This mistake went unnoticed for quite a time until it was spotted!

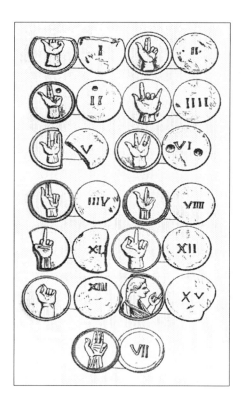

Bede's beads depicting signs for Roman numbers as used in his time.

Four pages from Johannes Aventinus' *Abacus atque vetustissima veterum latinorum per digitos manusque numerandi.* (Nuremberg, 1522). Also the two illustrations on the next page at top.

12

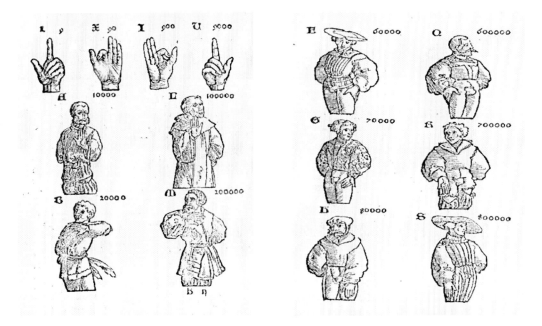

Bede's finger counting illustrated in Jacob Leupold's *Theatrum Arith-metico-Geometricum*, published in 1727 — a thousand years after Bede.

13

Cosma Rossellio's *Thesaurus artificiosae memoriae* (Venice 1579). Note the choice of handshapes to represent each letter of the alphabet, and the attempt to make the handshapes look like the letters they represent.

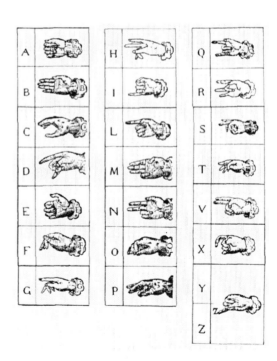

Melchor de Yebra (1526-1586) was a Spanish Franciscan monk who "created" a system of fingerspelling (above) to enable dying people who were no longer able to speak to make their confessions. His system was published in a small pamphlet, *Refugium Informorum*, seven years after his death. This alphabet was the forerunner of Juan Pablo Bonet's system below: note the striking similarities.

14

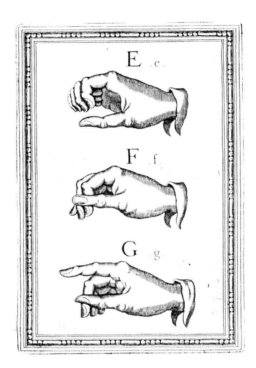

The manual alphabet from Bonet's *Reduccion de las letras y Arte para enseñar á habla los mudos* (Madrid, 1620). The handshapes are very similar to that of Yebra; Bonet seems to have adopted Yebra and made some improvements.

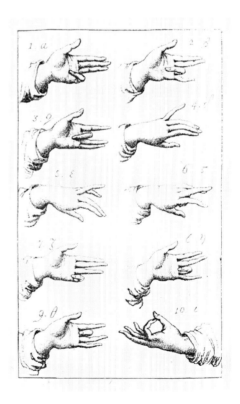

The two illustrations above are from Vincenzo Requeno's *Scoperta della Chironomia* (Parma, 1797).

Earliest Evidence of Use of the Manual Alphabet and Sign Language

There are accounts of deaf people having been educated, the earliest from Spain in the case of Pedro Ponce de Leon (c.1520-1584) who taught two deaf brothers, Francisco and Pedro de Valasco, to speak, but there is nothing on the use of signs. Another Spaniard, Ramirez de Carrion (1579-1652) taught the Marquis of Priego and Luis de Valasco between 1625 and 1629. Carrion initially used the one handed manual alphabet before proceeding to teach speech. This manual alphabet used by Carrion was recorded and described by Juan Pablo Bonet (1579-1633); Carrion himself, however, kept his teaching methods secret.

In France a deaf person named Etienne de Fay (1669-1747) was noted to have been successfully educated at the Abbey of Amiens. Deaf since birth and entering the Abbey when he was five years old, Fay grew up to become a noted architect, sculptor, librarian and teacher of the deaf. It is not known how he learned to sign, but he was recorded as always using sign language.

The earliest *documented* and *witnessed* use of the manual alphabet and sign language by Deaf people in Britain is not found until the 16th century when parish records in St. Martin's Church in Leicester gave a particularly interesting account of a marriage ceremony between Thomas Tilsye and Ursula Russel. In this ceremony, which took place on 5 February 1576, Thomas Tilsye took his wedding vows in signs.

After the description of the marriage ceremony described above, documented and witnessed accounts of the use of the manual alphabet and sign language began to appear more frequently.

Prior to this, there were hints in English law reports and in Scottish Royal Court records of the use of sign language though no actual witness accounts exist. In the Scottish case, these records related to Princess Joanna, the deaf daughter of King James I of Scotland, who lived from 1426 to c.1486. It was said that her sister, Princess Eleanor, acted as her interpreter. There was also a book published in 1450, *Anngiers History of the Zion Monastery at Lisbon and Brentford*, which gives descriptions of actual signs. Users of BSL will recognise that, with slight modification, quite a number of these signs are still in use in 21st century Britain. One example is:

Kepying (keeping) – *putte thy right hand under thy left*

Edward Bone and John Kempe

A book by Richard Carew (pictured right) entitled *A Survey of Cornwall* (1595) contains three different observations by the author on a deaf and dumb manservant named Edward Bone who lived in the Truro residence of the then local Member of Parliament, Peter Courtney. Carew records how Bone lipread sermons and news, and then signed the information he gained to his hearing Master who understood the form of signing used. Bone then when off-duty, went to meet his Deaf friend John Kempe who lived 8 miles away. The signed conversation between Bone and Kempe was on a different level from that which Bone used with his employer. These acute observations by Carew show that in 1595 the deaf Edward Bone was intelligent enough to use three different modes of communication, adapting them to suit his circumstances – lipreading where appropriate, using an early form of Signed English with his employer and using an early form of BSL with his friend Kempe. These observations also show that, in some localities anyway, sign language was in regular use by Deaf people.

Deviation from the Bedean System

Where Bede's one-handed alphanumeric system prospered and developed in Europe, it did not receive the same level of interest in England and Scotland. It is evident that in the late 17th and 18th centuries, a two-handed manual alphabet was being worked on in academic circles. It is believed that the awkwardness of placing one's fingers in position to denote every letter of the alphabet had put off many people. It was with this in mind that the Florentine monk and professor Cosma Rossellio offered people a choice of three digital positions for almost each letter of the alphabet in his great 1579 work, *Thesaurus artificiosæ memoriæ*, after which other scholars began to develop much more logical and easeful finger placements to denote letters.

In his 1648 book, *Philocophus: Or the Deafe and Dumbe Man's Friend*, John Bulwer (1614-1684 - pictured left) has a dedication to Sir Edward Gostwicke, a deaf baronet known to use sign language (see *The Letters of Dorothy Osbourne*), and mentions the existence of over 25 deaf people throughout England. In an earlier book, *Chirologia*, published in 1644, Bulwer includes a number of charts purporting to show signs, numbers and letters of the alphabet.

Sir Edward Gostwicke (1620-1671) was the elder of two Deaf brothers and it is possible that a clergyman educated him, although there is no proof of this. There are two separate sources showing that he was fluent in sign language. The first observation, made in 1637 when Edward was a young man of 17, was by John Hacket, Archdeacon of Bedford, who wrote: "(Edward)... is a sweet creature of rare perspicuity of nature whose behaviour, gestures and zealous signs have procured and allowed him admittance to sermons, prayers, the Lord's Supper..."

The second observation came much later in *The Letters of Dorothy Osbourne* in which she wrote of her frustration on being pursued for her affections by Sir Edward:

> *Just now, I was called away to entertain two deaf and dumb gentlemen. They have made such a tedious visit and I am tired of making signs and tokens for everything I had to say! Good God, how do those that always live with them?*

The gentleman accompanying Sir Edward on this visit was his younger brother William.

The Diaries of John Evelyn and Samuel Pepys

More independent evidence of the use of sign language in the 17th century comes from the papers of two renowned diarists of the time, John Evelyn and Samuel Pepys. These two men were also great friends but travelled and wrote observations in their diaries independently of each other, Evelyn travelling more than Pepys who tended to stay in London.

On one of his travels in 1677 Evelyn recorded an observation of another Deaf baronet of the time, Sir John Gaudy:

... there dined this day at my Lord's one Sir John Gaudy, a very handsome person but quite dumb, yet very intelligent by signs...

Pepys also liked to dine out and was on one occasion having supper with Sir George Downing, a government minister and the man who gave the name to Downing Street, when they spotted from their upstairs window a young man in the street below signing to them, signs which Downing understood though Pepys did not. Sceptical of the young man's ability to understand complex commands in sign language, Pepys challenged Downing to set the young man a task, which Downing proceeded to do and which the young man carried out successfully. How Downing understood or came to learn sign language is as yet a mystery to this day.

The Gaudy brothers

One of the most significant developments in the use of sign language and the manual alphabet in the 17th century, particularly with early deaf education, is contained in various documents relating to the two brothers, Sir John Gaudy (right) and Framlingham Gaudy, who were born deaf and documented as never having spoken in their lives. The two deaf brothers came from a wealthy family residing in Norfolk with ancestors who were at times Members of Parliament or High Sheriffs of Norfolk. Along with their hearing sister, they appear to have received an excellent education at home, being taught by John Cressener, the rector of West Harling, who is mentioned several times in correspondence which indicate the rector had access to books that contained manual alphabet and other sign charts, probably Bulwer's *Chirologia*. There is evidence that  Cressener's son, Henry, who was of the same age as John Gaudy, knew sign language. He grew up with John and later became his scribe.

Both brothers went on to study art (at different times) at the school in London run by Sir Peter Lely as they intended to become professional artists. When first John, then later Framlingham, started at this art school, they lodged with their Art Master, George Freeman who was the father of two deaf daughters. Freeman communicated with the brothers in sign language – this is clear from documents and also suggests that Freeman's daughters used sign language. The two brothers' education, both with Cressener and with Freeman, gives for the first time an account of the manual alphabet and sign language for educational purposes in Britain.

Sir John and Framlingham Gaudy were given to writing a lot of letters, to their father from London, and to their invalid sister and to friends. These two brothers are the earliest known born-deaf sign language users who were inveterate correspondents, and the use of signing is referred to in a number of letters. For example, in a letter written by George Freeman to Framlingham Gaudy's father when the boy was stricken with smallpox, said: *"... I should wish Mr. Bull to be carefull of him and gett him a good nurse who can signe...."*

Sir John Gaudy was the plaintiff in two separate Chancery Court suits, and family correspondence refer to his son and son-in-law being used as interpreters in these civil suits. The Gaudy brothers are an important part of Deaf history because of the clear evidence presented by many different sources of the development of and existence of an early form of British Sign Language in use in Britain.

John Wilkins (1617-1672, below) published his *Mercury, Or the Secret and Swift Messenger* in 1641. This book contained the first British published mention of the two-handed manual alphabet signs for vowels and consonants. In page 117, he wrote:

As for example: Let the tops of the fingers signifie the five vowels; the middle parts the five first consonants; the bottoms of them the five next consonants; the spaces betwixt the fingers the four next. One finger laid on the side of the hand may signifie T, two fingers V the consonant, three W, with the little finger crossed X, the wrist Y, the middle of the hand Z.

Deaf historians generally agree that this system was not "invented" by Wilkins, and it is adjudged to have been in use long before 1641.

The Arthrological method came to dominate debates on the subject of signs in academical circles after the publication of Bulwer's *Philocophus* in 1648. This method is the pointing to the joints of the fingers to denote letters of the alphabet and it was clearly a method that

would have been created by the hearing, not a method that would be used by the Deaf. The failure to seek out and consult with the Deaf by hearing academicians most likely caused people to shun the Arthrological method which they found quite difficult to read, especially from a certain distance or at a certain speed. However, persons of renown such as John Wallis (1616-1703), William Holder (1616-1698) and Christopher Wren (1632-1723) indulged themselves in attempts to create an acceptable national two-handed manual alphabet system, but without real success. Both Wallis and Holder taught deaf persons by the oral method and came into dispute with each other over claims of plagiarism in the

Christopher Wren

famous Royal Society debates. Wallis, however, was to comment in later years that the Deaf needed to be taught first through signs. George Dalgarno (c.1626-1687), a Scottish school-teacher, published his second work, *Didascalocophus, Or the Deaf and Dumb Man's Tutor*

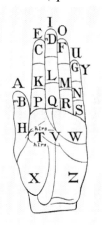

in 1680 and his work contained a manual alphabet (pictured left) that was a very slight improvement on John Wilkins' 1641 description, but it was not of much use. Dalgarno's system was not new, appearing to have been based on Christopher Wren's initial work. It did not lay the foundations for the birth of the present British manual alphabet as some scholars and writers have claimed. Dalgarno's system, although clear to read and understand on paper alone, was quite clumsy and difficult to read and follow in practice and the method was not taken up further. It was left to disappear into obscurity. The beginning of the modern dual-handed manual alphabet came about shortly after the publication of Monsieur La Fin's *Sermo Mirabilis, Or the Silent Language* in 1692 in which the author promoted the Paduan System, in which one pointed to parts of one's body to represent letters of the alphabet. The Paduan System was first mentioned in Giovanni Battista Porta's famous work on cryptography, *De furtivus literarum notis* (Naples, 1563). Then throughout the latter half of the century and the whole of the next century there was an interest in manual alphabets that depended on the pointing to parts of the body in which A = aures; B = barba; C = caput, etc. In 1698 an anonymous deaf person published a small pamphlet, *Digiti Lingua*, which contained manual alphabet charts that laid the foundations for present day usage.

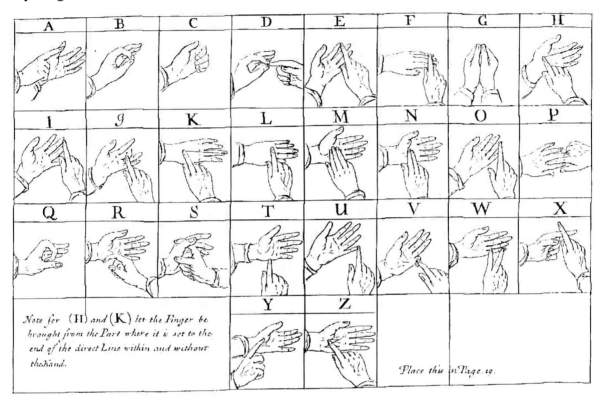

Manual alphabet chart - *Digiti Lingua*, 1698

In 1720 Daniel Defoe (1660-1731) published *The History of the Life and Adventures of Mr Duncan Campbell, Deaf and Dumb*. This book included a greatly improved manual alphabet chart that was nowhere as bad as those that the previous academicians tried to create. This chart was more closely associated with the Deaf and such signs would have been created by the Deaf, although the signs for the five vowels remained the same as that described by Wilkins in 1641.

Duncan Campbell

Manual alphabet in the mainstream

Contrary to false and twisted claims by most writers on Deaf history, in particular the Americans of the past, that Thomas Braidwood practised pure oralism, deaf pupils of the Braidwood Academy were not discouraged from communicating with each other using the manual alphabet and signs. Since Braidwood himself used the combined system, speech was used alongside signs and the system was not purely all-oral. Francis Green mentioned in page 152 of his 1783 work, *Vox oculis subjecta*, that when he visited his deaf son Charles during September 1782:-

Observing, that he was inclined in company to converse with one of his school-fellows, by the tacit finger-language, I asked him, why he did not speak to him with his mouth? – To this, his answer was as pertinent as it was concise, "He is deaf."

Many Braidwoodian pupils were proficient in the use of signs and they spread its use among friends (both deaf and hearing) and family members. From there, the use of the manual alphabet, rather than sign language, found its way among hearing people, especially those in position of authority and the landed gentry, through notable pupils such as Charles Shireff, Francis Humberstone Mackenzie, John Philp Wood, Sarah Dashwood, Thomas Arrowsmith, John Creasy, Jane Poole, Ann Walcott and Thomas Cooley, to name a few.

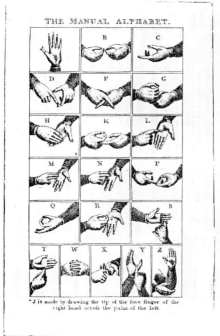

However, it was not until after the formation of the London Asylum in Bermondsey in 1792 that interest in the manual alphabet spread widely to members of the general public and printed sheets of manual alphabet charts were either issued free or sold for as little as a farthing for a small set to raise funds. Some wrote articles on the subject, but one anonymous author, known only as RR, published a book in 1809 entitled *The Invited Alphabet; Or, an address of A to B*. This delightful little book was intended for hearing children and interested adults with the aim of promoting an interest in signs. Joseph Watson (1765-1829), a kinsman of Thomas Braidwood, published his famous *Instruction of the Deaf and Dumb* in 1809 and included not only a manual alphabet chart (left) as used by his pupils at the London Asylum for the Deaf and Dumb in Bermondsey, but also pages after pages of useful information outlining the benefits of the use of sign language and its importance in the education of deaf pupils.

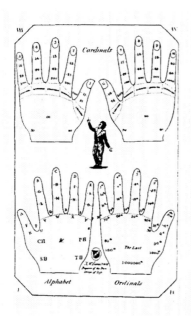

Despite the wonderful development of the manual alphabet in the mainstream since *Digiti Lingua* in 1698, academia failed to catch up with progress. It continued to publicise and extol the antiquated Arthrological method as late as the early 1810s, when books such as T. M. Lucas' *Chyrology; Or, the Art of Reading, Spelling and Ciphering by the Fingers, Designed for the Benefit of the Deaf, and For the Instruction and Amusement of Youth* (pictured left - pub: Harrison & Leigh, 1812), were published. The rapid progress in the development of the manual alphabet among the Deaf left academia standing and signalled the end of academic involvement.

The demise of academia's involvement in the development of the manual alphabet, and in some cases signs, demonstrates the futility of hearing people trying to make up sign languages for Deaf people to use. One recent example can be seen: the Paget-Gorman system, which quickly disappeared simply because the system cannot be accepted by those who were supposed to accept it, the Deaf. It was a system invented by hearing people and imposed on the Deaf who already had their own sign language which was much more intelligent, natural, powerful and acceptable.

The natural growth and development of sign, without intervention by hearing people but growing and developing like all languages, led the control of sign language away from the hearing into the hands of the Deaf.

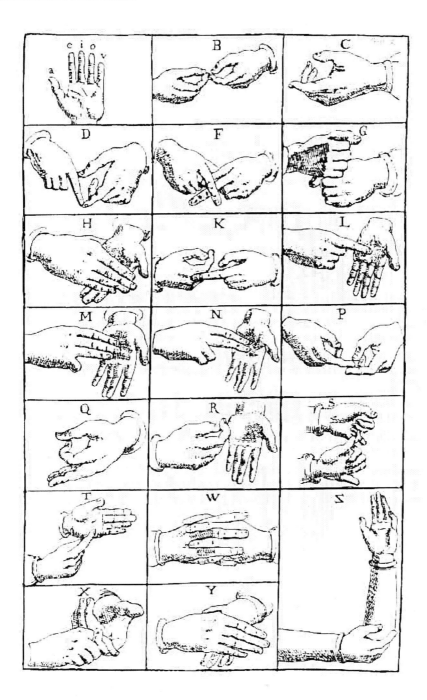

The first known modern manual alphabet chart. It appeared in the 1720 publication, *The History of the Life and Adventures of Mr Duncan Campbell, Deaf and Dumb,* by Daniel Defoe.

The growth of schools for the deaf

A naturalist by profession and a member of the Royal Society, Henry Baker (1698-1774, right) was credited with the invention and development of the microscope, and he was briefly a teacher of the deaf in a private capacity. His school had no base as Baker worked from his home. He was reported to have taught the Deaf to speak well, discarding those who were not capable of speaking well. He was said to have used the manual alphabet (as featured in Defoe's 1720 book on Duncan Campbell) to communicate with his pupils. The details on Baker are quite hazy and cannot be fully verified at present.

Thomas Braidwood (1715-1806) was a writing master running a private academy for young people at the foot of Canongate in Edinburgh when in the first quarter of 1760 a wealthy wine merchant from the Port of Leith, Alexander Shireff, approached him on an attempt to educate his 10-year-old deaf son, Charles. Braidwood undertook the task and within a few years was successful in this. Charles acquired a good command of not only the English language, but also the French language. Braidwood attempted to teach speech, but was not successful with Charles. However, Braidwood did achieve success in teaching speech to a good number of pupils during his lifetime. Braidwood was particularly interested in getting his pupils to acquire and master language rather than training them to speak well. To achieve this aim, he created a system of communication later to be known as the combined method through which he could teach deaf pupils. From that humble beginning, Braidwood's fame grew and his deaf pupils went on to become both famous and influential, in particular John

Braidwood Academy, Dumbiedykes

Philp Wood (1762-1838), Auditor of Excise in the Scottish Excise Office, editor of the prestigious *Peerage of Scotland* and author of both the *Parish of Cramond* and *John Law of Lauriston*; John Goodricke (1764-1786) who became both a renowned astrologer and the youngest member of the Royal Society; Francis Humberstone Mackenzie (1745-1815) who, as Lord Seaforth, became the first deaf Member of Parliament and Governor of Barbados, as well as a member of the Royal Society; John Creasy (1774-1855?) who not only became a teacher of the deaf, but trained other deaf persons to become teachers; and Jane Poole (1781-1860) who fought for the right of the deafblind to write their own wills. The original combined method, which involved the use of reading, writing, lipreading, fingerspelling and signing, is at present known as the Braidwoodian method.

Thomas Braidwood's success as a teacher of the deaf far outshone that of the Abbé de l'Epeé, who first established a shelter for the deaf and dumb poor in Paris in 1760 before going on to establish a proper school for the deaf around 1762-3 (*Bernard Truffaut*, 1998). Compared with the successful and renowned Braidwoodian pupils, l'Epeé's pupils were largely unknown and achieved nothing of note, even though l'Epeé himself achieved greater fame than Thomas Braidwood, possibly due to the fact that a "tale of a benevolent priest rescuing the unfortunate deaf and dumb wretches and providing them shelter and salvation" had greater appeal to members of the public at that time, generating an air of romance and benevolence which they associated and identified with sacerdotal works.

Braidwood moved his academy to Hackney on the outskirt of east London in 1783, ending the Scottish connection. From there, his kinsman, Joseph Watson, offered his services as the first head of the newly-founded public school for the deaf in England, *The London Asylum for the Education of the Deaf and Dumb*. This school was initially situated in Grange Road in Bermondsey and was opened in November 1792 by the Rev. John Townsend and the Rev. Henry Cox Mason. The chronology of the founding of the British schools for the deaf in the first half of the 19th century (along with the names of the head teachers) is as follows: -

The London Asylum	1792	Joseph Watson
Edinburgh Institution	1810	John Braidwood
Edgbaston (Birmingham)	1814	Thomas Braidwood
Glasgow	1819	John Anderson
Aberdeen	1819	Robert Taylor
Manchester	1825	William Vaughan
Liverpool	1825	John Anderson (transferred from Glasgow)
Exeter	1827	Henry Brothers Bingham
Doncaster	1829	Charles Baker
Belfast	1831	George Gordon
Newcastle	1839	Andrew Patterson
Bristol	1841	Matthew Robert Burns
Brighton	1842	William Sleight
Bath	1842	Jane Elwes
Dundee	1846	Alexander Drysdale
Aberystwyth (Swansea)	1847	Charles Rhind
Edinburgh (Donaldson's)	1850	Angus McDiarmid

Some teachers established private schools for the deaf, and amongst the most famous private schools were those run by Henry Brothers Bingham (1801-1875, bottom left) at Rugby and Thomas Arnold (1816-1897, top left) at Northampton. Bingham used the Braidwoodian method and Arnold used the oral-only method, but taught fewer pupils. Deaf people of note who hailed from Bingham's Rugby College for the Deaf included Arthur Henry Bather (1829-1892), George Frederick Healey (1843-1927) and Sir Arthur Henderson Fairbairn (1852-1915). Out of Arnold's Northampton School came Abraham Farrar (1861-1944), who was Arnold's first and only successful pupil. It must be noted here that Henry Brothers Bingham was a protégé of Thomas Braidwood (the grandson of the original Thomas Braidwood and the headmaster of the Edgbaston Institute) and along with Charles Baker (1803-1874) he was the last link with the Braidwood dynasty, having been trained in the Braidwoodian method by Thomas Braidwood. The number of schools for the deaf continued to grow until the 1950s.

The defeat of the Aristotelian dictum by sign language

The Braidwoodian approach to teaching placed great emphasis on language acquisition and this involved the use of all means of communication available to enable Deaf children to acquire language. Thomas Braidwood used the combined method, which embraced fingerspelling, signing, reading, writing and lipreading, and it was this method that enabled Braidwood to become a successful teacher of the deaf. Sign language slowly became recognised as a viable method of communication and was considered the best and most accessible means of communication with the Deaf, enabling many deaf children to receive an education. As a consequence, school after school was established all over Britain and education made available to the deaf children. Religious services and instruction were made accessible using sign language, and this defeated both Aristotle's and St. Augustine's mistaken insistence that the Deaf cannot be educated or receive religious instruction because of their deafness, a view that prevailed for over 1.300 years.

Deaf People as teachers

The rapid proliferation of schools for the deaf, especially between 1810 and 1830, meant that demand for suitable teachers trained both in the manual alphabet and in sign language outstripped availability. Several headmasters and teachers were so highly regarded that they were induced away from their first schools. This happened with people like John Anderson (Glasgow to Liverpool), Henry Brothers Bingham (Birmingham to Exeter, thence to Manchester) and William Vaughan (London Asylum to Manchester). Training older pupils of the schools themselves as Pupil Teachers and Assistant Teachers was the only answer to meet this severe shortage.

Although Thomas Braidwood began the practice of using Deaf teachers at his private academy in Hackney, Joseph Watson at the London Asylum took it up in earnest. Many other schools for the deaf were soon following the practice. Many pupil-teachers and assistant teachers stayed on to become full salaried teachers and often served for years in the same institutions. In the process, the use of the manual alphabet and sign language as educational tools became widespread in many public institutions and served to strengthen the cohesion of local Deaf communities.

Joseph Watson (right) became the first person to establish a professional training course for those wishing to become a teacher of the deaf. This course was initially of a five-year duration (which was later changed to three years) and many teachers of renown went through such a course. As more schools were established all over Britain, individual schools adopted Watson's teacher training course and opened up opportunities for people in different regions of Britain to train as teachers of the deaf.

27

The First Deaf Teachers of the Deaf

In the early days of the education of the deaf, those in charge of teaching deaf children began to see the advantages of employing certain gifted Deaf people as pupil teachers or assistant teachers in order that instruction might be given to school children in a language that they understood or could learn, the manual alphabet and sign language.

Braidwood's Academy in Hackney was the first school for the deaf to employ ex-pupils as teachers of deaf children, such as John Creasy. It was, however, the Asylum for the Deaf and Dumb firstly in Grange Road, Bermondsey, and later in Kent Road, that first trained and employed many Deaf people to become teachers of the children at the Asylum. William Hunter was the first teacher. He was trained by John Creasy and began teaching in 1804.

John Creasy (1774 –1855?)

John Creasy's exact date of birth is unknown but he was baptised at Deptford on 18 September 1774. The son of John and Mary Creasy, he was for almost ten years a pupil of Thomas Braidwood at his Academy, firstly at Edinburgh and then in Hackney.

Around early May 1792 John Creasy and his mother, Mary, met the Rev. John Townsend (right) the minister of a Congregational church in Jamaica Row, Bermondsey. During her conversation with Townsend, she suggested that a school should be founded for the education of poor deaf children. This had been the dream of Thomas Braidwood but he had failed to receive public encouragement in 1769. For the realisation of his dream, Mary Creasy presented before Townsend her tall and lean 18-year old deaf son John, for whom she had paid £1,500 in fees during his ten years of education at Braidwood Academy.

The new Asylum was founded on 14th November 1792 with the first six poor deaf children admitted to a humble building in Fort Place (right) in Grange Road, Bermondsey. This later grew into a large school that was to be famously known as the London Asylum for the Deaf and Dumb, located in Kent Road. As the school grew during its formative years, its principal Joseph Watson employed Creasy not only to teach his  private pupils, but also to train the bright Asylum pupils to become teachers. It is not known exactly where or when Creasy died but it is said that he lived on to a cheerful and active old age and died around his early to mid eighties (possibly around 1855). It is of interest to note that Watson was Creasy's teacher at the famous Braidwood Academy in Hackney.

William Hunter (1785-1861) and George Banton (1812–1879)

William Hunter and George Banton were just two of the pupils who went on to become teachers at the London Asylum for the Deaf and Dumb during the period when Joseph Watson and his son Thomas were headmasters.

William Hunter was in the second batch of pupils admitted to the institution in 1793 and, his talent having been noted by the school, he was trained by John Creasy to become a teacher of the deaf. Hunter completed his teacher training in 1804, and was still teaching when he died at the age of 76. His teaching career at the London Asylum for the Deaf spanned an incredible 57 years.

George Banton (left) first received a short private education before he was transferred to the London Asylum for the Deaf and Dumb in Old Kent Road, Southwark, as a "pay-list" pupil. Like Hunter before him, Banton's intelligence and talent were noted by the staff and, after being chosen to train as a teacher, Banton went on to serve the same school for 50 years before retiring in 1875, a year before his death.

These two Deaf persons were simply the first of many in the period between 1804 and 1880 whose intelligence and capabilities were noted by their schools and who were offered training as pupil teachers. Many former pupils who became teachers remained with the same schools throughout their working lives. Some, though, were more ambitious and wanted to run their own schools.

At least two schools were founded through the efforts of Deaf people at Dundee and Bristol.

Matthew Robert Burns (1798 – 1880) and Alexander Drysdale (1812-1880)

No writing on the history of the education of the deaf would be complete without mention of Matthew Robert Burns (left), the first born-deaf person ever to be a school headmaster, and the founder of several schools. Burns was initially educated by his mother but later attended a local hearing school where he began to become well educated. When he was 10, his family moved to London and enrolled him as a private pupil with Joseph Watson at the Asylum for the Deaf and Dumb in Kent Road, London.

The next date we have for Matthew Burns is 1830, in which year he appeared in Edinburgh and helped to form the church for the deaf in that city. In 1832 he opened a day school for deaf children in Carruber's Close Chapel, assisted by two other Deaf people, Charles Buchan and Alexander Campbell. He left after a short while to go to Dundee in 1833 to try and establish a Sabbath School. This did not last long as in 1834 he was appointed the headmaster of the Aberdeen Institution for the Deaf and Dumb where he remained for seven years.

In 1841 Matthew Burns went to Bristol where he helped to found the Bristol Institution for the Deaf and Dumb at Tyndall's Park as principal. He did not stay long at the school in Tyndall's Park – a mere two years. The cause of his leaving is a mystery. Matthew Burns would only say that the 'heathen Bristol' did not contribute much to the institution and to the instruction of deaf children.

Little is known of Alexander Drysdale's early years. He was either born deaf or became so at a very early age. He received his education at the Deaf and Dumb Institution in Edinburgh. After finishing school he became an assistant teacher, remaining at the Institution for just over ten years. In 1841, then 29 years of age, he began to look for a new position as he felt he could do better. He wrote to the directors of the Aberdeen Institution applying for the post that had been left vacant by Matthew Burns. To support his application Drysdale sent testimonials from parents, clergymen and directors of the Edinburgh Institution referring to the success of his teaching and cuttings from local newspapers, which showed that he often had exhibitions and examinations of his pupils, as was customary at that time, with the help of an interpreter. The perfection of the pupils' finger-language was noted, but signs were also used. The signs used by the pupils were seen to be very expressive, and the pupils' knowledge of all their lessons excellent.

Unfortunately he did not get the post in Aberdeen, but on March 9 1846 he and his wife, whom he had married in the previous year, opened the Dundee Institution for the Deaf and Dumb in Meadow Street. The school rapidly grew and after two years moved to another leased building. There blind and deaf children were taught together. After ten years a new building was opened for deaf children only in Dudhope Bank, Logie Den. He died suddenly in his chair after a heart attack in April 1880. He had been headmaster for nearly 35 years. He was succeeded by another Deaf man, James Barland, an ex-pupil of the school as headmaster.

Dudhope Castle, Dudhope Bank

By then, storm clouds were gathering over the education of the deaf. Drysdale died in the year of the Milan Congress, which saw a manipulated delegation pass resolutions calling for the banning of sign language. These resolutions were taken up by governments all over the western world.

Eliza Cockerill (b.1817), Mary Ann Cattermole (b.1821) and Alice Mary Vernon (b.1842)

A London-born orphan, Eliza Cockerill was admitted to the London Asylum in 1830 at the late age of thirteen years after a prolonged battle to gain admission. Her admission was initially refused under Rule 17 which stated that no child would be admitted to the Asylum before nine years of age and after eleven and half years of age. However, Eliza found at least 16 members of the committee of Governors willing to support her for admission under Rule 18 which stated that if sixteen members be in favour of admission of a pupil, the committee shall have the discretionary power to deviate from Rule 17! Eliza Cockerill turned out to be an extremely bright and talented pupil, and she was offered a teaching role at the school when she was due to leave in 1833. After training, she was officially employed as a teacher in 1836 and, as far as history stands at present, she is the first Deaf female teacher of the deaf in Britain. Eliza taught until September 1842 when she married a Deaf tobacconist, Francis Goodwin.

Following on Eliza Cockerill's footsteps, Mary Ann Cattermole became a teacher of the deaf at the London Asylum in 1838. Very little is known of her except that Mary Ann was born on 1 July 1821 to William and Ann Cattermole. Her father was a schoolmaster in Palgrave in Suffolk. Mary Ann entered the London Asylum as a pupil in 1832.

It was not until 1857 that Alice Mary Vernon, the third Deaf female teacher of the deaf would come onto the scene. Daughter of Thomas and Maria Vernon of Nottingham, she was born on 19 October 1842. Her father was a machine-smith with seven children of whom two were deaf. Alice Mary Vernon entered the London Asylum in 1854 and left two years later. She was taken on as a teacher of the deaf at the London Asylum in 1857.

Edward Alfred Kirk (1855-1924)

Edward Kirk (left) was born on 28 February 1855 in Doncaster. At the age of seven he fell victim to scarlet fever and eventually became deaf. In 1866 he was admitted as pupil number 708 at the Yorkshire Institute for the Deaf and Dumb (YIDD) under the headmastership of Charles Baker. Kirk progressed well, but when he left school in 1871 he found himself unemployed.

It was not long before Baker offered Kirk employment as an assistant teacher at the YIDD and this began Kirk's long and illustrious teaching career. After the death of Charles Baker in May 1874 there was a hiatus before James Howard became the principal of the YIDD in August 1874. He became determined to do away with instruction by sign method and to impose a speech-only approach. This caused a great upheaval among both teachers and pupils at the school and it affected Kirk badly.

Kirk's proficiency as a teacher of the deaf was noted by one Joseph Moreton, who eventually recommended that he be interviewed for the post as headmaster of the newly-founded school for the deaf in Leeds. Kirk attended the interview and was awarded the job – he was the only deaf person ever to be offered a job as headmaster of a school for the deaf by a local authority. Kirk commenced his duties on 6 January 1883 at a time when the post-Milan oralist craze was in full swing... and he died still the headmaster of the same school in 1924.

The appointment of Edward Kirk to the post of Principal at the Leeds School for Deaf Children in 1883 was unique. It was to be over 100 years before another deaf person was appointed Head of a school for deaf children in Britain.

Here and there, few Deaf persons continued to hold teaching posts. However, although they might have had the necessary qualifications to teach their chosen subjects, they struggled to qualify as *teachers of the deaf*. The main reason for this was the unfair and discriminatory criterion that, in order to teach, one had to be able to take any type of class and there was no way that an extremely high proportion of these Deaf persons could teach a *hearing class*.

British Deaf Teachers in Australia and Canada

The education which the Deaf of Britain received in its pioneering days before 1880 was of such a standard that the pupils were able to feel confident enough to become independent and hold their own in the wide world after leaving school. Certain pupils went on to achieve fame as pioneers in foreign lands, not least of all the MacLellan brothers who went on to become lawyers of renown in Canada. Archibald MacLellan (1831-1902) and Duncan MacLellan (1836-1920) were the protégés of one of the greatest British teachers of the deaf, Duncan Anderson of the Glasgow Institution for the Deaf and Dumb. However, it is to a band of few Deaf persons that some countries such as Australia and Canada are indebted for bringing the education for the deaf to their deaf children.

In Canada, the true founder of its education for the deaf was George Tait (1828-1904, right), a former pupil of the Edinburgh Institution for the Deaf and Dumb under the great Braidwoodian teacher, Robert Kinniburgh. Tait went to Canada via Maine (USA), eventually settling in Nova Scotia. He met a deaf girl, Mary Fletcher, and took to teaching her in his spare time. By a strange quirk of fate, Tait bumped into a Deaf person who was also educated at his former school in Edinburgh, William Gray (1806-1881). Gray was then poor and penniless, having fallen on hard times. Tait persuaded Gray to take up teaching deaf children in Nova Scotia and together they went on to found the first school for the deaf in Canada. Their friendship were later to be soured amid claims that each was the founder of the school ...

Another Kinniburgh pupil, John Carmichael (1803-1857), left Scotland for Australia to seek prosperity as an artist – he eventually ended up designing the very first Australian postage stamp. However, Thomas Pattison (1805-1898, right), another pupil of Robert Kinniburgh at the Edinburgh Institution, was to find greater fame in that he became the first Deaf person to open a school in Australia. Pattison left Scotland for Australia in 1858, and two years later on Monday 22 October 1860, he opened the first school for the deaf at 152 Liverpool Street, Sydney. Pattison taught at the school until 1866 when he retired.

Further south in Australia, a former private pupil of Joseph Watson at the London Asylum for the Deaf and Dumb, Frederick John Rose (1831-1920, right), established a school for the deaf in Melbourne on 12 November 1860, barely twenty days after Pattison established his school in Sydney. Rose became the school's first headmaster and superintendent and he retired in 1882 following ill-health. The Victoria School for the Deaf in Melbourne is still at present strongly associated with Rose: there is the legend that his spirit still wanders around the basement of the school, and when naughty or unruly deaf children were sent down as punishment in the past, many screamed to get out as soon as they got in. This brief "ten seconds" punishment was said to have worked wonders on them and their behaviour improved!

The Rise of Oralism

Running in tandem with the development of sign language (and manualism), attempts to teach the deaf to speak (oralism) were developed and practised by various people across Europe. The chronology of the rise of oralism is as follows:

1. Pedro Ponce de Leon (c.1520-1584). A native of Valladolid, Spain, he was educated at the University of Salamanca and went on to become a Benedictine monk. He was based at the monastery of San Salvadore at Oña, near Burgos, at which he spent much of his life. There exists a legal document of the year 1578, amongst other contemporary accounts, in which Leon said he had taught born-deaf pupils, who were children of the wealthy classes, to "speak, read, write, reckon and pray." He also taught them Latin, Greek and Italian, gave them an understanding of the doctrines of Christianity and showed them how to confess themselves by speech. One deaf pupil later was ordained and held office in the Church, performing services.

In 1550 a manuscript mentioned both the wonderful success of Pedro Ponce de Leon's oral method of education and two allegedly born-deaf deaf brothers, Francisco and Pedro de Valasco, as having learned to speak.

2. Ramirez de Carrion (1579-1652) was credited as the teacher who taught Luis de Valasco to "read, write, speak and converse with such success that he felt no other deficiency than that of hearing." It was said that Valasco became deaf at the age of two. Carrion's method was described by Juan Pablo Bonet (1579-1633) in his book, *Reduccion de las letras y arte para enseñar á habla los mudos* (Madrid, 1620). Interestingly, Carrion used the one handed manual alphabet in the early stages of teaching before proceeding to teach speech! Another deaf person to be successfully educated by the oral method by Carrion was the Marquise of Priego.

3. John Wallis (1616-1703, right). A Savilian Professor of Geometry at Oxford, Wallis with "much success" taught a 25 year old deaf person, Daniel Whaley, to speak in 1661. In 1662 John Wallis with likewise success taught another deaf person, Alexander Popham, to speak. Both pupils were paraded before King Charles II and the members of the Royal Society, and each deaf person gave an extremely short demonstration of their speaking abilities by way of questions and answers. The event was a great success for Wallis – but enter William Holder …

After a long-drawn dispute with Holder, Wallis withdrew from teaching the Deaf. In later years, in his letter of September 1698 to Thomas Beverly, he was to advocate the use of manual alphabet to instruct the Deaf!

4. William Holder (1616-1698), a clergyman and brother-in-law to Sir Christopher Wren, was connected with the study of music. While rector of Bletchington in Oxfordshire, Holder undertook to teach speech to Alexander Popham, the born-deaf son of Admiral Popham and Lady Wharton in 1659, two years before the very same deaf person was taught to speak by John Wallis. The method Holder employed to

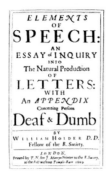

teach Popham was explained at length in his famous work *Elements of speech:... with an appendix concerning persons Deaf & Dumb*, published in 1669.

Holder was naturally infuriated when Wallis laid claim to teaching Popham to speak and accused him of plagiarism. The dispute encouraged scholarly interest in oralism and, as a consequence, the interest in oralism spread beyond the Royal Society circles. Historically speaking, Holder was England's first oralist teacher, not Wallis as some historians have assumed.

5. Francis Mercuris, Baron van Helmont (1618-1699) was the youngest son of a renowned Belgian chemist. He followed his father's footsteps to a lesser degree. Helmont resided in Sulzbach in Germany for most of his life. He published a book entitled *Alphabeti vere naturalis hebraici brevissima delineation* (*A brief description of the truly natural hebrew alphabet*) in 1667. He held that the Hebrew language was a natural language to men and that each character of the alphabet represented in some manner the sectional figure of the position of the vocal organs necessary to pronounce it. Helmont wrote that the born-deaf person was not deprived of all motion of his tongue, and that he could be taught to understand others by the motion of their mouths and tongues (e.g. lipreading). He described a method of teaching the deaf to speak and lipread in his work, and he claimed to have taught a deaf person to speak and lipread in only three weeks. Other than that, Helmont was in fact an obscure person who dabbled extensively in the occult and mysticism, but his 1667 work was a major boost for the oralists.

6. Johan Conrad Amman (1669-1724, left) was a native of Schaffhausen in Switzerland and was educated for the medical profession in Basle. Persecuted for his religious

views, he had to flee his country for Holland, where he found occupation as a physician and settled in Haarlem. There he commenced the oral education of his first pupil, Esther Kolard. The teaching was successful and Amman subsequently had more pupils which he taught with "much success." Amman published his views on the education of the deaf in his work *Surdus Loquens* (Amsterdam 1692). Amman published his second work, *Dissertatio de Loquela*, in 1700, in which treatise he added further details and information on his work in teaching the deaf to speak, read and write.

7. Jacob Rodriguez Pereire (1715-1780) was a Spanish Jew whose family was driven

by persecution to Portugal, and thence to Bordeaux where they settled in 1741. Pereire had a sister who was deaf and dumb and he took to educating her and teaching her to speak. In 1744 he took a deaf pupil from his own people and successfully taught him to speak so much that in 1746 he took another deaf pupil into his charge. This born-deaf pupil, d'Azy d'Etavigny, was then 16 years old and came from La Rochelle. The young man's progress under Pereire's teaching was rapid and he came to the notice of Caen Academy. In 1749 d'Etavigny was brought with Pereire before the French Academy of Sciences in Paris. Pereire was hailed for his work. The deaf Etienne de Fay had initially educated d'Etavigny before Pereire came on the scene, and d'Etavigny had by then acquired a good command of language, which more likely than not assisted him in speech training, but many people ignored this fact.

Pereire found fame through d'Etavigny and in 1750 this brought him to the attention of the Duc de Chaulnes, who had a 13 year old born-deaf child, Saboureax de Fontenay, whom Pereire successfully taught to articulate. In spite of the fact that Pereire publicised his proficiency in teaching speech, records show that he used the manual alphabet to a great extent to supply visual clues to aid speech, which is very similar to present day cued speech method which needs visual manual cueing to supplement speech.

8. Samuel Heinecke (1729-1790, right), born in Nautzschutz, near Weissenfels in Germany, first attempted to educate a deaf boy when he was a soldier stationed in Dresden around 1754. After leaving the army Heinecke went to Hamburg and became a private tutor of the children of a wealthy family. In 1768, Heinecke took a job as a teacher at Eppendorf. While there he met another deaf boy and was able to educate him with success. Following that event, several other deaf children were sent to him and his fame grew. In 1778 he was invited to found the first school for the deaf in Germany in Leipzig.

Heinecke used the oral method and was staunchly anti-signs as his correspondence with the Abbé de l'Epeé reveals, but there is some obscurity hanging about regarding his methods of teaching. This is due to the fact that Heinecke concealed his methods as far as he could. Heinecke's success influenced many German scholars and sowed the seeds for the spread of the oral method. Scholars and teachers of the deaf in Germany began to grow in large numbers, the most famous being Johan Baptist Graser (1766-1841), Victor August Jäger (fl.1825) and Fredreich Moritz Hill (1805-1874). Because oralism was strongly adopted and advocated in Germany the method of teaching deaf children by speech alone to the total exclusion of sign language became universally known as the German Method.

9. Thomas Arnold (1816-1897) is credited as the earliest and most successful English oral teacher. A native of Co. Antrim in Ireland, but of English extraction, Arnold developed an interest in teaching the deaf when he met a deaf neighbour and attempted to educate him. In pursuance of his wish to become a teacher of the deaf, Arnold became an assistant teacher at the Yorkshire Institution for the Deaf and Dumb in Doncaster under Charles Baker in 1840. While there, Arnold made some attempts to teach speech to a class, but gave it up as the combined method was very strong at the school, and he left after no more than two or three years at the school. After being away out of the country in Australia for some time in pursuit of his priestly activities, Arnold returned to England and in 1868 adopted the German Method when he established the Oral School for the Deaf in Northampton. Initially, he took on only one pupil, Abraham Farrar. Arnold's achievement with Farrar was resounding; not only was he successful with the oral method, but also he passed Farrar through both the Cambridge University Local examinations and

Abraham Farrar

London University Matriculation. Encouraged by this, Arnold took on more pupils (although extremely few in numbers) who became "successful", although none of them matched Farrar's achievements. This prompted Arnold to publish his methods, firstly in a pamphlet issued in 1872 on *The Education of the Deaf and Dumb, a Review of the French and German Systems*, which was followed in 1881 by his first major work, *A Method of Teaching the Deaf and Dumb Speech, Lipreading and Language*. In 1881, he published his famous *Education of Deaf Mutes: A Manual for Teachers*.

The Oral School for the Deaf's fine academic record produced the first deaf Fellow of the Geological Society and the first deaf Ph.D, besides a host of other academic successes, but neither Arnold nor his successor, N. H. Dixon, ever took more than eight boys at a time, and all of them were carefully selected to ensure the success of the oral method.

10. William van Praagh (1845-1907) was born in Rotterdam in Holland and became a trainee teacher under the oralist teacher of the deaf, David Hirsch, at his school for the deaf in Rotterdam. Following the spread of Arnold's success in the oral method of education, people of the upper classes who had deaf children began to crave for oral education for their children. One person, Sir Henry Isaacs, sent his two deaf children to the

William van Praagh

Rotterdam school to be educated in the oral method and he persuaded Baroness Mayer de Rothschild to give assistance in establishing oral education of the deaf in England. The Baroness had in 1863 founded a home for the Jewish deaf and dumb in Whitechapel. Following the Baroness' approach, David Hirsch was asked to send one of his pupils to England and in 1866 William van Praagh arrived and took charge of a little school in Mount Street. Initially, this school took only Jewish deaf children, but later admitted gentile deaf children. In 1870, Baroness Mayer de Rothschild founded the Association for the Oral Instruction of the Deaf and Dumb, with the object of establishing a training college for the teachers of the deaf, together with a school for deaf children of all classes. Under the direction of Praagh the Association acquired larger premises in Fitzroy Square, London, and the College was officially opened in 1872. From that place teachers were trained in the oral method of education and Fitzroy Square was soon established as the place where teachers of the deaf must be trained and qualified before they were to undertake employment as teachers of the deaf. Praagh went on to found the Union of Teachers on the Pure Oral System in 1894. Oralism was in full swing following the Milan Congress of 1880 and the country was flooded by a tidal wave of oralism that was to completely remove manualism and sign language from the classrooms and destroy the future of a very large proportion of deaf children who could not benefit from the oral-only approach. Praagh died in 1907 following a massive heart attack.

There were numerous oralists such as Arthur A. Kinsey (1849-1889), Susannah E. Hull (1845-1922) and Mary Hare (1865-1945) playing prominent roles in the development and enforcement of the oral-only approach in the training of teachers of the deaf as well as in the education of the deaf.

Arthur Kinsey was introduced to Benjamin St. John Ackers, a Member of Parliament, for the education of his deaf daughter, but firstly was sent to Osnabruck Oral School for the deaf in Germany for a year's training. After a year there, Kinsey travelled around Europe and the USA before returning to England in 1876 to take up teaching the deaf girl. Ackers established both 'The Society for Training Teachers of the Deaf and Diffusion of the German System in the United Kingdom' and in 1878 the Ealing Training College and School where prospective teachers of the deaf were trained in the oral method. He died on Christmas Day in 1889.

Susannah Hull was born with a silver spoon in her mouth. Her wealthy physician father introduced to her an uneducated and very disabled deaf and nearly blind lady. Susannah took up the challenge to teach her. From then onwards, she took to teaching the deaf in a private capacity and adopted the oral-only method. Her school was based in South Kensington in London and was later moved to Bexley in Kent. She was the first lady teacher to adopt the oral method in Britain.

Mary Hare (right) was a pupil of Kinsey at the Ealing College between 1881 and 1883. After successfully completing her course she became a teacher at the College and taught until around June 1884 when she left. In January 1885 she established a private school for the deaf in Upper Norwood and took on the role of an examiner in speech and language at Ealing College. Her school was moved to Brighton in 1894 before being transferred to Hove in 1909.

In 1916 Mary Hare transferred her school to Dene Hollow, Burgess Hill. She maintained very a strong oral-only policy of education and signing was strictly forbidden in her school. She died in November 1945. Her school at Burgess Hill was left as the foundation of a national grammar school as decreed by her will. The school was initially named 'The Mary Hare Oral School for the Deaf'. With the appointment of Edgar L. Mundin as headmaster, Mary Hare Grammar School for the Deaf opened in January 1946 and survives to the present day.

The Fitzroy Square College and Ealing Society for Training Teachers of the Deaf and Diffusion of the German System formed the Joint Examination Board of Teachers of the Deaf in 1907. There was later a decline in the intake of students for both colleges and this caused both colleges to merge into one training college in 1912. This later became the Faculty of Education in Manchester University in 1919 under the leadership of Irene Rosetta Goldsack.

Milan… and after

As schools for the deaf flourished and Deaf people found gainful employment as teachers, and in a few cases as head teachers, it was generally accepted that these developments were made possible by sign language. Even so, the practice of teaching speech to the deaf was not new; it was tried in Europe and Samuel Heinecke of Germany became a successful teacher off articulation. His fame soon spread across Europe and a small group of hearing people began after him to look to oralism as the tool to achieve a number of aims:

1. To eliminate the unsightly hand and arm-waving mode of communication.
2. To make deaf people appear "normal" and get them to talk like "normal" hearing people.
3. To establish regulations that would remove deaf people from teaching due to their inability to teach speech.
4. To monopolise Deaf education and decide the direction it should be moving.

It was not that long ago that the Aristotle - St. Augustine dictum on Deaf people being incapable of learning held sway. The new fact that Deaf people were not only able to be educated, but able to teach, hit those who held low esteem of the Deaf and who now felt nothing but shame that those who were once grouped those suffering from incapacity with idiots by Aristotle were now their equals. This group of people, all hearing teachers and their associates in government departments, got in touch with each other and agreed to meet in Paris in 1878. Twenty seven delegates, mainly French from the *Le Societé Peréire*, met at the French Universal Exposition of 1878 with the sole aim of directing the education of the Deaf through the oral method to the total exclusion of sign language and with the idea of promoting this aim in every European country. The meeting was successful and a national meeting was held at Lyon in the following year. It was entitled The First National Conference for Improving the Lot of the Deaf (*La Première Conférence Nationale pour Améliorer la Condition du Sourd*). More people from other countries attended and the delegates at the conference agreed to hold another in 1880.

That conference in 1880 was held at Milan in Italy, and the purpose of the Second International Congress (as it was called, the first at Paris in 1878) was to rubber-stamp the superiority of oralism over the sign method, and therefore to banish signs and Deaf teachers from schools for the deaf. The composition of delegates invited to attend the Milan Congress was carefully manipulated so that supporters of oralism were invited in large numbers to ensure resounding voting successes in favour of the abolition of sign language and Deaf teachers. The same course was taken for the officers of the Milan Congress – they were chosen to ensure that the outcome would end in favour of the oralists. The whole event was in essence a Franco-Italian conspiracy; there were 87 Italian and 53 French delegates. The only true representatives attending the Congress were the five delegates from the United States, as they were elected by vote earlier in the year in their own country to attend the gathering. The outcome of the Congress was inevitable. Eight resolutions were put before the Congress. Of the eight resolutions, the first two were the most important:

> *1. The congress, considering the incontestable superiority of speech over signs, for restoring deaf-mutes to social life and for giving them greater facility in language, declares that the method of articulation should have preference over that of signs in the instruction and education of the deaf and dumb.*

41

2. *Considering that the simultaneous use of signs and speech has the disadvantage of injuring speech, lipreading and precision of ideas, the congress declares that the pure oral method ought to be preferred.*

The first resolution was passed overwhelmingly by a massive 160-4 votes, and the second resolution was carried by another crushing 150-14 votes, fitting in and going the way the organisers of the Congress had planned from the outset by carefully selective invitations. When all the resolutions were passed and carried, a delegate at the Congress leaped up and shouted from the podium, *"Vive la parole!"* This became the slogan of the hearing oralist educators of the deaf.

In the aftermath of Milan pure oralism swept Europe, affecting many people, deaf and hearing alike, and schools. The consequences arising from the Milan Congress were truly appalling. Delegates from the Congress who were oral fanatics made representations to the government and authorities of their respective countries asking them to ban both signs and Deaf teachers in the education of the deaf, citing the Milan resolutions as evidence. Soon afterwards in Britain hundreds of Deaf teachers were to lose their jobs because they could neither teach speech nor hear so that they could correct deaf children's speech. Within a decade of the Milan Congress, it was estimated, nearly 2,000 Deaf teachers of the deaf, mainly in Europe and America, lost their jobs. It was not only Deaf teachers who found

B. St. John Ackers

Alexander G. Bell

Rev. Stainer

themselves out of work, but non-teaching Deaf members of staff, such as cooks, cleaners, housekeepers, gardeners and so on, were also excluded from working within schools for the deaf for fear that their use of signs might contaminate the deaf pupils undergoing a strict oral education. The consequences were truly terrifying. Many Deaf people were left unemployed and destitute, many forced to take lesser paid jobs than they had when the schools for the deaf employed them. The insistence on oralism and the abolition of sign language eventually reached alarming proportions during the oralists' quest to "abolish" deafness itself. One of the champions of oralism was the inventor of the telephone, Alexander Graham Bell, who campaigned vociferously for the ban on marriages between Deaf couples so as to prevent as far as possible deaf babies coming into the world. Bell touted his idea to various government authorities; in fact, Bell wrote a lengthy paper entitled *Upon the Formation of a Deaf Variety of the Human Race* and first presented it to the National Academy of Sciences at New Haven (USA) on 13 November 1883. Staunch British oralists such as Dr. David Buxton, Benjamin St. John Ackers, MP, Arthur Kinsey and the Rev. William Stainer, embraced Bell's idea about banning marriages between Deaf people. There was relief among the Deaf when the British government, although it noted Bell's proposals, steered clear of the issue, at least in public. Within 20 years of the Milan Congress, schools for the Deaf were converted to the oral-only method of teaching.

In the USA, there were 26 schools using sign language in 1850. By 1900 there were 139 schools, and sign language was forbidden in every one. The same went for France, where there were 160 schools using the oral-only method, and Britain, where its 87 schools were forbidden to use sign language at all times.

British deaf children suffered a reign of terror under oralist educators and teachers, who adopted cruel methods to suppress sign language. The oralists implemented everything they could to banish signs; they asked parents to stop their deaf children from signing and resorted to psychological as well as physical intimidation to stop signing not only in the classroom but outside the school.

Oralism created a large group of Deaf people who could neither read nor write. In spite of undergoing years of speech lessons at the expense of well-rounded educational provisions, many deaf children left school unable to speak in a way that ordinary members of the general public could understand them even a little, and they found well paid employment denied to them and they had to take on lowly paid menial work. The oral failures were many, but the oralists and their system were able to hide this fact.

The strength and influence of the move to oralism following the Milan Congress of 1880 can be seen in the fact that the oralists were able to include in the 1893 Elementary (Blind and Deaf Children) Act clauses that "gave every deaf child the right to two years' trial on the oral method."

The Milanese event was one of the greatest injustices ever done to Deaf people. This dark age of Deaf history began in 1880 and even at present has continued to affect the development of the education for deaf children in every country of the world, even where the education of the deaf is still in its early stages.

Early Voluntary Societies and National Associations for the Deaf

It is known that mission work among the Deaf was in progress in Edinburgh in 1818 with one Miss Elizabeth Burnside playing a prominent role. Miss Burnside noted that a number of Deaf men congregated each evening at the corner of Lawnmarket and Bank Street because they had no premises in which to meet. Miss Burnside therefore obtained a room for which she paid the rent, and acted as doorkeeper. She also preached at the meeting in a conversational way. She later consulted Robert Kinniburgh, the principal of the Edinburgh Deaf and Dumb Institution, who agreed to take over and organise the meeting under the name of the "Edinburgh Deaf and Dumb Meeting". Nothing much is known about what happened afterwards, and it is possible that this affair was short-lived.

It is generally acknowledged that the first true mission for the adult Deaf in the United Kingdom originated in Glasgow in 1822 when John Anderson, then headmaster of the Glasgow Institution for the Deaf and Dumb, held religious services in his own house. This gathering never broke up and continued to grow.

The one driving force that bound the Deaf together in the early years was their use of sign language as their primary means of communication, along with their need to socialise and communicate with each other through that medium. Church services, lectures and various group meetings were conducted in sign language, and this provided and created access to information for the Deaf.

1. The Institution for Providing Employment, Relief and Religious Instruction for the Adult Deaf and Dumb

Many former Deaf pupils who attended the London Asylum for the Deaf and Dumb in the Kent Road continued to socialise with each other during their free time, even though they did not have a base or a building in which to socialise and partake in activities. One day in 1840, a room was found where such Deaf people could meet together every Sunday for worship. This room was in Fetter Lane, and after the church services there the deaf worshippers moved on to a coffee house in Aldersgate for social intercourse. These meetings came to the notice of a man named George Crouch and aroused his interest, which stemmed from the fact that five of his children were deaf. Crouch later got in touch with Matthew Robert Burns (1798-1880) who had played a prominent role along with Alexander Blackwood (1805-1890) and Walter Geikie (1795-1837) in the establishment of the Congregational Church for the Deaf and Dumb in Edinburgh in 1830. Burns' work in Scotland led Crouch to consider the promotion of similar work in London, and so on the evening of 29 January 1841 Crouch and seven other gentlemen formed themselves into a committee, resolved to found a society to be entitled, "Refuge for the Deaf and Dumb", and set out to list its objectives and plans. After much work, a public meeting was held at the Crown and Anchor Tavern in the Strand on 29 August 1841 under the chairmanship of Lord Calthorpe. At that meeting *The Refuge for the Destitute Deaf and Dumb* was formed and the group secured premises at 13 Exeter Hall in September 1841. In March 1842 the group moved to a more spacious building, 22 Bartlett's Buildings in Holborn. The title of the society was changed in 1843 to *The Institution for the Employment, Relief and Religious Education of the Deaf and Dumb*. In 1845 the society moved to an even bigger building at

1 Red Lion Square in Bloomsbury. By 1846 however, the society was in debt by more than £292. The cause of the debt lay in certain seething differences between the Deaf and those who ran the society: one of the consequences of this tension was that the Deaf stopped contributing to or supporting the society and formed *The Society for the Propagation of the Gospel Among the Deaf and Dumb* with Matthew Robert Burns as its figurehead. Despite its great works, the society plunged into further financial difficulties, which continued until 1851 when the lease of the Red Lion Square premises expired. Deprived of its base and in dire financial difficulties to the amount of over £650, the committee of *The Institution for the Employment, Relief and Religious Education of the Deaf and Dumb* had no option but to call for a public meeting on 19 September 1851. The Institution was formally suspended at that meeting.

2. The Royal Association in Aid of the Deaf and Dumb (RADD)

The Institution for the Employment, Relief and Religious Education of the Deaf and Dumb was not entirely defunct. A solitary room used as an office was maintained at 1 Red Lion Square and the outstanding debts were eventually cleared within the next three years. In 1854 a public meeting to reorganise the society was held at Exeter Hall. The meeting resolved that, among others, the following be accepted:

1. For the present the attempt to maintain an industrial school or an establishment in the nature of a home for the Deaf be discontinued:
2. That in the future the society be carried on as an Association in Aid of the Deaf and Dumb;
3. The establishment of religious services for the deaf and dumb throughout the metropolis.

The first missionary of the Association was a former teacher of the deaf, Mr. Chalmers, who was appointed in 1854. Chalmers served only for a year as he returned to teaching in 1855 and was succeeded by Samuel Smith (left) who had been a teacher at the Yorkshire Institution for the Deaf and Dumb in Doncaster. Smith later attended King's College in London to qualify for Holy Orders and was ordained in 1861, after which he was appointed Chaplain to the Association.

In 1860 a group of seven deaf gentlemen formed themselves into a committee with the objective of forming a church for the Deaf. After much debate amid a stream of vociferous objections a Building Fund was started. Much of the work involved with this project was taken on by Arthur Henry Bather (1829-1892), the Honorary Secretary of the Association. Bather and the Building Fund committee's hard work culminated in June 1874 when St. Saviour's Church for the Deaf opened in Oxford Street on a piece of land which had been leased to the Association by the Duke of Westminster for a term of 60 years at a nominal rental of ten shillings per annum. The following year (1875) Queen Victoria consented to become a patron of the Association, whereupon it became *The Royal Association in Aid of the Deaf and Dumb* (RADD).

St. Saviour's, Oxford Street, London

The RADD's aims were both evangelical and welfare in nature. It expanded its activities into the provinces outside London and in the ensuing years it grew to such a size that in the 1980s it had ten centres exclusively devoted to the work of the RADD and a full time staff of 8 chaplains along with 17 lay-workers serving some 8,000 profoundly deaf people and 400 deaf-blind people. In addition, the RADD administered to some 900 to 1,000 deaf people in 22 psychiatric hospitals and nine hospitals for the mentally handicapped within the area of its operations covering Greater London, Essex, Kent and Surrey. The RADD became the largest regional voluntary society for the Deaf in Great Britain. While oralism in the education of the deaf reigned and the ban of sign language among deaf children was strictly enforced, the RADD stood as a beacon in its support for the use of sign language. RADD missioners and workers, whether volunteers or fully employed, were expected to achieve proficiency not only in sign language but also in manualism, and they had to integrate with the Deaf community. Wherever the opportunity or need presented themselves, the RADD advocated the use of, and campaigned for the acceptance of sign language among both the authorities and the public at large; this, however, had always played a minor role behind the major evangelical and welfare services that the RADD provided.

3. The National Deaf and Dumb Society (NDDS)

James Paul (1848-1918, right), a Scottish Deaf gentleman, founded the National Deaf and Dumb Society when he convened a meeting at the Knowsley Hotel, Manchester, on 13 July 1877. Delegates from all existing Deaf societies in Britain were invited, and over 20 representatives attended. A resolution was adopted "that a National Deaf and Dumb Society be formed at once, the objects of which will be to improve the social status of the deaf and dumb and to promote the establishment of missions at home under the designation of the National Deaf and Dumb Society".

A second meeting of the NDDS was held at Glasgow in 1878. The attendance was much larger and included the Rev. Samuel Smith, who agreed to become a member of the Committee. The objects of the NDDS at this conference were defined more briefly as being

George Frederick Healey

Henry Blenkarne Beale

Frederick L. Tavaré

Benjamin H. Payne

"to plant missions and to provide missionaries for the deaf and dumb". After that meeting, no information on the NDDS can be found but it appears that in 1880 it was resolved at a meeting in Dublin that the NDDS should be divided into English and Scottish sections under independent committees. From that point the records of the NDDS were lost, but it is known from various published sources that the aims and progress of the NDDS were stifled by a group of deaf people associated with the RADD, in particular Samuel Bright Lucas (1840-1919) and Thomas Davidson (1842-1910), who could neither see beyond their local interests nor fully comprehend the benefits that a national organisation could offer, and achieve for the Deaf of Britain. The stubbornness and intransigence of such myopic deaf persons from within the RADD caused ill feelings which led to internal tensions within the NDDS, which eventually met its downfall between 1884 and 1885. The collapse of the NDDS so badly affected its founder, James Paul, that he took to local missionary and welfare work instead of serving the Deaf nationwide.

The National Deaf and Dumb Society was the first attempt by a group of Deaf people to create a national organisation to improve the social status of the Deaf, and among its achievements were the founding of both the Durham and Cleveland Mission for the Deaf under the patronage of the Bishop of Durham and the Ayrshire Mission for the Deaf and Dumb, and it was instrumental in forming the Hampshire Mission under the patronage of the Bishop of Winchester. The very existence of the NDDS, however, laid the ground for the foundation of another national organisation for the Deaf. Deaf people such as George Frederick Healey (1843-1927), H. B. Beale (1845-1921) and William Agnew (1846-1914), all of whom were involved with the NDDS, continued to stay in touch and discussed possibilities of re-establishing a national association for the Deaf.

4. The Deaf-Mute Association (DMA)

The rise of oralism following the Milan Congress of 1880 and deaf people's dissatisfaction with the Royal Commission of 1886 on the Blind, Deaf and Dumb as it included only two hearing persons, the Rev. Charles Mansfield Owen and the Rev. William Blomfield Sleight, who had any practical experience of work with the adult Deaf, and the Commission was indifference to the views of the Deaf themselves, led to the founding of that "other national association for the Deaf". The Royal Commission report ignored both the needs of the Deaf and dismissed signs as merely a method of communication in the education of the deaf, and cryptically banning signs by leaving open the method adopted to individual schools' own decision and choice, which was for oralism, oralism and nothing but oralism.

The collapse of the NDDS hit a group of Deaf people very hard, notably George Frederick Healey of Liverpool, Benjamin Hill Payne of Swansea, Frederick Lawrence Tavaré of Manchester, John Thomson Maclean of Greenock, William Agnew of Glasgow, Henry Blenkarne Beale of London and Alexander F. Strathern of Glasgow. This group of Deaf people were determined to maintain contact in the sure hope that one day they would form a national association of the Deaf. They began the *Deaf and Dumb Correspondence Association* (DDCA) in 1886. Around that time an Irish Deaf man, Francis Maginn (1861-1917), left America for Belfast upon the death of his father and became involved with the affairs of the Deaf community of Britain. He joined the DDCA and became active in corresponding with various Deaf people and was more interested in promoting a national organisation to represent the Deaf. He saw the DDCA as the springboard for the creation an organisation of the Deaf. Maginn and Maclean both pushed for the establishment of a new national association.

First issue of The Deaf-Mute

Towards the end of 1887, members of the DDCA agreed that a proper national organisation of the Deaf should be formed, and following various discussions through letters, they decided to set up *The Deaf-Mute Association* (DMA), which was formally instituted on 1 February 1888. It was acknowledged by all involved in this venture that both Maginn and Maclean were the co-founders of the association. Its primary aim was "to further and advance the interests of the Deaf and Dumb throughout the United Kingdom and the World." Strangely, both Maginn and Maclean never met each other in person, let alone keeping in contact through letters. Maginn was elected President and Maclean the Secretary and Treasurer of the association, and as the editor of its monthly magazine, *The Deaf-Mute*, which ran from I July 1888 until 1 August 1889 when its publication abruptly stopped .

Very little is known about the actual activities of the DMA. Reading the pages of its magazine, one gains very little information apart from the list of members of the association. It reads like a roll call of names that represent not only the best in the British Deaf community, but foreigners of renown from the world over. Names of members, both Deaf and hearing, include Thomas Widd, Ernest Abraham, Alex McGregor, W. R. Roe, William Raper, George Frankland, Elizabeth Jane Groom, the Rev. Edward Rowland, James Paul, George Edward, Saul Magson, William Woodall, MP., Thomas Francis Fox, Miss W. Tredennick, Richard Elliott, George E. H. Hogg, W. S. Bessant and Frederick J. Rose.

In its vol.2, no.1 issue of *The Deaf-Mute* dated 1 January 1889, there is a mention of membership numbers: 48 from Scotland, 47 from England, 18 from Ireland, 15 from Wales, 5 from USA and one each from Canada, China and Australia. This gives a total of 136 members after a year. In the very last issue of the same magazine in August 1889, the total rose to 238.

The DMA had a problem in that it attracted the cream of the Deaf world, but could not appeal to the grass-roots Deaf. This was mainly because the DMA relied largely on correspondence, and personal interaction and public meetings were seemingly non-existent. Deaf people in various cities spoke out against the DMA, accusing it of elitism and ignoring their needs and aims. Whether the organisation itself was to be blamed for such a state of affairs remains to be verified, but it can be gleaned from the pages of *The Deaf-Mute* that there was friction between the co-founders, Francis Maginn and John Thomson Maclean, about a month or two before Maclean moved from Greenock to London in April 1889. It appears that these two persons had strong differences of opinion on the name and structure of the organisation.

"Notes from Ireland" was a regular feature of *The Deaf-Mute* and it was contributed by Maginn. This feature was noticeably absent in the March, April and May 1889 issues. It returned for the June 1889 issue, but it appeared to have been published with great reluctance on the part of the editor, Maclean. The clash between Maclean and Maginn centred on Maginn's obsession that both the American system of education was far superior to that of the British and his continual insistence that Britain adopt the American system. Maclean and his allies rejected Maginn's opinion and felt that the British system of education was far superior. Thus a division was created.

A good number of members of the DMA were to meet each other in July 1889 when they all went to Paris for the International Congress of the Deaf. The return train journey from was to change the course of history – the *Deaf-Mute Association* was finished.

Francis Maginn

5. The British Deaf and Dumb Association (BDDA)

Francis Maginn felt that it was high time that Britain formed a national Deaf association and he set about to meet others who would assist him with his idea. He was not the only one with the idea for it, and this idea was already being floated around and discussed by those formerly associated with the NDDS and who were then involved with the DMA. A stroke of luck was to bring everyone together to trigger off the new national association for the Deaf, and this came in the form of a train journey to Paris for the International Congress for the Deaf and Dumb in 1889. The British delegates converged in London to catch a train to Dover and from there they took a ferry to Calais, where they again caught another train to Paris. On that train journey James Paul and Francis Maginn were among the British delegates, and they took to discussing the founding of a new association for the Deaf with other delegates in the party and they all agreed on the need and urgency to establish a national Deaf association. The then existing *Deaf-Mute Association* died on that journey, even though its last issue of *The Deaf-Mute* was published a month later. This might have been because the co-founder, secretary-treasurer and editor, John Thomson Maclean, was totally unaware of the meeting on the train.

On 16-18 January 1890 a National Deaf Conference was convened in the Lecture Hall of St. Saviour's Church in Oxford Street for the purpose of enabling the Deaf to discuss the recommendations of the Royal Commission of 1886 and of its hostile attitude to the manual system of communication and its veiled recommendation in certain passages that both the association and intermarriage of the Deaf should be discouraged. After much discussion and after the presentation of a paper by Francis Maginn entitled *The Proposed National Association of the Deaf*, the meeting unanimously passed a resolution:

> *"In the opinion of this Conference it is advisable that a National Society should be formed, the chief objects of which will be the elevation, education and social status of the deaf and dumb in the United Kingdom."*

A Steering Committee of six hearing men and six Deaf men, which included Maginn, Healey and Agnew, was formed on that day. This Steering Committee met only twice, and each time they met they meticulously planned the way to the official founding of the new organisation and agreed on the proposed constitution and the venue for the first Congress. The title of the new association was open to much debate; Maginn wanted it to be *National Deaf Association*, but the Steering Committee and would-be members decided unanimously on the *British Deaf and Dumb Association* (BDDA) to Maginn's dismay.

William Agnew

The inaugural venue for the new association was the small Lecture Hall of the Church Institute in Albion Place, Leeds, on 24 July 1890 and it was attended by thirty-six (of which four were females). After a short church service, the meeting commenced and was unanimous in adopting the proposals. Those present then paid their entrance fees and first annual subscriptions to the acting treasurer. The Steering Committee was disbanded and the first official election of officers of the BDDA took place.

Charles Gorham

William Blomfield Sleight (hearing) was chosen as the first President and then four regional vice-presidents, all deaf, were elected: Wales - Benjamin H. Payne (1847-1926); England - G. F. Healey; Ireland - Francis Maginn and Scotland - William Agnew. Then James Paul (Ayr) was elected as Honorary Treasurer and Charles Gorham (1861-1922) as Honorary Secretary. Eight members of the executive Committee were also elected on that day to complete the organising body.

Between its foundation in 1890 and 1902 the BDDA saw a rapid expansion of diocesan mission work for the Deaf as a result of representations made by its officials to the bishops of several dioceses. Not only that, new missions and centres for the Deaf (known as Deaf Clubs) sprang up all over the country following the BDDA's efforts and approaches to various bodies. Annual congresses were held and BDDA members were able to participate in discussions of their affairs and pass resolutions for the BDDA to act upon, as well as socialise with each other.

Branches and Regional Councils of the BDDA were established and grew as the years went by. Contact and interaction between the Deaf in various cities of Britain were made easier by participation in the BDDA's national, regional and local activities, which were frequently arranged. Sports, mainly in the form of football and cricket matches, provided opportunities for social gatherings after matches. The Deaf of Britain were more united than never before, and through the BDDA, their views were heard and presented to the authorities.

A mention of the historical link between the BDDA/BDA and sign language must be made here. The pioneers who formed the Association over a century ago were all highly articulate men, very proficient in their use of written English (as can be judged from letters written in *The Times* and other newspapers and magazines of the day). These people were also proud to be known as fingerspellers and sign language users and because of their beliefs and their anger over the way many of them were treated by the Royal Commission, the Association has always had sign language at the forefront of its aims and objectives. Indeed, the very first BDDA Congress in 1890 passed only one resolution:

Members of the BDDA at the 1893 Swansea Congress

"That this Congress of the British Deaf and Dumb Association, held in Leeds, indignantly protests against the imputation of the Right Hon. Earl Granville, in his recent speech in London, that the signer and sign language was barbarous. We consider such a mode of exchanging our ideas as the most natural and indispensable, and that the Combined System of education is by far preferable to the so-called Pure Oral. We are confident that the Combined System is absolutely necessary for the welfare of the deaf and dumb."

The Association never wavered in its resolution and strong conviction that sign language was the best method to be used in the education of the deaf.

A final word on Francis Maginn must be added here. Since he was educated at the National Deaf-Mutes College in Washington D.C., he held the American system in awe and made a lot of effort to have it adopted in Britain. Upon joining *The Deaf-Mute Association*, he tried but failed to create change to the American system. Maginn was so disappointed at the indifference to his desire for change that he went on to create yet another organisation with the help of some other Deaf persons but that too failed. His proposal for the name *National Deaf Association* was also rejected outright. He was later never to play any major role, taking up local missionary work in Belfast and Northern Ireland, and he eventually faded into oblivion for much of his later life.

[In 1971 members of the BDDA voted overwhelmingly to drop the word "Dumb" from its title and the association is now known as the British Deaf Association (BDA).]

6. Royal National Institute for the Deaf (RNID)

In 1909 a deafened and retired banker, Leo Bonn, chanced to meet a teacher of the deaf, Miss Mary Hare (1865-1945), and was persuaded to consider getting involved with a scheme to establish a national institution for the Deaf. Becoming interested, Leo Bonn offered to found and maintain the new organisation for a period of two years. On 9 June 1911 Leo Bonn held a meeting with representatives concerned with the education and welfare of the deaf at his home. At that meeting it was resolved that an organisation to be entitled the National Bureau for Promoting the General Welfare of the Deaf (NBPGWD) should be established with three main objects:

1. To get into touch and co-operate with all existing agencies and charities for the improvement of the deaf.
2. To collect all information available from annual reports, periodicals, daily papers and Government publications and to classify such information and keep it available for members of the public.
3. To make special studies of any problem affecting the deaf and recommend reforms.

The organisation duly established, its first council of management comprised 14 teachers of the deaf, 2 representatives from the National League for Physical Improvement, 2 from the Social Welfare Association, 3 from the BDDA and one from the RADD. The composition of the council had a profound impact on the course the Bureau would take in steering its way into the future – the low number of missioners for the adult deaf on the committee was taken to mean that there was a covert opposition to their presence by teachers of the deaf, who belonged to the oralist cause and who opposed the missioners' sympathy and support for signs. The work of the Bureau suffered greatly from the First World War of 1914-1918, although there exist four Annual Reports for 1912, 1913, 1914 and 1916 which detail the Bureau's activities.

After the war, in 1923 the Bureau was in need of re-organisation to meet the changing demands and needs of the deaf, and its committee applied for the free use of income from a trust fund established by Leo Bonn. The trustees of the fund, however, considered that the Bureau had insufficient support for its work from the various national organisations and consequently refused to pay the Bureau the income from the trust fund. A row ensued and the trustees of the fund gave formal notice to the Bureau that after 31 March 1924 the income from the trust would no longer go to the Bureau.

Faced with possible closure, the Bureau was saved by a BDDA stalwart and a great supporter of sign language, Ernest Ayliffe who was also then the superintendent of the Liverpool Adult Deaf and Dumb Benevolent Society. Ayliffe recommended that a "Conference of Committees" be convened to consider the question of a National Committee to create interest in the work.

On 19 May 1924, at a meeting attended by some 250 representatives at Kingsway Hall in London, two resolutions were passed. The first declared the need for the reconstruction of the Bureau so that the claims of the deaf would be authoritatively expressed and nationally met. The second resolution changed the name of the Bureau to "The National Institute for the Deaf" (NID) and made interim arrangements relating to the management of the newly constituted body. The Bureau's acting secretary, A. J. Story, had successfully secured the agreement of the trustees of the National Bureau to pay the income from their funds to the new NID for a period of three years, and then permanently if the NID's progress justified the payment.

As from 31 March 1924 the NBPGWD became defunct and from 1 April 1924 the NID came into existence. Later, in the same year, A. J. Story accepted an invitation to become the permanent secretary of the NID and retained the position until his death in 1938. The NID became an incorporated body in 1948. In 1961, on the occasion of the 50th anniversary of its establishment, H.M. Queen Elizabeth II commanded that the NID should incorporate the word "Royal" into its title and it became known as the RNID.

<u>Growth of Provincial Local Voluntary Societies and Missions for the Adult Deaf</u>

The chronology of the growth of missions and voluntary societies for the Deaf in Britain up to the end of the 19th century is as follows:

Glasgow Mission to the Deaf & Dumb	1822
Edinburgh Deaf & Dumb Benevolent Society	1835
Association for the Deaf & Dumb	1840
Manchester & Salford Deaf and Dumb Benevolent Association	1846
Manchester Society for the Promotion of Temporal Welfare of the Adult Deaf and Dumb	1850
Leeds United Institution for the Blind, the Deaf and the Dumb	1850
Oldham (then a branch of the Man. & Sal. D & D Benevolent Assoc.)	1851
Dundee & Tayside Mission to the Adult Deaf & Dumb	1853
Doncaster (then just a group of former pupils of the Yorkshire Institution)	1855
Kinghan Mission to the Deaf & Dumb, Belfast	1857
Ashton (then a branch of the Man. & Sal. D & D Benevolent Assoc.)	1857
Bolton & Bury (then a branch of the Man. & Sal. D & D Benevolent Assoc.)	1860
Halifax (then a branch of the Leeds United etc.)	1860
Sheffield (then a branch of the Leeds United etc.)	1861
Hull	1864
Bradford (then a branch of the Leeds United etc.)	1864
Liverpool Adult Deaf and Dumb Benevolent Society	1864
Birmingham	1867
Stoke on Trent	1868
Nottingham	1868
Cardiff (with branches at Merthyr, 1872; Aberdare, 1874; Pontypridd, 1881)	1869
Greenock (then a branch of the Glasgow Mission)	1870
Derby	1873
Lewisham (originally St. Barnabas Church, a branch of the Assoc. of the D & D, St. Saviour's)	1873
West Ham (a branch of the Assoc. of the D & D, St. Saviour's)	1873
Paisley (then a branch of the Glasgow Mission)	1874
Bristol	1876
Northumberland & Durham	1876
Winchester Diocesan Mission for the Deaf & Dumb	1878
Southampton	1879
Nottingham Mission to the Adult Deaf & Dumb	1880
Ayrshire Mission for the Deaf & Dumb (Kilmarnock)	1881

Deaf Sport, Deaf Drama & the Deaf Churches and their links with BSL

Deaf sport, Deaf drama and the Deaf church all pre-date the formation of national deaf organisations, and are largely responsible for providing many participants with a sense of Deaf identity that they lacked in the hearing world. The common denomination for participation in these activities was the ability in fingerspelling or knowledge of sign language.

Deaf Sport

Although the history of Deaf Sport is difficult to trace with absolute certainty, it is likely that Deaf sport had its origins in the first schools for deaf children. For example, school records show that pupils in both the Glasgow Institution for the Deaf and Dumb at Langside and the Manchester Institution for the Deaf and Dumb were taking part in sports activities in the 1860s. The Yorkshire Institution for the Deaf and Dumb at Doncaster had introduced gymnastics, soccer and cricket to the school-children by the early 1870s. These sports activities had originally been introduced for the purpose of building up pupils' strength as many of the children who attended the schools were poor and physically deficient.

Manchester Deaf School Athletic Club 1874

There is no dispute, though, the first adult deaf sports club. This honour belongs to the Glasgow Deaf and Dumb Football Club which began in 1871. Its first matches were played against hearing teams. It was not until 1888 that it started to play against other Deaf teams. It is the oldest Deaf sports club in the world still in existence.

Also in 1871 an adult rugby club comprising school staff and older pupils was formed by the Manchester Institution but the first proper adult deaf

Liverpool Deaf & Dumb Cricket Club, 1878

sports club was not formed until 1876 as the Manchester Deaf and Dumb Sports Club. In the same year the Derby Deaf and Dumb Cricket and Football Club was established. These two adult sports clubs were set up directly as a result of close links with the schools in those cities. A similar situation took place in Liverpool with the formation of Liverpool Deaf and Dumb Cricket and Football Club in 1878.

The *first organised* inter-club sports match was a cricket match in 1882 between Derby and Sheffield, which was won by Derby by one run!

The first organised tournament or competition was in Scotland by the newly formed Scottish Deaf Football Association in 1889. Edinburgh beat Glasgow in the final by 3-1 in front of 2000 spectators at Falkirk.

The first international sports event was a football match between Scotland and England in 1891. In reality, all the players were drawn from northern English Deaf football clubs, as London at that time had no Deaf football teams except in schools. The novelty of the first international sports match proved attractive to many Deaf people starved of popular pastimes, and special excursion trains were put on to transport supporters to Glasgow from Manchester, Nottingham and Yorkshire. Many were willing to put up with a slow eleven hours journey. It must have been quite an experience to see so many deaf people signing away on those trains. They were rewarded by excellent weather conditions on 28 March 1891 when the match finally got under way at Ibrox Park, Glasgow, the current home of Glasgow Rangers FC, in front of a crowd exceeding 3000. The result was a 3-3 draw between the two teams.

Deaf sport reached out to thousands of deaf men, women and children and was largely responsible for the development of BSL into a socially acceptable language and helped to foster a cohesive and strong sense of community.

Deaf Drama

Like Deaf sport, drama activities originated in the early residential schools for the deaf, usually arising from the desire of various headmasters to mount exhibitions or performances by their pupils in public to demonstrate their intelligence and as a means of securing donations to keep their schools going. As Deaf people left schools and joined social activities organised by adult deaf missions or societies, drama activities came into being as a form of entertainment.

From the 1850s onwards many adult deaf missions held regular soirees, readings or performances of essays in which the audiences enjoyed being entertained in fingerspelling or sign language.

Because many adult deaf people enjoyed dramatic performances conducted in sign language, influenced the British Deaf and Dumb Association was influenced to hold Drama competitions as regular feature of its congresses.

The interest in drama or theatrical performances continues to this day with performances in mainstream theatres interpreted in sign language, thereby giving to Deaf people access to plays and opera.

Deaf Churches

The influence of the Deaf Churches, particularly in the early 19th century, may have provided the strongest support on sign language as a means of participation. When deaf people finished their education many sought out the company of other fellow ex-pupils in order to keep up their contact. Their social interaction using sign language was limited to gatherings in streets (hence introducing the lamp-post into deaf folklore; meetings around lamp-posts were common because their light enabled visual communication to take place in the dark). It is equally true that places for the Deaf to gather as a social unit were few in number and many Deaf people met in public houses and took to drinking.

Liverpool

The first 'official' gatherings of deaf adults were generally termed 'prayer meetings' at which (usually) a former teacher or headmaster would provide bible readings or lessons in the scriptures, taking up from where these had been left off in school. The first such gathering was held in Glasgow in 1822.

The first Deaf church to be established was the Congregational Church for the Deaf and Dumb in Edinburgh in 1830. This is still in existence today, and is the oldest church for the Deaf of any denomination anywhere in the world.

In 1840, St. Saviour's Church for the Deaf and Dumb was established in Oxford Street, London. This developed during the 19th century into a popular meeting place for Deaf people and its services were always conducted in fingerspelling/sign language. Many prominent deaf people of the time attended regularly; occasionally, the church services were graced by the attendance of Royalty. Princess Alexandra, as Princess of Wales, attended frequently, enjoying the sermons and prayers in a language she could follow.

Many members of various Deaf churches scattered around Britain formed local and national Teetotal Societies and launched campaigns to "rescue deaf people" from public houses and introduce them to the more "sober and gentlemanly" environment of the church. Members of the Teetotal Societies, both deaf and hearing, were fiercely anti-drink and preached strongly against the "demon drink". The original National Deaf and Dumb Teetotal Society was a fearsome and overzealous movement, where members often entered public houses to drag out Deaf people in order to convert them to their "Christian" ways. This national organisation, however, collapsed as its members were unable to devote as much time as was

needed to enforce its aims. In 1879 John Jennings (1833-1884, top left) revived and re-organised the movement under the title of "Anchor of Hope", of which he was President and Samuel Bright Lucas (1840-1919, bottom left) was vice-President. This organisation adopted a gentler and more humane approach and was in many ways successful. Its success enabled over 100 deaf people to leave the public houses to join other Deaf people to help Jennings set up the South London Mission to the Deaf and Dumb, which was established in Ossery Road, off Old Kent Road, in 1882.

History, however, records that the success of many campaigns by the Teetotal Societies was minimal, and many deaf people continue to enjoy meeting in public houses as venues of social interaction.

Nowaday the various Deaf churches that sprang up have evolved a specialised form of sign language that is relevant to only church services, and which is not commonly found outside the church. The Deaf Christian Fellowship has produced many videotapes in BSL and some sects such as Jehovah's Witnesses and the Church of the Latter Day Saints have re-formed the bible reading classes and prayer meetings that were very popular in the 19th century. These classes have a large proportion of hearing people as well as Deaf people. Many hearing churchgoers are learning sign language so that the classes can be conducted in that medium.

Taken altogether, Deaf sport, Deaf drama and Deaf churches are some of the main reasons why the Deaf community remained strong during the oralist years and also why BSL could not be eradicated.

The Deafblind and Additionally Handicapped Deaf

It is difficult to chart the early history of Deaf persons who were both blind and educationally challenged, especially in the area of learning difficulties. In the case of the Deafblind, there was an excellent book published in 2000 entitled *Touch, Touch and Touch Again*. Sponsored by SENSE and written by Doreen Woodford, the book outlines the lives of Deafblind individuals and their teachers between the 18th century and the beginning of the 20th century.

Of all deaf-blind individuals, James Mitchell (1796-1869, right) of Nairn, Scotland, is the most famous. He was born deaf and blind and never attended a school. His family guided him throughout life, allowing him to learn and develop by touching and feeling. Mitchell was taken to London to be operated on by the then eminent surgeon, James Wardrop. The operation was doomed when Mitchell writhed and shook in agony and could not be held still. Mitchell lived until he was 73 years old and he was a very well-known and popular local character.

There were attempts to educate the deaf-blind in school settings, and the earliest known moves were made in Scotland at the Royal Blind Asylum in Edinburgh and at the Glasgow Blind Asylum where there exists reports of individual deaf-blind children being successfully educated, albeit to a certain limit.

In England, the Manchester Institution for the Deaf and Dumb took in a number of deaf-blind pupils under the headmastership of Andrew Patterson during the period 1841-1883. The most famous of these pupils were Mary Bradley (c1840-1866, right) and Joseph Hague (1844-1879). These two pupils were taught by Patterson who was able to make them aware not only of things surrounding them, but of communication and language. Patterson's pioneering work with his deaf-blind pupils opened up opportunities for the deaf-blind to be independent to a large extent. It was reported that Joseph Hague was quite a stubborn and determined person who insisted on doing what other non-blind deaf pupils did.

The Edgbaston Institution for the Deaf and Dumb also took on deaf-blind pupils along the same line as that of Manchester, and eventually a good number of schools for the deaf took on deaf-blind pupils who were able to enjoy almost the same conditions of living as the non-blind deaf pupils.

For many of those deaf children who were mentally challenged life meant confinement in mental hospitals, along with Deaf people who were wrongly diagnosed as mentally handicapped when their only problem was deafness. Deaf children whose only problem was that they "learned slowly" were often wrongly classified as "idiotic" and "mentally retarded". Specialised schools to cater for such children did not exist until 1899 when

education authorities held discussions on the classification and groupings of deaf children in various London Board schools. It was decided that a special school should be established to cater for those Deaf children who were "on account of their mental deficiency unsuitable for instruction in the oral classes and who had to be taught on the sign system." This school was established at Homerton College in Hackney in 1900 and Frank G. Barnes (1866-1932, left) was appointed headmaster.

These *"defective"* deaf children, as the authorities of the day labelled them, were to find a great friend in Frank Barnes and members of his staff, for they were great pioneers in the education and care of the additionally handicapped deaf children. All children were encouraged to mix with each other, communicate with each other and study together. The sighted and the blind communicated through the deaf-blind manual alphabet, the fast learner patiently showing the slow learner the ropes, everyone encouraged to help each other outside of class as well as inside, and they were educated as far as could be humanely possible. To broaden their outlook of life school trips were arranged, and these children travelled often. Barnes and his teaching staff devoted their efforts to prepare them for life and employment outside school.

Ivy Swann (deaf) & Albert Criscuoli (deaf-blind) of Homerton College at a school outing, communicating using the deafblind alphabet..

The work at Homerton showed that the additionally handicapped deaf could have a good quality of education and life rather than being dumped into local mental asylums. Frank Barnes and the school teaching staff received acclaim for their work and this gave a lot of hope to the Deaf who needed such education along with special care. Homerton College closed in 1921, and the school moved to "Rayners" in Penn, Buckinghamshire.

There was later another school catering for the same kind of additionally handicapped deaf children in Yorkshire. This was Bridge House School near Harewood. It was established in 1949 under the headmastership of William Edward Wood who later went on to become the first headmaster of Burwood Park Technical Secondary School for the Deaf in Walton-on-Thames in 1955.

Around the 1950s the increasing number of additionally-handicapped children finding places in the residential schools led to several of these schools specialising in the education of these children. Margate grouped together its existing "C" classes (in the A, B, C stream) into an Opportunity Department, which eventually became famous throughout the UK and elsewhere. Today it has become the totality of the school, which takes in every kind of multi-handicapped deaf children, and includes specialised work with the deaf-blind. Manchester (Cheadle Hulme) followed a similar path with similar results. Many other schools found themselves with a class, or a whole department, additionally-handicapped Deaf children. Some schools "specialised" gaining experience with one group. The work of schools for children with language disorders and cerebrally palsied should be noted, as these had expertise with deaf children.

The development of Makaton, primarily intended for deaf children, though it was not wholly successful, led to it being of inestimable value to all children with learning problems.

The lack of specialised teacher training of deaf children with other disabilities was a constant concern, and still not yet totally resolved at present. The work of two parents of deafblind children in first encouraging teachers to train in the USA and then in getting formalised training in the UK is noteworthy, as are workshops and courses run by the British Association of Teachers of the Deaf (BATOD) and other organisations. It was parents who, striving for provision for their deafblind children, founded the National Association for Deaf and Blind Rubella Handicapped Children. Strengthened by the work of Peggy Freeman and Margaret Brock, themselves parents of deaf-blind children, a parent group pushed for the development that would benefit deaf-blind children, and formed a society, SENSE, now an influential force.

The number of special schools for deaf-blind children suddenly declined in the 1980s as various local authorities planned their own educational provisions

Right - a class of deafblind children at the turn of the 20th century.

Left - two deafblind girls, Isabelle Birrell seated at the typewriter.

Ear Trumpets

These instruments were basically simple ear horns of conical shape. They developed over time and became more sophisticated and practical before the advent of electrical and battery-powered hearing aids. The earliest reference in literature to an ear trumpet and its practical application is found in the work of that astute observer and chronicler of scientific progress, Athanasius Kircher, who in one of his important volumes, *Phonurgia Nova* (1673), described several interesting developments of sound-trumpet or simple hearing device. This was an elliptical double-ended tube, with the speaker's voice transmitted through one end and the listener's ear applied to the other end.

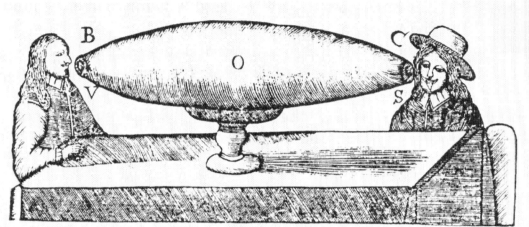

Ellipsis Otica—Earliest form of hearing device.

In Britain, ear trumpets were sold by two renowned companies: F. Charles Rein & Son of London and T. Hawksley of 357 Oxford Street, London. Ear horns, trumpets and speaking tubes were often beautifully crafted and decorated as well as being practical. The examples shown here are taken from the 1895 catalogue of T. Hawksley of 357 Oxford Street, London.

CLASS B (Series 1).—SIMPLE RIGID CONES.

Made of cardboard, ebonite or gun-metal, with sound collectors of various sizes and shapes, gradually tapering to the ear-pieces.

63

CLASS B.—CORNETS.

The CORNET is a very convenient and elegant hearing instrument. It consists of a cone with expanded orifice accurately fitting around the ear, the small end coming *under* the lobe to the *front*, and then turning into the ear; *no other support is required*. They are made upon wax models which have been moulded to the ear and side of the head of the wearer. The material is copper, silver or vulcanite, which may be either gilded, plated, bronzed or japanned. Single or in pairs.

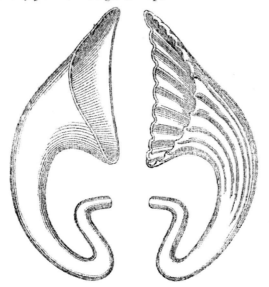

The above cornets made in vulcanite of various colours are much lighter and *acoustically* more perfect. For ladies they afford the most ready means of concealment, as the hair or cap may be easily arranged to hide them, and for gentlemen either kind is readily put on or taken off.

CLASS B.—CORNETS—*continued*.

vulcanite, which render the articulation of a speaker with greater purity than those made of metal; though the latter where durability is required are to be preferred. Vulcanite cornets will not withstand falling on stone floors, or being sat upon if carried in the pocket.

As seen in the above illustrations these self-supporting cornets may be rendered works of art by being tastefully decorated with repoussé work, engraving, or embossing, and the sound collector covered by a grille. Parts may be enamelled a flesh tint, or to match the colour of the hair.

Of various shapes and sizes, tastefully trimmed in Leather, Black Silk and
Lace to disguise their appearance, and named after their designers.
Suitable for use in public.

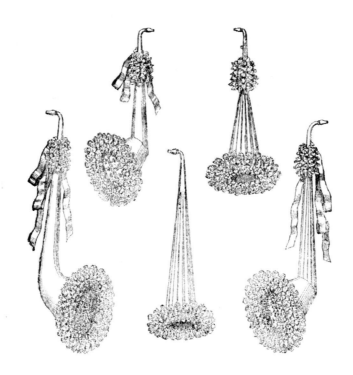

CLASS B.—AURICLES.

The AURICLE is a very powerful form of hearing instrument. The
principle is a metal cone having a large sound-collector doubled
on itself. They are covered in silk or japanned, and attached
by an adjustable spring, going over or behind the head; they
require to be carefully fitted to the ears so as to avoid undue
pressure; are light in weight and easily concealed by the hair,
wig, &c.

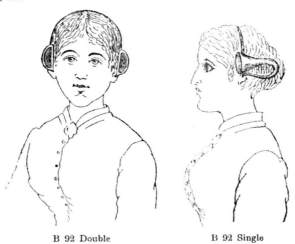

B 92 Double   B 92 Single

When only one auricle is required the spring attaching it to the
ear must pass over the head; those with a spring at the back of
the head are in all cases double. The advantage of the spring
being at the back of the head is that the weight of the auricles is
sustained by the soft ribbon which alone passes over the head, and
the spring keeps the nipples in contact with the ears.

CLASS F.—REFLECTORS.

Consists of appliances by which sound is *reflected* to the entrance of the external ear, without the intervention of any nipple or tube fitting into the auditory canal. They form an efficient substitute for the hand, and are made in ebonite, metal, &c.

Ear Shells in
use.

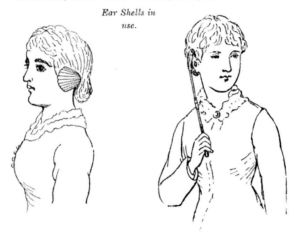

CLASS D.—PORTABLE RESONATING INSTRUMENTS.

"Adjusted" or "adjustable" to certain notes; in gun metal, plated or japanned.

Adjusted Instruments.

D 51

D 51 " Rawlins' " Resonator, consists of a large flattened oval collector which may be suspended to the coat or watch pocket by means of a hook, and a thin flexible tube passing to the ear. This instrument need not be conspicuous, it may be covered by the coat or gown and is extremely powerful

G 510 A powerful board-room or dining-table instrument, consisting of an inverted parabolic collector supported on a heavy brass base, with a long conical tube fitted with either single or bin-aural ear-mount. The collector may be either parabolic or hyperbolic, and of any size, finished to special designs, and, when used for the dining table, adapted for the reception of flowers, fruit, &c.

"THE STANILAND," in use as a *Table Instrument.*

"The Staniland."

G 425 This instrument is one of the most powerful and durable that is made, and is specially suitable for the Colonies, where a nice adjustment between speaker and listener is not always obtainable. It is a resonator in principle, and may be used by resting its flat side on a table, where it will receive sounds from an area of 180°, *i.e.* half a circle, or carried by a leathern strap over the shoulders as a race glass, which in size and shape it somewhat resembles. From one side an elastic tube, which is easily moved in any direction, conveys the sound to the ear, or it may be made bin-aural and self-supporting, as shown in illustration, which, leaving both hands free, adds greatly to its power and usefulness. At committee meetings the single tube may be kept fitted

to the ear by means of a spring passing over the head, or, as described above, both ears may be used. It is equally useful in the domestic circle, in walking or in the saddle, as the leather-covered collector only requires to be brought to the front of the body and the tube raised to the ear.

"THE STANILAND" in use as carried on the person.

G 425

On removing the strap used to suspend the instrument in walking, the collector may be laid in the lap or on a table, or on the book rest when used in church, chapel, &c. The elastic tube is fitted to the side of the collector by means of a long screw, so that it is easily turned in any direction, and for packing removed altogether. The collector is flat in section, and, as before stated, much resembles in shape an ordinary field glass.

CLASS A. CONVERSATION TUBES.

Wood, and Horn Mouth-Pieces.

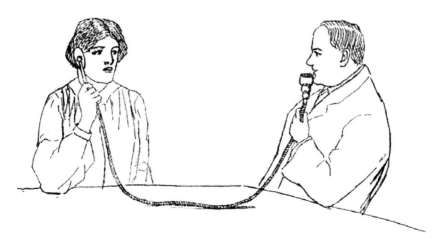

The illustration shows the most efficient and comfortable way of using these tubes. A disc ear-piece is shown, and the speaker should hold the mouth-piece so that he speaks across not into it.

All fitted with rotating ear-pieces and Hawksley's prepared conical and cylindrical tubes.

CLASS G.—TABLE INSTRUMENTS

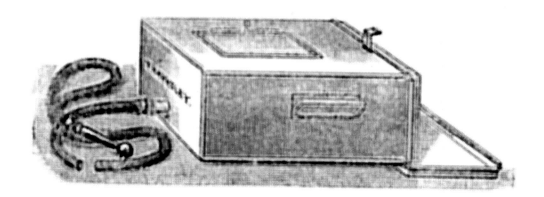

Improved Hearing Appliance (Budgen's Patent).

This appliance is designed for severe forms of deafness, where the maximum of loudness and clearness of voice sounds is required, and the least instrumental resonance. In form it resembles a camera, being square, covered with leather, and with a handle for carrying it. At one end is a hinged door which serves for closing the instrument, or, to increase or to diminish the amount of sound admitted. At the other end is a plug mount to receive the tube which conveys the sound to the ear.

This tube may be from three to five, or more feet in length, is removable, and when not in use may be stowed in a chamber on one side of the box as shown in the illustration.

One construction of this instrument is suitable for listening to the voice when there are no disturbing external sounds, the other when the noise of street or other traffic is present. Various shapes and sizes are adopted, as to imitate a deed box, or small handbag, or camera. Instead of a tube from the sound collector, a microphone and telephone may be adapted, which together with the dry cells may be stowed in the case enclosing the collector.

This appliance was invented by Mr. Budgen to enable him to carry on his office work with ease, he keeps it on his writing desk, and using it, he can hear ordinary conversation. It should be of great use to solicitors, if defective in hearing, and those engaged in seeing clients. An apparatus can be fixed in church or chapel, in the office, and at home, one tube only being necessary for the three receivers. The inventor says, that " this appliance makes just this difference to me—that with it I can hear, without it I cannot, and there must be many situated like myself."

The above is one of many arrangements for enabling one severely deaf person to hear conversation at the table. The figure to the right is addressing his hostess by a form of sound-collector that is self-supporting, the other collectors on the table require to be *held* to the mouth and are placed between guests on either side. The fruit dish on the table has no acoustical properties but simply holds the tubes steady, under other circumstances weights are used. A *bin-aural* ear-piece, which is self-supporting, may be used, thereby leaving the hands free. Price according to number of tube mouthpieces attached.

During the late 19th century, when developments and improvements of table instruments were being made, schools for the deaf both adapted and used them for speech and aural training among deaf pupils.

Speech and aural training at Homerton School in 1904

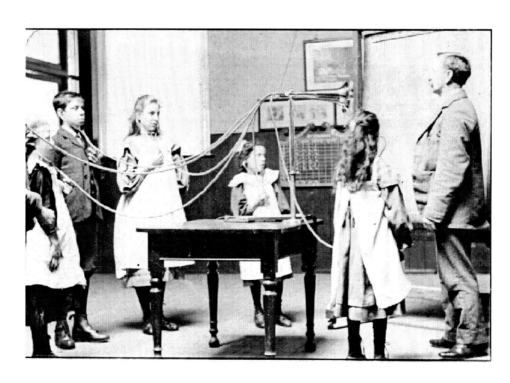

Speech training in a school for the deaf around the turn of the 20th century

Deaf People in Workhouses

One of the most interesting aspects of census returns from 1841 is that they give Deaf historians the ability to gauge the socio-economic status of a large number of Deaf people. This is particularly true if one looks at the returns from individual workhouses throughout the country. These give a good indication of the numbers of Deaf people out of work and living in poverty, which necessitated their entitlement to Poor Law Relief.

On 29 July 1861 a paper, "Index to Paupers in Workhouses 1861", was submitted to Parliament. This paper came from *"Returns from each Workhouse in England and Wales, of the Name of every Adult Pauper in each Workhouse who has been an inmate of the Workhouse during a continuous Period of Five Years; stating the Amount of Time that each of such Inmates shall have been in the Workhouse, and the Reason assigned why such Persons are unable to maintain themselves...."*

This index of paupers in workhouses names some 14,200 adult paupers aged 16 years and upwards in England and Wales, who had been in receipt of parish relief for a continuous period of five years or more.

From a statistical point of view the value of the report cannot be overstated. It was submitted to parliament on 29 July 1861, and was ordered to be published the following day. The information it contains dovetails nicely with the 1861 census returns. The census that year was conducted on Sunday 7 April, so it is may be that the information-gathering processes for the report and the census would have overlapped. The accuracy of the information contained in the report can be proved quite simply by comparing it with the census returns.

It is interesting to note that approximately 42% of the 14,200 were in the workhouses mainly because of old age and infirmity; about 35% were there because of insanity or mental disease, and of the rest (about 23%), among the unusual (or least common) reasons was that of being orphaned. It is interesting, at this late date, to note there are a few cases of wives having been admitted because their husbands had been sentenced to transportation.

What is more pertinent to Deaf History is that a 10% sample of the full index has been published. This has thrown up 27 names of persons described as 'deaf and dumb' or 'very deaf' as the cause for their being in the workhouse, so of the full number of 14,200 persons, there would in proportion be at least 270 who were 'deaf and dumb'.

It should be remembered that this Parliamentary Report only covered people over the age of 16 and who had been in a workhouse for 5 years or more, which meant that deaf children and those having temporary or short stays were excluded. The figure of 14,200 was only 20% of the total workhouse population of 70,000, meaning that the other 80% were short-term inmates or children. If we apply the same percentage of Deaf people in the sample to the total, this would mean that there could have been as many as 1,300 Deaf people (including children) in workhouses throughout the country – quite a large group living a tough life. If one sets this figure against the total Deaf population figure of 19,501 for 1861 in the book *Deaf Mutism* written by W. H. Addison and J. Kerr-Love (1896), this indicates that at least 6.7% of the total Deaf population above the age of 15 were institutionalised in workhouses.

To back this up, a small survey of a number of workhouse census records for 1861 was conducted. Those workhouses that were surveyed came from (a) St. Pancras Workhouse in London; (b) four of the Manchester area workhouses and (c) 5 of the 15 workhouses in Shropshire. The results of this small survey are shown below:

St. Pancras Workhouse: 4 Deaf and Dumb inmates
Chorlton, Oldham, Ashton-on-Lyne and Salford workhouses: 6 in total (one had none; Ashton had a married couple!)
Shrewsbury and other Shropshire workhouses: 3 in total (three had none)

The census records are not always legible or easy to read, nor were some of them very informative. Shrewsbury workhouse census records did not even list the names of the inmates, just their initials. In addition, a check on the Manchester Institution for the Deaf and Dumb's Pupil Roll for 1860-2 showed that just four new pupils in that period were directly admitted to the institution from workhouses. It is therefore fair to make an assumption based on available records that the poorhouses/workhouses in the 19th century had quite a number of inmates classified as Deaf and Dumb who were there because they were unable to support themselves.

This assumption is borne out by a second Return of Blind and Deaf-Mute Persons (England, Wales and Ireland) presented to the House of Commons in September 1887. This shows that in England and Wales alone there were 1289 Deaf and Dumb people in workhouses, plus another 586 not in workhouses but having poor law relief. The 1901 census returns were more specific in how people were classified and counted, and this classification was further clarified in 1911 to include the totally deaf as well as deaf and dumb, and gave a total of 41,771 deaf people in England and Wales.

The actual numbers of deaf people in workhouses will never be known because there were many individuals who were truly deaf but were wrongly classified as imbeciles or lunatics. By trawling through the census return, one could come close to obtaining more pertinent statistics. The known numbers from the 1901 census return for English and Welsh workhouses are given here on a county-by-county basis rather than on individual workhouse basis.

ENGLAND

Bedfordshire	79	Berkshire	147
Buckinghamshire	96	Cambridgeshire	81
Cheshire	302	Cornwall	163
Herefordshire	51	Huntingdonshire	29
Kent	545	Lancashire	2064
Lincolnshire	188	London	2057
Middlesex	309	Norfolk	203
Northamptonshire	129	Nottinghamshire	211
Rutland	8	Shropshire	112
Somerset	214	Staffordshire	604
Suffolk	179	Surrey	256
Sussex	316	Warwickshire	607
Westmoreland	39	Wiltshire	105
Yorkshire	1665		

WALES

Breconshire	15	Caernarvonshire	58
Carmarthenshire	88	Monmouthshire	105
Montgomeryshire	35		

The above sample counties give a total of 11,060 deaf workhouse inmates in 1901. This figure, consisting of 10,759 deaf inmates in England and 301 inmates in Wales, is merely the minimum known figure, but if applied to an estimated population figure of 40,000 deaf people in 1901, it produces the astonishing figure of 27.7% of the total deaf population being subject to poor law relief.

Workhouse Life

Although they were not prisons, workhouses were a painful experience for many people.

Upon entering the workhouse, paupers were stripped, bathed, and issued with a workhouse uniform. Their own clothes would be washed and disinfected and then put into store along with any other possessions they had and only returned to them when they left the workhouse.

Husbands, wives and children were separated as soon as they entered the workhouse and could be punished if they even tried to speak to one another. (In 1847 this was relaxed slightly in the case of married couples over the age of sixty who could request to share a separate bedroom.) For a Deaf family dependent on sign language communication, being separated from fellow sign language users was an extra hardship. In the case of the married couple discovered in the Ashton-under-Lyne workhouse census records, there is an additional disadvantage for the husband as he was listed as Deaf, Dumb and nearly Blind and, no doubt, he would have relied on the Deaf-Blind manual alphabet. If he was separated from his wife he would most likely be isolated.

Once inside the workhouse, an inmate's only possessions was an uniform and a bed in a large dormitory. Beds were simply constructed with a wooden or iron-frame, and could be as little as two feet wide. Bedding, at least in the 1830s and 1840s, was generally a mattress and cover, both filled with straw. Blankets and sheets were later introduced. Bed-sharing, particularly amongst children, was common though it was prohibited for adult paupers in the late nineteenth century.

For vagrants and casuals, the 'bed' could be a wooden box rather like a coffin, or even just a raised wooden platform, or the bare floor serving as the bed.

The inmates' toilet facility was often a simple privy – a cess-pit with a simple cover having a hole in it on which to sit – shared perhaps by as many as 100 inmates. Dormitories were usually provided with chamber pots or, after 1860, earth closets (boxes containing dry soil, which could afterwards be used as fertiliser).

Once a week the inmates were bathed (usually superintended – another assault on their privacy and dignity) and the men shaved.

The daily routine for inmates proposed by the Poor Law Commissioners during the 1840s was as follows:

	Hour of Rising	Interval for Breakfast	Time for setting to work	Interval for Dinner	Time for leaving off Work	Interval for Supper	Time for going to Bed
25 March to 29 September	6 o'clock	From ½ past 6 to 7	7 o'clock	From 12 to 1	6 o'clock	6 to 7	8
29 September to 25 March	7 o'clock	From ½ past 7 to 8	8 o'clock	From 12 to 1	6 o'clock	6 to 7	8

The ringing of the workhouse bell announced meal breaks during which the rules required that "silence, order and decorum shall be maintained".

One source of insight into life in the workhouse comes from the lists of rules under which the workhouses operated. These were often printed and prominently displayed in the workhouse, and also read out aloud each week so that the illiterate could have no excuse for disobeying them. Workhouses inmates were fed on diets that were very detailed and rigorously enforced, although children were given a slightly better diet with more meat and milk.

Life for children in workhouses, although tough, was mainly short term in that they were almost always sold off by the workhouses to factories and mills. Workhouses needed to earn money and, apart from materials made in their workshops such as oakum, the most valuable commodity that workhouses had were their children.

Many textile, cotton and silk mills were desperate for labour, which was in severe shortage, especially in rural areas where there was competition from agriculture. To overcome this labour shortage factory owners had to find other ways of obtaining workers. One solution to the problem was to buy children from orphanages and workhouses. This involved the children signing contracts that virtually made them the property of the factory owners. Owners of huge textile mills purchased large numbers of children from workhouses in all the towns and cities and transported them hundreds of miles to where they were needed.

Often these children were sold without the knowledge of their parents. Because of the system of separating husbands from wives, children from parents, it might be some time before parents found out their children had been sold, and workhouse officials would never tell them where they had gone. It seems likely that some of these children included deaf children, especially if they were strong and able-bodied.

Although schools for the deaf such as the Manchester Institution for the Deaf and Dumb accepted children from workhouses, there were long periods or gaps between children being sent to such institutions from workhouses. For example, only 5 deaf children were sent to the Manchester Institution from Cheshire workhouses between 1823 and 1893 compared with 12 in 1893/4 after the introduction of the Elementary Education (Blind and Deaf Children) Act of 1893, which made it compulsory for deaf children to receive an education.

These statistics clearly tell an unknown story of deaf children being sold into the "care" of mill owners and being separated from their parents. Is it any wonder that in 1823 numerous deaf workers were found in cotton mills in Manchester and Salford? Were these workers there as a result of being sold into the employ of the cotton mill owners?

Some children might be sent miles away from where they had lived. It was not uncommon for "cartloads" of pauper children to be taken from the Bristol workhouse to work in mills in Derbyshire or from the St. Pancras workhouse to Nottinghamshire. Indeed, there still exists a contract between the St Pancras workhouse and the owner of a great cotton mill in Nottingham to supply him with their workhouse children. There is a story written by a female ex-inmate of a workhouse, whose children were sold without her knowledge, on her search to find them after getting herself out of the workhouse. (Lavalette, 2001).

To be sold into virtual slavery must have been a terrible experience for the deaf child and we can only be thankful that the practice no longer exists. It would be marvellous for Deaf History if one could find a true-life account of a workhouse deaf child.

Among the famous Deaf people who lived in workhouses were the deaf-blind Joseph Hague (1844-1879) and the renowned biblical scholar John Kitto (1804-1854, right) who entered The Hospital of the Poor's Portion in Plymouth in 1819 and did not leave until 1824, when he was trained in dentistry.

School Records and Stainer's Homes

A further indicator of the socio-economic status of Deaf people in the 19th century comes from an examination of school admission records combined with an account of the brief existence of what has come to be called 'Stainer's Homes', a series of boarding establishments for deaf schoolchildren from very poor families in London.

Many of the surviving admission records (or pupil rolls) of 19th century institutions for the deaf or schools contain a wealth of detail about the family backgrounds of the children who were admitted to these schools.

For many years, deaf school-children at the old, great institutions were mainly from poor family backgrounds and their fees were often paid by their fathers' employers, or Boards of Guardians, or in some cases they were sponsored by local benefactors. A few deaf schoolchildren had their fees paid by their own families,

Rugby College for the Deaf

and in most cases these families had members in well-paid occupations such as solicitors, farmers and businessmen. A number of these private fee-paying deaf schoolchildren became the private pupils of various headmasters or were sent to small private schools set up for this purpose, such as Henry Brothers Bingham's Private School at Rugby which educated many of those who were later to become leading personalities in the late 19th century Deaf community. These included people like George Frederick Healey, who was Treasurer of the BDDA for over 25 years, and Sir Arthur Henderson Fairbairn, the Deaf baronet (right).

Children whose parents were paying their school fees faced an hazard: it was not unknown for parents to remove their children from school so as to avoid paying fees when the family fell on hard times. In a minute made by the Manchester Institution for the Deaf and Dumb on 31 March 1833, it was stated that:

Mary Curbishley was clandestinely removed from the school during the night hours.

Generally children whose fees were paid privately were the lucky ones. Parents who were boatmen, washerwomen, servants, farm labourers or general labourers, woollen or cotton mill workers, roadmen (workmen responsible for the repair of roads), and low-paid, menial trades were often so poor that they could not afford the school fees. Children of these poor families might be sent away to the great residential schools, and thus relieved their families of the cost of maintaining them at home. In the 1887 Return of Blind and Deaf-Mute Persons (England, Wales and Ireland) presented to the House of Commons, it was reported that there were a total of 672 deaf and dumb children in England and Wales between the ages of 5 and 15 who were being supported by poor law relief. Of these, 575 were in special schools for the deaf and 35 in workhouse schools. 8 children were said to be in other public elementary schools, while the rest (56) were receiving no form of education at all. The situation was no better in Ireland. In fact, given the respective sizes of the populations, it was somewhat worse in Ireland with 321 children between the ages of 5 and 15 being assisted by poor law relief. Of these 321 children, 298 were in special schools for deaf children.

London Asylum for the Deaf and Dumb, Kent Road, circa 1871

In London a different situation existed. Prior to 1871 deaf children of London had no school set up specifically for them. True, the London Asylum for the Deaf and Dumb Poor was in existence, but this school was accepting children from all over the country, not just London itself. When the London Schools Board was set up in 1871, it decided to find out the numbers of deaf children in London. Four hundred and fifty deaf children between the ages of 5 and 13 were found; of these approximately 150 were receiving education in institutions both in and outside London while the other 300 were receiving no education at all as they came from very poor families, many of whom were not eligible by one means or another for poor law relief. This led to the London Schools Board deciding to do something about the situation. It would not, however, build a special school but where enough deaf children were living close to each other, a class was to be established in a local school for hearing children.

In 1873 the London Schools Board decided that the "Reverend William Stainer of the Royal Association in Aid of the Deaf and Dumb be appointed to initiate a system of deaf-mute

instruction at the Wilmot Street, Bethnal Green (Permanent) Board School from 10 a.m. to 12 noon for five days a week". When the class started in September 1874, there were five children to begin with, but numbers soon grew and a second school was quickly opened at the Winchester Street School in Pentonville.

Despite the success of these schools, Stainer (left) had a problem. The fact that so many of the children came from impoverished families meant that attendances fluctuated so much when these families could not afford to send their children to school that some children were receiving patchy education. Even when they were being sent to school, they were often underfed and poorly clothed. A solution to this problem was needed, and Stainer decided that one way to overcome this was to set up Homes for deaf children near their schools so that they could attend more regularly and also be properly clothed and fed. The children were to reside in the Homes from Mondays to Fridays when they were attending classes, and the first Home was set up at 74 Pentonville Road. Later, houses numbered 70, 72 and 75 were added to the Home.

Stainer was eventually to have four Homes in various parts of London, and at one time there were up to 500 deaf children living in the Homes. Stainer relied mainly on charitable donations though parents and guardians paid a small contribution. Stainer appears often to have dipped into his own personal funds to sustain the Homes.

What started out to be a scheme of good intentions and high hopes eventually became a very unsatisfactory state of affairs. Although the London Schools Board found favour at the beginning with the establishment of these Homes, the Board never - perhaps wisely - actually took over and ran them despite Stainer's frequent persuasions that it should.

The beginning of the end came in 1895 when the London Schools Board set up its own Hugh Myddelton classes in Camberwell Road. With the board's approval, staff at these classes set up their own boarding-out scheme with carefully selected foster homes for individual deaf children, in contrast to the Stainer Homes where deaf children were boarded together. Following the withdrawal of authorisation for the Homes in 1895, the London Schools Board began to withdraw children from the Stainer Homes and placing them under their own care.

In March 1898 the London Schools Board received a damning report presented to them by two inspectors who had come without warning to the houses in Pentonville Road. They found that the houses were in a very dirty and dilapidated condition; night supervision arrangements were unsatisfactory, with no proper ventilation and no fire escape. Children's clothes were very ragged and dirty, and the food was of poor quality. The report went on to list many faults. It must have come as a shock to William Stainer, who died very shortly afterwards, leaving a most unsatisfactory mess, and the last of the Homes were closed in 1904.

The First World War… and After

When Britain declared war on Germany on 4 August 1914, the nation's young men made a Gadarene rush to the recruiting centres to join the armed forces. This euphoric response to the call to arms did not bypass the Deaf people. A good number were known to have applied to join the armed forces and somehow succeeded despite their deafness. Profoundly deaf people, who were proficient at speech and lipreading, were known to have tricked the medical profession into thinking they were hearing. Records of such deaf persons seem to have largely disappeared with the passage of time, but a few survive to the present day. Two of those known are Harry Ward and Gower Jones.

Harry Ward (right) was born deaf in Cardiff in 1887. He possessed no speech and it was over ten years before he was able to utter a word; he was taught at the Oral School in Cardiff under the tuition of one Miss E. Young. Harry then was educated under Joseph Hepworth, the famous Deaf superintendent of the Glamorgan and Monmouthshire Mission for the Adult Deaf and Dumb based at 25 Windsor Place, Cardiff. After leaving school Harry was apprenticed as a shoemaker.

Harry's three hearing brothers were in the armed forces and, being the son of a soldier, Harry developed an urge to join the armed forces. How he took and managed to pass a stringent army medical examination still remains a great mystery to this day. The only information recorded about this event was when Harry's father, Edwin Ward, commented to a *British Deaf Times* reporter, "Oh, there's nothing to tell. He simply came home here one day and said, 'I've enlisted – and I'm off to the front'." Harry Ward in fact joined the Munster Fusiliers in 1914 and was sent to the Curragh Camp in Ireland for training and from there he was sent to the war front in France. Nothing more is known about Harry Ward and on what happened to him.

Gower Jones (right) was an extraordinary Deaf person – he was born not only stone deaf, but blind in his right eye. He attended the Llandaff School for the Deaf and applied to join the army after leaving school. His application was successful. The *British Deaf Times* of Nov.-Dec. 1918 featured an article on Gower Jones and reported that in spite of being one-eyed he was one of the best shots in his company. Jones drilled and marched so smartly that no one was able to pick out the profoundly deaf man. Jones admitted in the article that his soldier pals often asked him via pen and pad mode of communication if he were really deaf and dumb and how he managed to hear officers' orders. Jones did not seem to have answered their questions. It is doubtful if Jones actually saw war service, and his company was most probably engaged in "Home Guard" duties. After several years in the army Private Gower Jones left to become a missioner with the Deaf.

Many Deaf people were easily rejected after undergoing very strict medical examinations. Many Deaf people of working age were engaged in essential war work, especially in the munitions and armoury manufactures, besides farming. Many Deaf tailors were called upon to work on uniforms and essential pieces of clothing for the armed forces, such as overcoats.

Some schools for the deaf were taken over by the military for the duration of the war, in particular the Yorkshire Institution for the Deaf and Dumb in Doncaster, Dudhope Castle in Dundee and Clyne House, a part of the Old Trafford Schools for the Deaf in Manchester. Despite the hardship caused by war conditions, very few schools experienced horrors arising from the war itself. There were a series of near misses that happened to several schools. Amongst those was the East Anglian School for the Deaf at Gorleston which avoided being hit by shells from the massive guns on German warships off the coast of Norfolk and

Donaldson's Hospital (now Donaldson's College)

Suffolk. A good number of bombs narrowly missed Donaldson's Hospital in Edinburgh during the Zeppelin raids in April 1916. In fact, the Germans tried to bomb Donaldson's on two visits in the same night but to no avail apart from intensive damage to its windows.

Deaf people did face some problems at home during the war when strict controls were being enforced, such as the sentry system. Lack of training or awareness of the Deaf on the part of the soldiers and civilian authorities often led to tragic shootings of innocent Deaf people. Examples of such incidents can be seen in the case of one James Waddell, a Deaf employee of the town council. While on duty in Grangemouth Public Park, he was shot by a guard of Kerse Parish Church Hall. Waddell was going his rounds following a flooding, when he was challenged from the opposite side of Grange Burn. The sentry called out three times to Waddell to stop and identify himself. Being deaf, Waddell did not respond. After the sentry's final call Waddell was lighting his pipe when he was shot through the hand and the heart. He died, leaving a widow and family. There were many reports of Deaf people falling victim to the shots of sentries – some died and many were wounded. Many Deaf people were shot at whilst cycling and failing to stop when the sentries called out at them three times. Many were shot in the leg and, equally, many lucky ones escaped being shot when the sentries missed.

Even Deaf people who managed to find themselves employed by the army were not immune to being shot at by their own fellow soldiers. There is the case of one David Bedwell, a deaf driver in the Army Service Corps based at Woolwich in Southeast London. Bedwell's level of deafness was described as "very hard of hearing". He was approaching a compound around 11.15pm on a December night in 1915 when a sentry called out and challenged him to identify himself. Receiving no reply and with Bedwell still walking on ahead, the sentry called out twice more, but still received no reply. After the third call, the sentry raised his rifle and fired, hitting Bedwell who was some 18 yards away. Bedwell was severely wounded and died later in the hospital. An inquest was held in Greenwich. The jury exonerated the sentry, bringing in a verdict of "justifiable homicide". The coroner remarked that it was a clear case of a sentry obviously only doing his duty.

Being a Deaf person in one's own country during the war was not easy, but if coming from another country, life was even harder for a Deaf person. Francis Maggin of Belfast was canvassing for subscriptions in Scotland when he was arrested at Highlaw Station on suspicion of spying for the enemy. He was eventually released.

The great Deaf entrepreneur Arthur James Wilson had his motor boat, "The Splash", fired on three times whilst trying to enter Southampton. One of the shells came within a length of the boat. Fearing the worst, the boat's engineer turned back to the open sea and entered Poole Harbour. The next day the boat was brought around again, but was seized at Sandown in the Isle of Wight. The crew was detained for 20 hours, after which a permit was given to proceed into Southampton. Strangely enough, the Admiralty borrowed the boat and the crew for the duration of the war.

Arthur James Wilson (1858-1945) was a great Deaf businessman and entrepreneur, whose hobby was philanthropy. Under difficult wartime conditions Wilson, as a businessman, raised funds for thousands of workers who had hit hard times and who were unable to gain much in unemployment benefit. Wilson was touched by the wounded soldiers brought home from the battlefields and took pity on their sufferings. He launched the Hospital Motor Squadron and became its Commandant, a position he held for five years. He organised transport for half a million war wounded from London hospitals for health drives and taking them to various entertainments on the river and to golf courses and to theatres. Wilson once filled the Albert Hall with 8,000 war-wounded men for an afternoon's concert. Much of Wilson's time and money went on this enterprise. Despite all the hard work, Wilson remarked that these five years of exemplary and bountiful labour were the best years of

Arthur J. Wilson

his life. For these five years he was made a Freeman of the City of London on 5 December 1916.

Wilson was a man of many talents. On 26 July 1918 he agreed to chair a meeting of representatives of eight London Deaf Clubs in his company premises at 154 Clerkenwell Road and this meeting led to the foundation of the Federation of London Deaf Clubs (FLC). Wilson became its chairman and William Baird the Honorary Secretary. This organisation was the first organised Deaf sports association in Britain.

After the war ended in November 1918, the social situation improved considerably for the Deaf, but bitterness over those who were killed or wounded by sentries remained.

Deaf people's social life and interactions during the first 30 years of the century were almost on par with those of the hearing with the exception of music and the newly developed telephone.

Deaf people enjoyed going to the movies alongside hearing people since every film was supported by captions and there was no sound, apart from accompanied piano music. Every film was silent and classic films such as David Wark Griffith's "Intolerance", Erich von Stroheim's "Greed", F. W. Murnau's "The Last Laugh" and Abel Gance's "Napoleon" were enjoyed on an equal basis with hearing people in the cinema. Charlie Chaplin, Buster Keaton and Mack Sennett gave fun to all, Deaf and hearing alike, who went to see their films and had their lives lightened with bursts of laughter.

Group of Deaf ladies from Liverpool on an outing

Television was then an invention for the future and many Deaf people participated in sport and social events that revolved around many Deaf centres and Missions. Local and regional travel by trams was cheap and this enabled many Deaf people to visit places of local and historical interest that broadened their knowledge.

The post-World War I era was also a period of adjustment for many Deaf people who had to adapt themselves to fit in with changing social trends. One example is the simple matter of responding to the knock at the door. Many Deaf people left their front doors open when they were at home so that visitors such as friends, postman and council officials, could walk in and announce their arrival. This was quite risky because there were also thieves around, but Deaf people were able to judge the appropriate times of the day for leaving their door open. Some Deaf people adopted new innovations, no matter how crude, such as the golf ball and spoon method of answering the door. Using this method, one attached a piece of string or soft wire to the doorbell knob and strung it along to whichever room the occupant frequently used. The end of the wire or string in that room was tied to a spoon, on which a golf ball was seated. When the doorbell knob was pulled, the spoon would also be pulled and the golf ball dropped onto the wooden floor with a thud, making everyone jump. The spoon would then swing like a pendulum and the Deaf occupants made aware of someone at the door. This system was in much use until the World War II.

Another original, similar in intention, was the tennis ball bounce.

Despite the fact that poor attitude and discrimination against the Deaf on account of their handicap were rife, Deaf people were in the main gainfully employed and enjoyed regular and steady income. They were in want of very little… until the Wall Street Crash of 24 October 1929, an event known as Black Thursday.

The Great Depression Era

The Great Depression, known as the Great Slump, commenced in the United States following the Wall Street Crash of 24 October 1929 and the event caused worldwide economic collapse that precipitated commercial failures and mass unemployment. Britain was badly affected by the depression and many factories and businesses folded. Many workers went on the dole. This paid a measly weekly amount that was only just sufficient to keep one's family above the borderline of poverty.

Deaf workers suffered the same fate. Deafness was not kindly tolerated during these days, and whenever there were few jobs available, very often the Deaf people lost out. When bad times sank in, Deaf people looked to each other for help and support. All over Britain, many unemployed Deaf people thronged their local Deaf Missions for assistance in obtaining employment.

Employment was secured on a day to day basis and people very often crowded outside factory gates, hoping to obtain tickets that would guarantee them work. It was intensely difficult for the Deaf to hear their own names being called and they consequently lost the opportunity to work. Some missioners with the Deaf, such as the Rev. T. S. Blakeman of Newcastle-on-Tyne, would queue outside factory gates at 6am to get tickets from the foremen when workers were required. Another missioner who worked for the RADD in London, a small stout man named Parmenter, at one time managed to find about 100 jobs for Deaf people in a period of five days! Despite these brief and incredible feats, many missioners met with small success, but they nevertheless showed great altruism and managed to obtain jobs for a few Deaf people. Some schools for the deaf tried to ameliorate the bad times to help their pupils. The Northern Counties Institution for the Deaf and Dumb (Newcastle) always trained pupils in trades such as tailoring, carpentry, boot making, gardening and dressmaking. Employers who were experiencing a slump tended to hire these deaf school-leavers on low wages, enabling them to dismiss highly paid staff. This was practised all over the country.

Deaf ladies often found employment as either dressmakers or housemaids whenever these occupations were available. During that era two Deaf ladies had the honour to work on Queen Mary's dress made to mark her Silver Jubilee.

Between 1925 and 1936 there were in many cities soup kitchens which attracted many of the impoverished. Some Missions for the Deaf launched soup kitchens and some chose to keep a low profile by having food delivered to the needy Deaf people's houses. The RADD launched a soup kitchen at the old St. Barnabas Church and Mission in Deptford, Southeast London. Although only bowls of soup and hunks of unbuttered bread were handed out, many Deaf people came and praised the scheme.

Deaf people who were at school during the time of the Great Slump spoke of dreadful and meagre school food; one said he became so hungry at one time that he felt compelled to eat toothpaste, and few others recalled eating grass and were afterwards ill. The ordeals these Deaf people went through were hard enough, but a good few went on to celebrate their centuries!

Despite the starvation diet the children did well in sport; and some schools, particularly the Northern Counties School for the Deaf in Newcastle-Upon-Tyne, had cadet forces that won

Deaf cadets from the Northern Counties School for the Deaf - 1930s

several honours by beating better-equipped and well-fed hearing teams! These deaf cadet forces often travelled to other parts of the country to participate in competitions with other cadet forces.

Parents with large families tended to struggle to obtain sufficient food to feed their families and obtaining clothes for their children always turned out to be a financial burden. Many tended to send their deaf children to residential schools so that each child became one mouth less to feed and one person less to clothe. Even children who had very slight and negligible deafness were not spared and they were packed off to residential schools for the deaf.

For unmarried Deaf men the Great Depression was a particularly atrocious period in that regular income was hard to come by and many were forced to sleep outdoors on occasions when they had no money. When they had money, they were able to afford staying in certain doss-houses. When they were able to earn a little bit more, they would stay in a slightly "superior" accommodation, such as London's Rowton Houses, which cost a shilling per night, or six shillings and sixpence for seven nights. In a Rowton House, each resident occupied a cubicle containing a bed with clean sheets and blankets, a cupboard and a chamber pot. There were large dining rooms and washhouses, but no baths. There was also the Church Army's doss-houses in London. These doss-houses provided board and work, which was mostly making wooden cloth pegs, chopping and bundling firewood. For the work inmates were given food vouchers instead of money. Very few Deaf men frequented those places.

In some parts of London, Bristol and Edinburgh unemployment for the Deaf was so bad that they were driven to take desperate measures to lodge their protests. In 1933, from a pub at the corner of Green Lanes and Seven Sisters Road, one Deaf man in his early thirties named Blake persuaded at least forty Deaf people to join the notorious Blackshirts, the nickname for members of Oswald Mosley's British Union of Fascists (BUF). Sonny Blake, who was educated at Anerley School for the Deaf, was a feared local bully who took to beating up any person, Deaf or hearing, who stood in his way. Blake, strangely, was in full employment at that time and therefore had no reason to protest about the unemployment situation. He was in short a ruffian. A Maltese Deaf man, Pandolfino, known by his sign name "Shoulders" (because he was employed as a tailor stitching in shoulder pads) filmed Blake and his Deaf followers taking part in a Blackshirts march in Cable Street in 1936 and showed the film to Blake's Jewish employer. After seeing the film, the employer fired Blake from his job.

Sonny Blake

There were Deaf Blackshirts actively participating in BUF marches in Edinburgh. These Deaf people joined the Blackshirts for exactly the same reasons as their London counterparts – to register their protest at the unemployment situation. In the case of Bristol, there is an account of a Deaf man who joined the Blackshirts and tried to persuade other members of the local Deaf centre to join. Failing in this, he brought in some Blackshirts ruffians with him to intimidate Deaf men to join, but still to no avail. A group of Deaf men gathered together and attacked the Blackshirts, running them out of the Deaf centre into the arms of the police who had earlier been called out by the local missioner.

Following the Blackshirts' notorious Cable Street Riot in the East End in October 1936, where 7,000 Blackshirts taking part in a march through a poverty-stricken working class area were confronted by an opposition of nearly 100,000, Parliament passed the Public Order Act, which act banned people in uniforms from participating in marches. Certain Deaf people's involvement with the BUF after this Act grew less and they faded into oblivion.

In some parts of the Midlands such as Sheffield, Deaf people had electric doorbells that were first installed in the early 1930s. Many of these doorbells were connected to batteries from which wires were run to small torch bulbs, which would light up whenever doorbells were pressed. According to James Mountcastle, the batteries went flat too quickly and they were replaced by transformers. Deaf people admitted that it was difficult to see the tiny bulbs flashing and as a consequence many a caller went away thinking they were not at home. These altered doorbells were of very little use during the night hours when everyone was asleep.

When Franklin Delano Roosevelt, the President of the USA, announced his famous New Deal in 1934, hopes for Britain's commercial recovery were boosted albeit very slowly. The scene did brighten up after the mid-thirties, but it was not until Britain's declaration of war on Germany in 1939 that there was a sudden glut of jobs.

As reported in publications such as the British Deaf Times, a reasonably large number of Deaf people managed quite well despite the gloomy economical climate. Visits to Deaf clubs, travel to other cities for sport and social events continued, but visits to the cinema began to become less frequent for the Deaf with the Talkies growing in popularity and the slow demise of the silent films continued. The introduction of sound and music in films gained great popularity with members of the general public; these films had little or no appeal to the Deaf.

The Peak of the Growth of Schools for the Deaf – 1930-40

The growth of schools for the deaf reached its peak in the 1930s and there was a staggering count of 31 Residential and 40 Day schools for the deaf in Britain, including the Republic of Ireland. The following known schools were as recorded in 1933-1934, a period taken merely to quote an example. (The number of pupils where known follows the name of the school at that time and the date of foundation of the school is given in the last column).

Residential Schools

Anerley School for the Deaf (LCC), Versailles Road, Anerley, London.	90.	1902.
Cabra, St. George's Street, Dublin, Ireland.		1846.
Claremont Institution, Dublin, Ireland.		1816.
Donaldson's Hospital Deaf School, West Coates, Edinburgh.	108.	1850.
East Anglia School for the Blind & Deaf Children, Gorleston-on-Sea.	160.	1912.
Glasgow Institution for the Deaf & Dumb, Langside, Queen's Park, Glasgow.	200.	1819.
Inst. for the Education of the Deaf & Dumb, Dudhope Bank, Dundee.	40.	1846.
Institution for Deaf Children, Kingstown, Bristol.	45.	1898.
Institution for the Deaf & Dumb, Eastern Road, Brighton.	101.	1842.
Jewish Deaf & Dumb Home, Nightingale Lane, Balham, London.	80.	1865.
Northern Counties Inst. for the Deaf & Dumb, Newcastle-on-Tyne.	180.	1838.
Northern Staffordshire Blind and Deaf School, Stoke-on-Trent.	112.	1897.
Oak Lodge School (LCC), Balham, London.	76.	1905.
Rayners, (LCC), Penn, Bucks.	79.	1900.
Royal Cambrian Inst. for the Deaf & Dumb, Swansea, Wales.	98.	1847.
Royal Cross School for the Deaf, Preston, Lancs.	90.	1894.
Royal Inst. for the Education of the Deaf & Dumb, Henderson Row, Edinburgh.	150.	1810.
Royal Institution for the Deaf & Dumb, Edgbaston, Birmingham.	185.	1812.
Royal Institution for the Deaf & Dumb, Friargate, Derby.	165.	1873.
Royal Residential School for the Deaf, Stretford.		
Royal School for the Deaf, Margate.	401.	1792.
Royal School for the Deaf, Old Trafford, Manchester.	363.	1825.
Royal West of England Inst. For the Deaf & Dumb, Exeter.	120.	1826.
School for the Deaf, Blenheim Walk, Leeds.	132.	1881.
School for the Deaf, Oxford Street, Liverpool.	200.	1825.
St. John's, Boston Spa, Yorkshire.	228.	1870.
St. Joseph's, Rochfort Bridge, Westmeath, Ireland.		1892.
The Ulster Society, Lisburn Road, Belfast, Northern Ireland.	92.	1831.
Thomasson Memorial Council School, Devonshire Road, Bolton.	20.	1909.
Tollcross Blind & Deaf R.C. School, Shettleston, Glasgow.		1872.
Yorkshire Institution for the Deaf & Dumb, Doncaster.	170.	1829.

Day Schools

Ackmar Road (LCC), Fulham, London.	75.	1898.
Birmingham School for the Deaf, Gem Street, Birmingham.	80.	1894.
Bradford School for the Deaf (formerly Odsal House), Bolton Royd House	54.	1885.
Bristol School for the Partly Deaf, New Street, Bristol.	40.	1910.
Burnley School for the Deaf, Oak Mount House, Burnley.	40.	1897.
Cadzow Street School for the Deaf, Aberdeen.		1911.
Cardiff School for the Deaf, Howard Gardens, Cardiff,	40.	1895.
Clarendon Street School for the Deaf, Nottingham.	64.	1883.
Deaf Council School, Stockton-on-Tees		1932

Gower Street Council School for the Deaf, Oldham.	40.	1890.
Dudley School for the Deaf, Deaf Dept., Higher Elementary School, Dudley.	20.	1897.
Frederick Road School for the Deaf, Custom House, London.	20.	1893.
Glasgow, Ibrox Special School, Ibrox		1878.
Glebe Oral School for the Deaf, Greenock.	35.	1883.
Goran School for the Deaf, Copeland Road, Glasgow.	30.	1886.
Harcourt Street Deaf & Dumb Public School, Dundee.	60.	1885.
Hearnville Road (LCC), Balham, London.	45.	1913.
Hugh Myddelton School (LCC), Sans Walk, Clerkenwell, London.	110.	1892.
Kingston-upon-Hull School for the Deaf, Osborne Street, Hull.	48.	1894.
Lady Hamilton School (Special Class), Charlotte Street, Ayr.	12.	1896.
Leicester School for the Deaf, Church Gate, Leicester.	50.	1884.
Liverpool School for the Deaf, Crown Street, Liverpool.	200.	1904.
Maud Maxwell Day School for the Deaf, Easthill, Sheffield.	84.	1921.
Moorfields School for Semi-Deaf Children, Bristol		1910.
Mosley Road School for the Deaf, Birmingham.	55.	1895.
Newington Green (LCC), Islington, London.	15.	1915.
Oakshaw Deaf School, Paisley.	43.	1894.
Old Kent Road School (LCC), Bermondsey, London.	99.	1903.
Phillip Lane School for the Deaf, Tottenham, London.	70.	1895.
Randall Place School (LCC), Greenwich, London.	40.	1906.
Renfrew Special School Semi-Deaf Class, Glasgow.	90.	1910.
School for the Deaf, Nelson Terrace, Stockton-on-Tees.	40.	1895.
School for the Deaf, Woodburn, Hamilton.		1911.
St. Jude's School for the Deaf, Salisbury Road, Plymouth.	40.	1895.
Stanley Street (LCC), Deptford, London.	42.	1913.
Surrey Lane School (LCC), Bridge Road, Battersea, London.	40.	1899.
Barbara Priestman Council Deaf School, Tatham Street, Sunderland.	30.	1926.
The "Tollet" (LCC), Mile End, London.	80.	1914.
Water Lane (LCC), Stratford, London.	40.	1895.
Westburn Road School for the Deaf, Aberdeen.	50.	1904.
William Morris School for the Deaf, Walthamstow, London.	20.	1900.

Private Schools for the Deaf

Mill Hall School, Cuckfield, Sussex	10.	1934.
Miss Blanche Nevile's Private School, Regent Park, London NW1.		
Miss E. M. Andress' Private School, Streatham Common, London.		1929.
Miss M. Mills' Private Oral School, Worple Road, Wimbledon, London.		1890.
Miss M. Wehner's Private School, Carshalton, Surrey.		1900.
Miss Mary Hare's Oral School, Burgess Hill, Brighton.		
Miss M. M. Taylor's Private School, Redhill, Surrey.		1914.
Park Hill High Class Residential School for the Deaf, Hemel Hempstead, Herts.		
Private School for the Deaf, Spring Hill, Northampton.		1868.

World War II

When the British Government declared war against Germany in September 1939, notices went out to many people requiring them to report to recruiting centres for assessment of their fitness to serve in the armed forces. Many deaf men went; and many were rejected and received their discharge papers. Two discharge certificates are shown, both issued to Herbert Colville of Hove, Sussex.

With many men called up, Britain was soon in dire need of workers not only to contribute towards the war but to replace men called up by the armed forces. Many willing and able hands were found in the form of Deaf workers. While many workers continued in their employment during the war, there were many others who were requisitioned under Essential Works Orders (EWO) and instructed to report to factories elsewhere to carry out work essential to the war. Deaf females had to do ammunition work, as well as welding and heavy riveting work in armoury divisions along with males. Deaf women were generally so impressive in their war work that they were in much demand. Some Deaf ladies were called to the Land Army. Carpenters were also in great demand and they were posted all over Britain, in particular in naval yards where new ships were being fitted out and existing ships altered for the war. Deaf tailors and seamstresses were kept busy making not only uniforms and clothing materials essential for the war, but utility clothes that were cheaply bought during the war. Farms and poultry farms were other places to which Deaf people were posted for the product of essential food supplies. Once an EWO had been issued instructing a Deaf person to do a particular job, there was no refusing it. One Deaf carpenter had to go into a factory making candles and soap for the forces until the war was over. Another Deaf man, who was a tailor, was ordered to work as an aircraft fitter. He had to do shift work, and even when the air raid sirens were sounding, he was forbidden to stop and had to continue working.

A very large number of Deaf people were trained and engaged to do some professional and supervisory tasks, mainly as air raid wardens (ARPs), firewatchers, casualty and decontamination workers and were also in rescue teams.

The situation in Britain during the Second World War was different to that of the First War in that warfare technology had made great leaps during the intervening years. Warplanes were faster and more powerful than biplanes - there were single winged speed terrors and massive flying fortresses capable of dropping huge bombs that would destroy not one house, but twenty or so per drop. A state of highest alert was on at almost all times and air raid sirens frequently blared out. For the Deaf, they had to keep their eyes open and make a dash for the safety of air raid shelters the moment all hearing people made for, even though not all air raid shelters were safe. There was a Deaf couple with six children. One day the air raid sirens went and the couple were notified by neighbours of the situation. The father for some unknown reason decided to head for his house with all his six children, but his wife went for the shelter which was destroyed when a Nazi bomb hit it.

Blackouts and the Sentry System

Blackouts and the dreaded sentry system were put into force in Britain during the war. Blackouts were necessary to prevent the enemy on night time bombing missions spotting targets by picking out lights on the streets or from the houses. Casualties among the Deaf during the blackouts and sentry system were quite alarming and a short account of selected events occurring in 1941 and 1942 illustrate this.

1941

A 65 years old Leeds Deaf man, Patrick Cosgrove, a former pupil at St. John's, Boston Spa, died on January 19 after he was knocked down by a tram during the blackout on January 15. He was unconscious for four days before he died.

A Deaf man, Henry Holland, had to be rushed to hospital when local Stockport Corporation bus knocked him out during the blackout as he was returning home from work. He was pronounced dead on arrival.

On December 23 Alfred Powe was walking with a group of Deaf men on a ship during a blackout when he fell nearly 40 feet down into the hold of the ship. Powe survived the fall but suffered spinal injuries.

1942

A 56 years old Deaf electrician from Gillingham (Kent) named Thomas Sidney Pearce went out in the darkness to post a letter near a sentry post in Southport. The sentry spotted him and challenged him thrice to stop, but Pearce continued to walk towards the letterbox, whereupon the sentry fired. Severely wounded, Pearce was rushed to Southport hospital where he died 24 hours later.

In Wakefield Martin Dalton, a Deaf man, was knocked down during the blackout by a Special Police car. He was rushed to hospital, but never regained consciousness and died four days later.

In Rye in Sussex, the famous Deaf artist, A. R. Thomson, RA (right), was making his way home after visiting his friend Lord Davenport. Walking past a sentry point near an army encampment, Thomson did not hear the sentry calling him thrice to halt three times. The sentry fired and Thomson went down. He was shot in the shoulder. Thomson clutched his shoulder and staggered up while the sentry came running with his bayonet aiming for his stomach. Thomson gesticulated by pointing to his ear and shouting "Deaf!" whereupon the sentry halted and lowered his rifle. The shot alerted the commanding officer who came in a car. When they found out who Thomson was, the soldiers were very apologetic and drove him to hospital. Thomson was discharged from hospital two days later with the bullet still in his arm. The surgeon had told him he would be paralysed if the bullet was removed.

Two Deaf men were walking home along the Woolwich Tunnel footpath during the blackout, communicating with each other in sign language. The sentries patrolling the area spotted them. Despite the fact that the two Deaf men were using their hands and arms for communication the sentries could not perceive the movement and they called out for them to halt, and they called out twice more, but to no avail. Volleys of shots rang out and down went the two Deaf men. They were both seriously wounded but survived the terrible event.

The imposition of strict blackout regulations severely disrupted the adult Deaf Club activities and many were forced to cancel long-arranged social events and to re-arrange social club hours. The circumstantial dangers to the Deaf were not restricted to the blackout and the sentry system. In Britain almost everyone was seemingly a suspect first and foremost until proven otherwise. This is illustrated by two examples out of numerous actual events:

1.   In Warrington, a Deaf man decided to pay a visit to a relative he had not seen for

some time, and set off to cycle there. Unfortunately all road signposts having been removed, he soon lost his way and had to ask someone for directions. Because of his speech impediment he was mistaken for a German spy and was arrested. He spent some uncomfortable hours in custody before being released.

2. In Manchester a Deaf tramp, who had roamed the country for nine years, was arrested as a spy because he had 55 Ordnance Survey maps in his possession as well as two compasses and twenty crisp £1 notes. He was eventually released.

The greatest danger to the Deaf came from the air: falling bombs and debris from shot-up planes. A number of Deaf people, including children, lost their lives during air raids by German warplanes, including a family of eight killed when a bomb scored a direct hit on their dugout. In the Tyneside area, one huge bomb hit and blew up a small, humble public convenience that contained an elderly Deaf man who had gone in and sat down in answer to the call of nature.

Southampton Deaf Centre after being bombed

Although a number of Deaf people, especially in London, Coventry and Southampton, lost their homes, Deaf institutes, churches and schools seem to have received more damage. Deaf centres destroyed by enemy action included Southampton, Coventry, Clapham St. Bede's, Great Yarmouth, Manchester's Roman Catholic Centre and the premises of the National Deaf Club. Other centres that received some damage were Norwich and Birmingham, whilst in Bristol the square in which the Deaf centre stood was reduced to rubble except for the Deaf centre itself, which was unscathed apart from blasted windows. In Manchester the Church of All Saints was reduced to rubble whilst the Deaf institute remained unscathed.

St. Bede's, Clapham before the bombing

There were attempts by the authorities to help the Deaf overcome circumstantial difficulties created by the state of war. Deaf people in Hull were issued with whistles that would enable them to call for help should they get trapped under rubbles. Deaf people in London were issued with round white badges with the word DEAF in blue to enable people, in particular the sentries, to identify their handicap. The National Institute for the

St. Bede's after the bombing

Deaf manufactured these badges, but many Deaf people avoided wearing them because they had no wish to parade their deafness in public and become embarrassed.

The Reverend Vernon Jones (right) was so concerned about the situation of the Deaf under the sentry and blackout systems that he wrote and produced a booklet entitled *The Challenge of the Sentry* and distributed it among the authorities and armed forces. His opening paragraph simply read:

> *A deaf woman was walking near a factory recently and was unaware that she was in a prohibited area. The sentry on duty challenged her. She did not hear, and walked on. She was shot, and died. This tragedy was entirely due to deafness.*

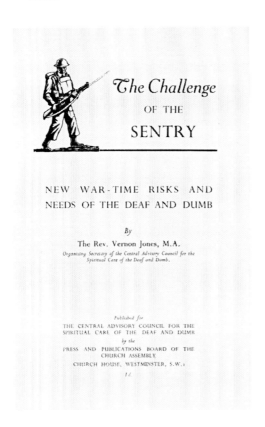

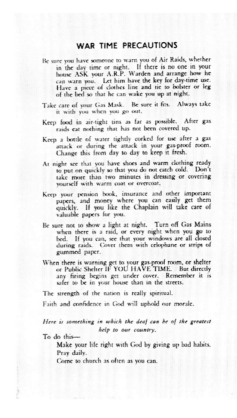

Jones included a list of "War time precautions" in the booklet. Whether his efforts to promote awareness of the Deaf among the hearing under wartime conditions succeeded or not has yet to be verified.

Food Rations

When the government introduced rationing, Deaf people became alarmed because there was no accompanying information explaining the rules of the system. Once they understood the system, their frustrations did not end there. Food was in scarce supply and people had to queue for hours with ration books outside shops. Deaf people were very often the losers – there was many a time when hearing people in the queue would suddenly rush off to other shops upon hearing shouted announcements that certain foods were out of stock and that other shops had opened. Being deaf, the Deaf were left standing behind. Learning this lesson, many Deaf parents brought along their hearing children to the queues, using them as their ears so that they would not be left out in their quest to obtain rationed food.

There was a great spirit of camaraderie among those within local Deaf communities in various cities and towns. Many would help each other by queuing outside various shops and then meet up later in the Deaf centre to swap and sort out the food according to each family's needs. Birthday parties and special celebrations were not spared because of rationing; everyone contributed a little bit of saved rationed item of food and this enabled a mini-feast to be organised for the special event.

The Baedeker Raids

Perhaps the greatest amount of damage done to Deaf centres within a short span of time occurred during the Baedeker raids of May 1942 in Southwest England. This was an intensive bombing campaign by the Luftwaffe that really had little to do with the war. The air raids during this particular campaign were commonly known as the Baedeker raids, after a publishing house that produced travel guides, because the Germans made a sudden switch from bombing major cities, industrial and military targets to bomb cities that did not have anything remotely connected with any major war effort. All six of them in fact were what might be called tourist towns: Torquay, Exeter, Bath, Weymouth, etc. – the very towns which had travel guides on them published by this firm Baedeker. The firm was a casualty of the raids and never published again.

There was first a minor raid on a Thursday night on Exeter, followed on the next night by a much larger raid, which caused great damage to parts of the town. Amongst the buildings damaged was the Church Hall, where the Deaf of Exeter met and where the missioner (Canon A. Mackenzie) had his offices. Then the Germans left Exeter alone for one full week, during which they bombed, amongst other towns, Bath, Weymouth and Torquay.

The Deaf Institute in Bath was totally destroyed and all its archives and records were lost. Torquay Deaf Club suffered some minor damage, but nothing which could not be easily repaired. In Weymouth, one of the casualties was the Toc H building, which amongst other things was home to the local Deaf club. This building was totally destroyed, causing the Deaf of Weymouth to be without a club for some months.

One week after the second raid on Exeter, the Germans returned in force, and devastated the centre of Exeter. Already previously damaged, the Deaf centre was made totally uninhabitable. Another casualty of this second bombing raid was the Royal West of England School for the Deaf at Exeter, which at that time seemed a safe haven, not only for the children of the area the school served, but also for the 52 children and staff of the Anerley School for the Deaf, London, who had been evacuated there on 14 September 1939. Blasts from high explosives caused substantial damage to all buildings of the school and no room escaped damage. Fortunately, the tedious but sensible arrangement of all the children sleeping on the ground floor instead of in the bedrooms paid dividends; there were no serious casualties. Within four days all the children had returned home, and the school was closed for two months to enable repairs to be carried out.

The 1943 Raids

During the Baedeker raids, there were no human casualties in any of the Deaf centres, although a few Deaf families were made homeless when their homes were hit. The Deaf in Exeter occupied temporary premises for a few weeks before settling into another building near the centre of the town, but not for very long. In early 1943 four Heinkel 111s made a low-level sneak raid on the town in broad daylight. The raid took less than five minutes, but the damage suffered by Exeter was greater than it had suffered in the Baedeker raids and there was greater loss of life, over 250 people killed. One of the buildings totally flattened was the new home of the Deaf in the town. Within the space of one year, the Deaf in Exeter had to find a new club premises. In the same raid, Torquay was also again bombed. The Deaf centre escaped with minor blast damage when a bomb fell on the St. Mary's Church building a few yards along the road, killing 18 children who were in the building.

The Bristol Deaf Centre had a very near miss when much of the square round it was reduced to rubble in a heavy bombing raid. The local society later took the opportunity to build the new deaf centre on the bombed site.

The Bombing of Schools

The first bombs to fall on any British school for the deaf came the day the war broke out, at Margate on 3 September 1939 when a number of incendiary bombs landed in the school grounds. The school was to be subjected to a number of air raid attacks, but the greatest loss the school suffered was when the Allen Homes were totally destroyed in 1942. These Homes were used to accommodate boarders at the school and their destruction severely hampered the school's capacity after the war. The headmaster's house in the school grounds was also destroyed, and the main building hit.

Other schools which suffered wartime bomb damage included the East Anglian School at Gorleston-on-Sea, which also had its headmaster's house destroyed, the Royal West of England School at Exeter as previously stated, and the Royal Cambrian School for the Deaf in Swansea. In London the Old Kent Road and Anerley Schools for the Deaf, which were both occupied by the civil defence and military authorities at the time, were also substantially damaged and needed major repairs after the war before they could be reoccupied.

In Manchester the Clyne House Nursery School, then occupied by the military authorities, was also severely damaged and the main school building was hit by a bomb, which went through its roof but fortunately failed to explode.

In Edinburgh the grounds around Donaldson's Hospital in West Coates were badly shaken by a series of bombs exploding. Fortunately for the deaf pupils at the school, the destruction stayed outside and the building, although badly shaken, was left intact. Donaldson's Hospital was later taken over by the military and used to house Italian prisoners of war until 1945.

Deaf People's Circumstances and Contributions

During times when the blackout and sentry system were at their highest state of enforcement, Deaf people were in the main afraid to venture out lest they were shot at and many stayed at home. In many cities and towns the opening hours of Deaf Centres were altered so that Deaf people could meet during the daylight hours. Attendances were small since many had to do war work. In Deaf clubs and institutes throughout the country there were many activities such as fundraising and knitting for the armed services. Deaf women in Wakefield, Birmingham and Belfast produced hundreds of knitted pullovers, socks and other woollen articles for the soldiers. One club in London, the Spurs Club, raised £760 in three years for a variety of armed services' benevolent funds.

Many Deaf people were commended for their contribution towards war work and Civil Defence, but received almost nothing. In Manchester it was found that over 50 Deaf men from the Manchester Institute for the Deaf were entitled to the Defence Service Medal for their work with the Civil Defence. This could be repeated throughout the country, but many never got to receive their medals.

The activities and contributions of some Deaf people brought them renown, in particular those serving as ARP wardens. One of these was Herbert Street, an air raid warden and a sergeant in the Home Guard. He did sterling frontline work in Southampton, a principal port that was always subjected to repeat bombing raids. Herbert Street developed an uncanny knack in spotting approaching enemy aircraft before most of his fellow wardens were aware of them. He was always in the thick of rescue work for which he was later awarded the British Empire Medal. Another ARP warden was Harry MacDonald of Truro, whose work was praised by many people. Mary Swain of Oldham was awarded the B.E.M. for her work in a tank factory.

The warning system alerting people to incoming air raids or telling them to put out the lights in their houses was mainly geared to the hearing. Deaf people generally kept their eyes open and followed whatever they saw as an activity on the part of hearing people that conformed to the warning system. Deaf families with hearing children were informed by them of any alarms being sounded. There were numerous Deaf people who, after tying strings around their wrists and toes, ran the length of strings to outside the windows. ARP wardens acquainted with Deaf people in their areas would pull the strings and so catch the attention of the Deaf persons in the houses. Some reported that the wardens pulled so hard that they were flung onto the floor, and some nearly out of the windows. The egg and spoon doorbell method was also used during that period.

Schools for the deaf continued to provide education, but many were evacuated to safe places .

Wartime Evacuations of Schools for the deaf in WWII

Name of School	Evacuated to:
Birmingham, Gem Street	Stansfield Camp, Headington, Oxford
Birmingham, Moseley Road	Youth Hostel, Shottery, Stratford-on-Avon, Warwickshire
Bradford	Youth Hostel, Gisburn, Lancashire
Brighton Institution	Coldharbour, Wivelsfield Green, Surrey
Dundee	Belmont Castle, Meigle, Perthshire
Edinburgh, Henderson Row	Redcroft Hotel, N. Berwick
Edinburgh, West Coates	Dunglass House, Cockburnspath, Berwickshire
Glasgow, Langside	Dalquharren Castle, Dailly, Ayrshire
Glasgow, Renfrew Street	Lumsden Home, Maybole, Ayrshire
Hull	Fairview Hotel, Scarborough, Yorkshire
Leeds	James Graham Open-Air School, Old Farnley, Yorkshire
Liverpool	1. Underlea, N. Sudley Road, Aigburth, Liverpool 2. Birkdale Residential School for Deaf Children
London: Ackmar Road School	1. Nyetimber Holiday Lido, Bognor Regis, Sussex 2. Fir Tree Road, Banstead, Surrey
Anerley	1. Royal School for the Deaf, Exeter, Devon 2. Fir Tree Road, Banstead, Surrey 3. Maltby, Yorkshire 4. Warmsworth, Yorkshire
Blanche Nevile, Tottenham	Gileston Camp, St. Athenes, Glamorgan
Hugh Myddelton, Clerkenwell	Gileston Camp, St. Athenes, Glamorgan
Jewish Deaf School	1. School for the Deaf, Eastern Road, Brighton, Sussex 2. Havering House, Milton Libourne, Wiltshire
Oak Lodge School	Nyetimber Holiday Lido, Bognor Regis, Sussex
Old Kent Road	Gileston Camp, St. Athenes, Glamorgan
Oldridge Street	Gileston Camp, St. Athenes, Glamorgan
Randall Place	Cuckfield House, Cuckfield, Sussex
Tollet Street	Gileston Camp, St. Athenes, Glamorgan
Walthamstow	Gileston Camp, St. Athenes, Glamorgan
West Ham	Fyfield School for Evacuated Deaf Children
RSD Margate	Goring-on-Thames, Surrey
Middlesbrough	Lewisham, Yorkshire
Northern Counties School, Newcastle	North Seaton Hall Camp, Northumberland
Royal Cambrian Institution	Newbridge & Rhayader, Wales

Ewingism

There was a period of some 50 years when a campaign of "fitting the deaf child into the system" at all costs was enforced in Britain. That system was based on speech and hearing only to the exclusion of everything else, including fingerspelling and sign. The main inspiration behind that movement was one woman – Irene Rosetta Goldsack (1883 – 1959).

Irene Goldsack qualified as a teacher of deaf children in 1907 and she started to teach at the Royal Schools for the Deaf in Manchester. After five years, she established the Henry Worrall Nursery School within the same grounds. It was the first nursery school for deaf children in Britain. Irene Goldsack rejected the formal articulation lessons current at that time, and replaced them with language through lipreading and speaking and also through play and everyday activities. She emphasised the importance of parents in playing a role in their young children's speech and hearing development. She forbade signs and fingerspelling, and concentrated on using any residual hearing that the pupils might have. This interest was based on the findings of James Kerr Love (1858-1942), who reported in 1893 that only 10% of the pupils of the Glasgow Institute for the Deaf were totally deaf and that the residual capacity of the pupils in the institutions for the deaf to hear could be a decisive factor in their speech improvement.

Irene Rosetta Ewing
(*nee* Goldsack)

Irene Goldsack coincidentally was losing her hearing and eventually became profoundly deaf. She however developed excellent lipreading skills, and her first book was "Lipreading" (1930) which was to be many times revised and republished.

The chairman of the Board of Governors of the Royal Schools for the Deaf, was a parent of a deaf boy named Ellis Llwyd-Jones, who was a very clever pupil. Ellis became the first profoundly deaf undergraduate at Oxford University, but died in 1917 before completing his studies. In 1919 his father Sir James Jones campaigned for a University course for training teachers for deaf children, and the first course was started under the Education Department of Manchester University. Irene Goldsack was placed in charge. The students met in a small room at the top of one of the buildings, and the course began with about six students. The Royal Schools for the Deaf was appointed the sole teaching-practice school. Irene Goldsack trained all her students in her method, that of talking and listening, and from there an increasing number of students carried this method into the schools.

Alexander Ewing (1896-1981, right) came under Irene Goldsack to be trained as a lecturer in the education of the deaf. His original expertise was in aphasia, and he had a medical and highly scientific background that was put to much use to add weight to the developing theories on the education of deaf children. The pair started a romance that led to their marriage in 1922 and formed a team that was to become both famous in the hearing world and infamous in the Deaf world. Their association was also the beginning of a period of tremendous scientific development in hearing aids, in hearing testing, in intelligence testing, and so on.

In the year they married, 1922, the first audiometer in Britain was bought from the Bell Telephone Laboratories in New York.

T. S. Littler at work on the Two-Valve Microphone Amplifier Unit in 1936.

In 1931 Thomas Simm Littler, a pupil at Wigan Grammar School and later on a coalminer, who went on obtain a physics degree and then his M.Sc. at Manchester University, joined the Department and developed very sophisticated and efficient apparatus, gaining the Department renown for this side of the education of the deaf. The approach to deaf children became more scientific, more tests were devised of speech, sound perception, lipreading skills, intelligence and developmental patterns and so on. Children were being tested continuously and relentlessly up to the stage where speech and hearing dominated the educational curricula and all other subjects were seemingly allocated a lower status.

Deaf children who could not hear or perceive the meaning of the sounds and who could master neither lipreading nor speech were losing out educationally. Hearing aids were not helping the profoundly deaf – sounds became an irritant to a good number of deaf

Typical class of deaf children with headphones

pupils and that caused them to be bad-tempered. Their educational standards did not improve because they could not understand their teachers without the help of signs.

For the profoundly and signing deaf, instead of enjoying the happiest days of their lives, their schooldays were living hell at times. Many children who were caught signing had their hands caned by a ruler or a slipper; they were also beaten on the bottom with a variety of implements: plimsolls, bamboo cane, cricket bat, wooden rule, the open palms of the teachers' hands, and so on. Those deaf children who could not resist using their hands to accompany and supplement their speech were forced to sit on their hands or have their hands tied behind their backs. Communication in their chosen language was forbidden at all times on pain of punishment. To these deaf children, the era of Ewingism was known as a reign of terror.

The only beneficiaries of the Ewings' method were mainly the partially deaf, the postlingual deaf, the very hard of hearing and the few talented prelingually deaf children who were able to master lipreading, let alone hearing. Hearing aids helped this group of deaf who had useful residual hearing; educational standards rose for these children. Classification of children and separate provision according to need was introduced and enforced. Deaf children who benefited greatly from hearing aids ran into many thousands as opposed to the smaller number of profoundly deaf children, and therefore in the main hearing aids served a very useful and valuable purpose for those who could use them.

One of the biggest Ewing-inspired achievements was the grading of children with defective hearing. In June 1934 a committee was appointed by the Chief Medical Officer of the Board of Education "to inquire into and report upon the medical, educational and social aspects of the problems attending children suffering from defects of hearing not amounting to total deafness." The Committee's published report suggested that children suffering from deafness should be classified in three grades – of which Grade III consisted of children for whom education in a school for the deaf was essential. The report continued on about educational grades:

Grade I

Children with defective hearing who can, nevertheless, without special arrangements of any kind, obtain proper benefit from the education provided in an ordinary school – elementary, secondary or technical.

Grade II

Children whose hearing is defective to such a degree that they require for their education special arrangements or facilities, but not the educational methods used for deaf children without naturally acquired speech or language. These facilities range from a favourable position in an ordinary school classroom to attendance at a special class or school.

> *Grade IIa*
> Those children with Grade II who can make satisfactory progress in ordinary classes in ordinary schools provided they are given some help, whether by way of favourable position in class, by individual hearing aids or by tuition in lipreading.
> *Grade IIb*
> Those children with Grade II who, even with the help of favourable position in the class, individual hearing aids or tuition in lipreading, fail to make satisfactory progress in ordinary classes in ordinary schools.

Grade III

Children whose hearing is so defective and whose speech and language are so little developed that they require education by methods used for deaf children without naturally acquired speech or language. This grade includes the totally deaf.

Alexander and Irene Ewing went a bit further and created a subdivision of Grade III. They "suggested" that the new classification was one which teachers of the deaf might usefully adopt for general use in the schools. This creation of a subdivision of Grade III led to the following definitions:

Grade IIIa
Hearing Capacity – Pure tone audiometer:
Can hear a sound over a frequency range of not less than 4 octaves.
Ability to benefit from the use of Class Hearing Aid:
After practice, can distinguish most vowels and at least a few consonants without lipreading. Combined use of hearing aid and lipreading therefore facilitates language development and acquisition of correct pronunciation.
Grade IIIb
Hearing Capacity – Pure tone audiometer:
Can hear sound over a frequency range of less than 4 octaves.
Ability to benefit from the use of Class Hearing Aid:
Use of hearing aid facilitates hearing and therefore language development and progress in school subjects. It helps in voice training but only to a limited extent, if at all, in the

improvement of pronunciation.
Grade IIIc
<u>Hearing Capacity – Pure tone audiometer:</u>
Totally deaf.
<u>Ability to benefit from the use of Class Hearing Aid:</u>
None.

One question was never ever answered – "Why were those deaf children classified under Grade IIIc still forced to wear hearing aids against their will when it was proved that they could never benefit from hearing aids?"

One thing did not change, however. Because of the Ewings' domination of teacher training courses at Manchester University, oralism was the order of the day and all prospective teachers were trained in the pure oral method of the Ewing brand and approach. Ewingism grew to dominate the education of the deaf in many ways, both directly and indirectly. A few schools had a separate class, often concealed and taught by an older long-serving teacher, for deaf children who could not cope with the oral/aural method. These children were taught through signing and fingerspelling, but they were seen as "stupid", "backward with learning difficulties" and "unworthy of society."

To strengthen their grip on the Ewing approach, the oralists brought in parents of deaf children to bear some responsibility for their upbringing and education. These parents were put under intense pressure to teach their children and to rely entirely on speech. This approach contribute towards the success of Ewingism first and the education of the deaf child second. Both teachers and parents, not the Ewing method, were seen as failing if the children did not talk. Ewingism dictated that speech was a sign of intelligence and the absence of speech was seen as a sign of mental-inability. Ewingism dictated that, because deaf children lived in a speaking community, they must speak. Ewingism had a ruthless approach, devoid of any sentiment for those deaf children who could not benefit from the oral/aural approach. These deaf children, often labelled failures, were hidden away from the public eye and only the oral successes were paraded to publicise the "wonderful" approach to the education of the deaf as devised by Alexander and Irene Ewing. The deceit was so good and well manipulated that no one was aware about the rejected signing deaf. Alexander Ewing was knighted for his work in February 1959.

Ewingism was much more than the "Hear! Hear! Speak! Speak!" approach. The Ewings' work was diverse within the strict oral-only environment and established a variety of educational provisions:

1. Parent guidance programmes
2. Units for Partially hearing children
3. Integration/mainstreaming programmes
4. Developing peripatetic services for the deaf
5. Emphasis and development of audiological services

The fact that the training of teachers of the deaf was exclusively oral completely and deliberately severed the link between deaf adults using sign and the education of deaf children. Ewingism prevented educated Deaf persons from becoming teachers of the deaf. The warnings of the adult Deaf and also those of the missioners that Ewingism was not the right way to educate many of the very deaf children went unheeded while Alexander and

Irene Ewing were basking in the glory of their work and system by travelling across the world, particularly to the USA, Australia and New Zealand, where they received many honours.

Perhaps it was human nature that led to the spread of the philosophy taking on the nature of a crusade, with strongly felt expressions. According to Ewingism oralism was the only right gospel; any use of signs was pernicious and would blight the chances of deaf children for ever. There was no child that did not have some useful hearing, and there was no child that could not be helped by hearing aids provided as early as possible, by good testing, and within a well-arranged acoustic environment. The introduction of even a few signs would stop the children working hard to speak. There was a profound failure to separate speech from language. Many inexperienced teachers gained the idea that surrounding deaf children all the time with speech would lead to them talking in correct language. A typical catchphrase was "language is like gravy – pour it over the children all the time and it will stick."

Books written and published by Alexander and Irene Ewing contributed a lot to their work and philosophy, and included "The Handicap of Deafness" (1938), "Opportunity and the Deaf Child" (1947) and "Speech and the Deaf Child" (1954). Not only that, their work inspired Hilda Lewis (1896-1974) to write a novel about a deaf child at the Royal Schools for the Deaf in Manchester. Lewis' novel, "The Day is Ours", was dedicated to Irene Ewing – "… she makes the deaf to hear, the dumb to speak." In 1952 her novel was turned into a film entitled "Mandy" with Jack Hawkins, Phyllis Calvert and Mandy Miller in it.

In 1945 Lady Ewing retired from her work. She died on 16 July 1959, five months after her husband was knighted, and was succeeded by her husband, Sir Alexander, who eventually became the first Professor of what by then had became a separate and independent department. Barely two years after his wife's demise, Sir Alexander married her niece, Ethel Constance Goldsack (1899-1981, right) who had been in charge of the Clyne House nursery at the Royal Schools for the Deaf since 1937.

Ethel Ewing

Sir Alexander and the second Lady Ewing together revised or re-wrote many of their books, added others and continued the work of a world-famous and highly influential department, promoting strict oralist principles and approach. Their revised books include "Teaching Deaf Children to Talk" (1964), "Hearing Aids, Lipreading and Clear Speech" (1967) and "Hearing Impaired Children Under Five: A Guide for Parents and Teachers" (1971).

Like many empires at their peak, Ewingism began then to lose its grip. Deaf children who were oral failures began in the late 1960s to voice their grievances and concerns and a growing interest in sign language as a part of the Total Communication package emerged. People and employers were beginning to question why the deaf oral failures were not educated to an acceptable standard. Many issues came to light and were raised, and the blame rested with… Ewingism.

Typical school for the deaf assembly under Ewingism - note the great distance between the teacher and the deaf pupils in the rear who were unable to lipread from such a distance.

For all the significant advances in audiology and advancing technology in amplification, which were notable, a deep rift between the Deaf community and the medical profession grew. Ewingism was inhumane in that its philosophy insisted that within the aural/oral environment the system should fit the child, and denied the emergence of a system that benefited the signing deaf to whom the aural/oral only approach was of no benefit. Ewingism discriminated against the profoundly and signing deaf child; Ewingism deprived every deaf child of his/her right to a fully rounded educational provision – and Ewingism caused every deaf child to suffer a future after school in lowly paid menial jobs with very few opportunities to achieve better paid occupations. In short, Ewingism destroyed five generations of deaf children, their education and their future.

Hearing Aids

Hearing implements for the deaf and hard of hearing have come a long way since days long ago. Great leaps began in the 19th century. First of all, there were ear trumpets and subsequent variations of ear trumpets before the onset of electric and battery hearing aids. The chronology of improvements in hearing aid technology is as follows:

1876 – Telephone invented
1895 – First electric hearing aid
1906 – Triode vacuum tube invented
1923 – Vacuum tube hearing aid
1925 – Carbon wearable aids
1932 – Valve aids in carrying cases
1940 – Printed circuits developed
1947 – Transistor invented
1948 – Hearing aids with printed circuits
        Free valve aids on the NHS
1953 – All-transistor hearing aids
1960 – Integrated circuits developed
1964 – Hearing aids with integrated circuits
1966 – Behind-the-ear (BTE) aids on the NHS
1970 – House (Los Angeles) & Hochmair (Vienna) introduced single-channel cochlea
        implants with limited success.
1975 – Very large scale integrated circuits developed
1976 – In-the-ear (ITE) aids available
1983 – First UK deaf adult given a cochlea implant
        In-the-canal (ITC) aids
1985 – Multichannel, Inneraid & Nucleus implant devices introduced
1987 – First deaf child in the UK given a cochlea implant
        Completely-in-the-canal (CIC) aids
1995 – Digital aids created in Denmark
2001 – First digital hearing aids available on the National Health Service

Hearing aids developed to the stage that many deaf people with residual hearing and deafened people were able to benefit from them, and continued to participate in society as if their deafness was did not exist. These equipments have restored to millions of people the pleasures of hearing and listening that would otherwise be impossible without hearing aids.

For the profoundly deaf, though, many were able to hear sounds but derived no great benefit from using hearing aids because they very often encountered difficulties in picking out what was being said, or what sounds they were hearing. There was, and still is, a certain category of deaf people who had no wish to hear sound at all due to the fact that they find sound an irritant and an interference to their natural state of being deaf. Such deaf persons become short-tempered and seemingly violent when forced to wear hearing aids.

Battery operated hearing aids were sold as early as the late 19th century by the reputable ear trumpet company, T. Hawksley of 357 Oxford Street, London. In the following are examples of hearing aids from the 1890s to the present. The development from bulky set of equipment to a tiny behind-the-ear aid is shown and presents a fascinating study of hearing aid development.

THE "ACOUSTICON."

This is the invention of Mr. Hutchinson, of New York, U.S.A., and is the most perfect of the numberless attempts made to aid the deaf by Electrical means. It consists of a very sensitive microphone, a waistcoat-pocket battery, and a telephonic ear-piece. The illustration conveys an idea of the instrument when used conversationally.

The **telephonic ear-piece** may be held to the ear by means of its sliding handle as shown, or kept in position over the ear by means of a spring passing over the head, thus leaving both hands free. **The receiver.**—The receiver may be held in the hand towards the source of sound, but the better way is to attach it by its clip to the waistcoat, or front of the dress. The **small battery** is carried in any convenient pocket or receptacle. For ordinary conversation one receiver is sufficient, but for extreme deafness or for use in church, theatre, or large halls, from two to six receivers may be required. The battery, consisting of three dry cells, is put into action by inserting the two plugs at the end of one of the wires into two holes in the casing of the battery. If, however, greater power is required, one of the plugs may be inserted into the third hole in the casing.

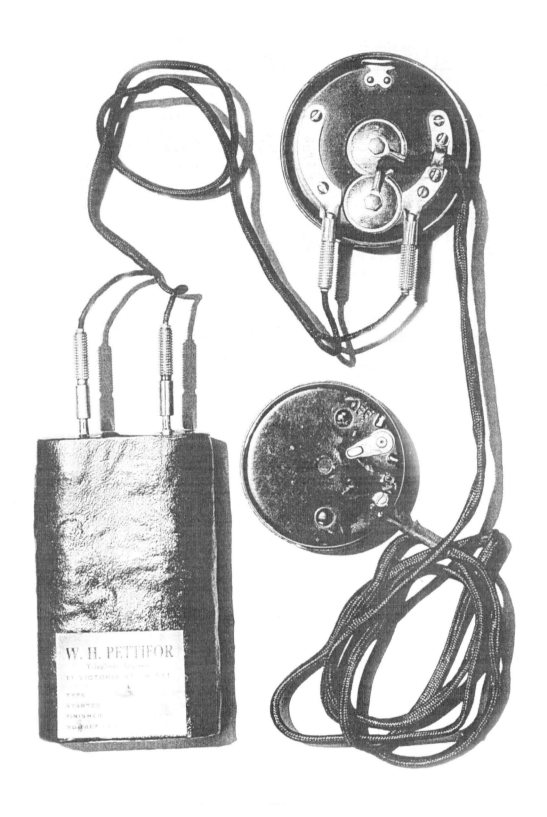

Stoltz - c 1900

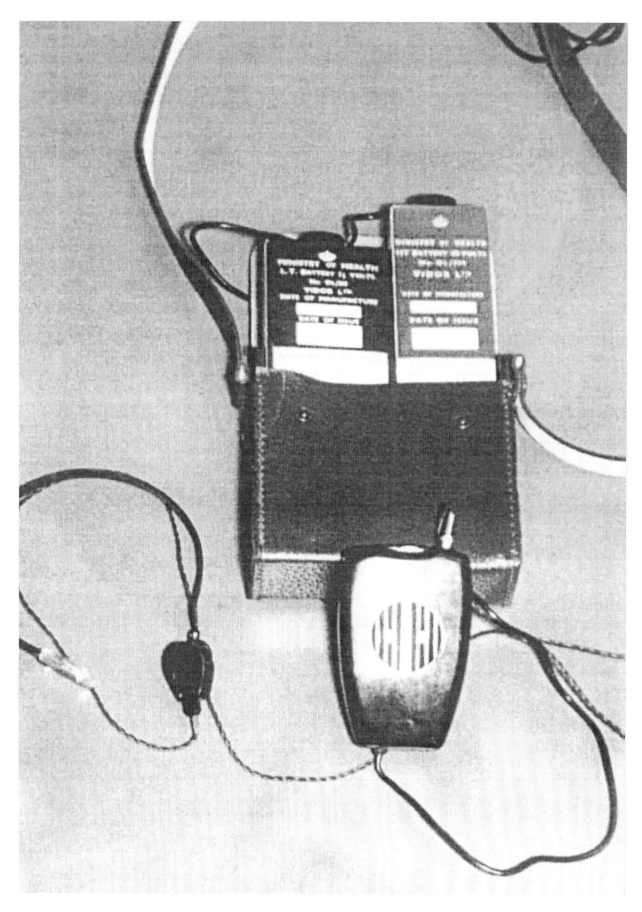

Medresco - 1948

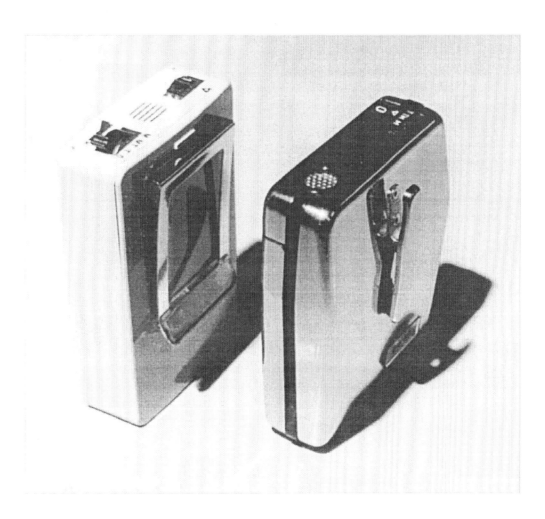

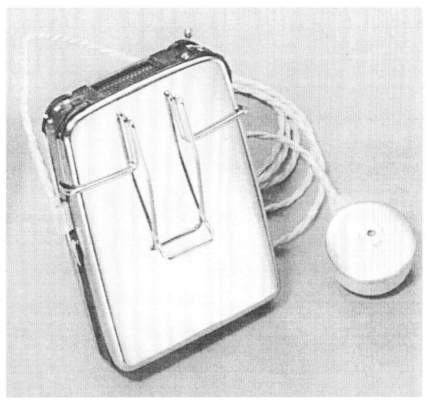

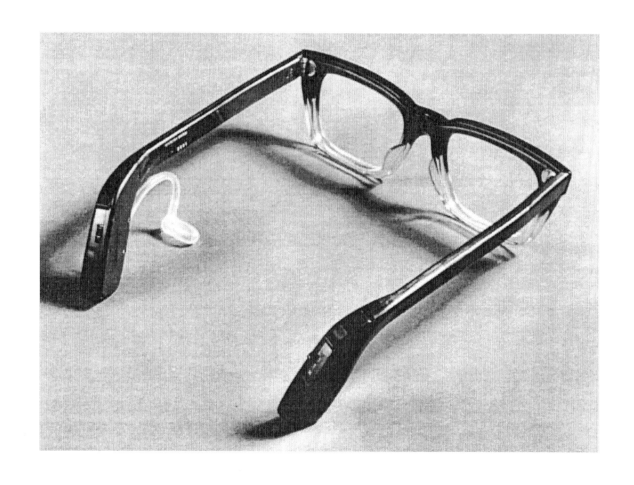

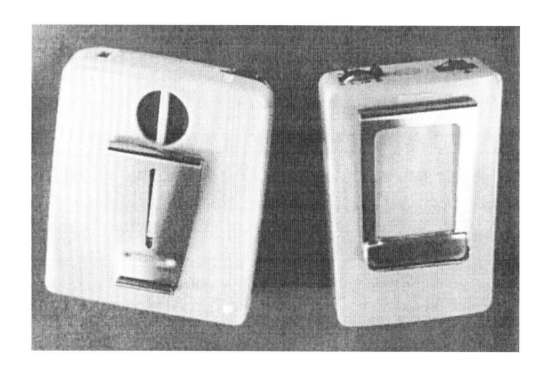

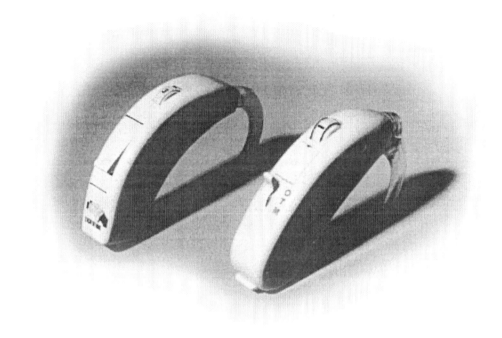

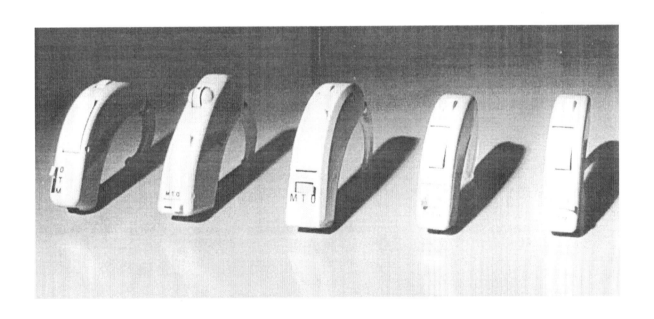

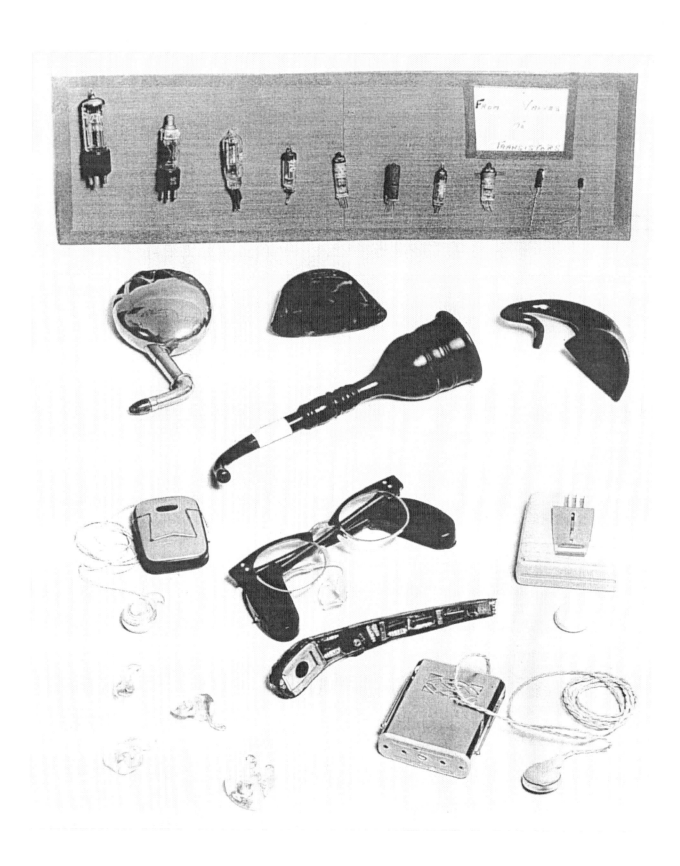

Cochlea Implants

A cochlea implant is sometimes known as the bionic ear. The device comprises a microphone, speech processor, transmitter, transmitting coil and a cable, all worn externally.

The implant, which is a transmitting coil, is placed underneath the skin by means of an incision made behind the ear. The skull is drilled and the implant placed in the skull and threaded into the cochlea. The operation takes about three hours. Once the incision has healed (in about 3-4 weeks) the cochlea implant can be activated.

A functioning ear converts sound waves to electrical signals in the inner ear. If the inner ear is damaged, the signals cannot get through to the brain. The implant takes over the role by producing an electrical signal that stimulates the auditory nerve and bypasses the damaged part of the ear on its way to the brain. This is different from a hearing aid, which simply amplifies the acoustic signal. Cochlea implants are particularly aimed at those profoundly deaf persons who cannot benefit from hearing aids.

There are approximately 60,000 cochlea implant users worldwide, of which 1,900 are in the United Kingdom. The average rate of cochlea implant operations in England and Wales is around 400 per annum. Unlike hearing aids which are easily obtainable either via the National Health for free or through private hearing aid dispensers at prices between £300 and £2,500, cochlea implants a involve lengthy assessment and a testing process before one can be adjudged suitable to receive an implant. This is because of the high costs involved. The costs of cochlea implantation are as follows:

Adult

Assessment	£ 3,000
Full treatment	£27,500
Annual Support Charge – 2nd year	£ 4,000
Annual Support Charge – subsequent years	£ 2,000

Child

Assessment	£ 4,000
Full treatment	£31,000
Annual Support Charge – 2nd year	£ 5,000
Annual Support Charge – subsequent years	£ 2,500

The above costs are approximate and are as in March 2001. The charge for full treatment includes assessment, device, surgery, hospital stay, rehabilitation and support for the first year after implantation.

Although many of the implantees have reported that they are benefiting enormously from the implantation, there is a number of cochlea implant users who stopped using their cochlea implant devices because they were of no or little use. In one paper published in the *British Medical Journal* (31 August 2002; 325:471) the researchers found that in Wales only, out of 116 people traced from a total of 176 people who had implants between 1986 and 1994, 66 were not using their cochlea implant devices and had given them up. This little piece of information, amongst others, gives rise to the question why balanced information outlining the pros and cons of cochlea implant is strikingly absent and in favour and in praise of implantation.

Cochlea implantation has the same surgical risks as other procedures conducted under general anaesthesia and other routine surgeries of the middle or inner ear. Other risks include:

1. During surgery any remaining hearing in the treated ear will be permanently lost.
2. Because the surgery is done in the vicinity of the nerve that belongs to the face, there is a remote possibility that temporary or permanent facial paralysis may occur after surgery that disturbs or affect the nerve.
3. There is a slight risk that the patient may experience taste disturbances, such as a metallic taste, following implant surgery.
4. There is the risk that the surgical site may become infected, which might require removal of the device.
5. The patient may experience pain at the wound following surgery; this is typically temporary.
6. There has been a reported infection of meningitis in at least 25 known implantees worldwide.

The issue of cochlea implant is not without controversy. Some members of the Deaf community see deaf babies and children with cochlea implants as representing the "ultimate invasion of the ear; the ultimate denial of deafness; the ultimate refusal to let deaf children be deaf; the ultimate proof that deaf children have no rights of their own." The medical profession generally insists that the earlier deaf children are given implants, the better their chances of hearing.

Although cochlea implants have benefited many deaf people, there is a large number who found no benefit and subsequently discarded their devices. For the Deaf community, the main issue is that of human rights of deaf children. The Deaf community feel that no implantations should take place until the child becomes old enough to decide if he or she wants to have an implant. The Deaf feel that literature and information on cochlea implants are one-sided and in favour of the implants and also that, since many deaf children are born of hearing parents, the medical profession is taking advantage of the desire of the hearing parents to make their children hearing.

On 21 June 2003 UNISON, the largest trade union in the UK with 1.3 million members, passed a motion at its annual delegates conference supporting the opposition to cochlea implants in children. UNISON acknowledged that a cochlea implant would not make a Deaf person "normal and hearing", and he or she will remain deaf.

In 2004 a new method of restoring or curing deafness was introduced by the House Hearing Institute in Los Angeles in the USA. This is the brainstem implant, a device designed to restore hearing by directly stimulating nerves. This brainstem implant has been under research for 15 years and it was not until the early months of 2004 that it was finally tried on two deaf women.

The issues of both cochlea and brainstem implants are at present still being hotly debated.

Deaf Population Figures

Recording the exact number of deaf people in Britain has been a task much avoided or ignored by the British authorities for nearly 100 years since 1911. There have been some attempts, albeit poorly thought out, to verify the numbers via censuses between 1851 and 1911. Taken from W. H. Addison and J. Kerr-Love's *Deaf Mutism* (1896), the figures from each census between 1851 and 1891 gave the following:

1851 – 17,300
1861 – 19,501
1871 – 18,072
1881 – 19,430
1891 – 19,692

In each of the above censuses according to Addison and Kerr-Love, about 75% of deaf children under the age of 5 years escaped counting, and it was reported that a good number escaped who were over 5 years of age. These numbers put together amount to 12% of the deaf population recorded and the numbers given above should be increased by that percentage to give the final minimum figures – to take an example, the 1891 census should read 22,055 instead of 19,692. The figures for the 1891 census are further confused by the fact that the *Return of Blind and Deaf-Mute Persons in England, Wales and Ireland who are Assisted from the Poor Rates*, ordered by the House of Commons on 12 September 1887 and published in March 1888, showed the following figures:

England and Wales

In workhouses,	1,289
Not in workhouses but having poor law relief	586

This gives an additional figure of 1,875, but whether that was recorded in the 1891 census or not is open to argument.

The drop of nearly 1,500 recorded in the 1871 census cannot be explained, but it is possible that certain enumerators failed in their tasks or parents failed to declare their deaf children. It is well known that in the early years of the census people were suspicious of its purpose and did not take kindly to listing everyone, especially members with criminal backgrounds, disabled children and travellers taken in as lodgers.

The censuses between 1851 and 1901 had columns for the recording of handicapped people and the 1911 census amplified this requirement to include the totally deaf or deaf and dumb. The returns for England and Wales for 1911 showed a total of 26,649 totally deaf and 15,122 deaf and dumb. The last figure included 1,695 stated to be dumb but not deaf. This particular census gave a total of 41,771 deaf people, but this figure fell short of the true numbers and this total must be taken with care.

Moving onwards in the 20th century, the Registrar General, who was responsible for the census, decided to scrap the section asking about disability beginning with the 1921 census. He stated that "the census inquiries respecting infirmities were discontinued because of the difficulty of finding a suitable definition understandable by the general population and the knowledge that any figures obtained through the census would be incomplete owing to the reluctance of parents to record the information on the schedules."

The 1930s yielded the best available deaf child population figures one could find, even though these figures represent nowhere near the maximum. The Board of Education issued a publication in 1933 entitled *The Report of the Board of Education* and in this report the following information for the year 1930-1931, ending on 31 March 1931, read:

> *The number of special schools for the deaf in England and Wales is 50. Of these schools, 30 are Day schools with accommodation for 1,893 and 20 are boarding schools accommodating 2,731, a total accommodation of 4,624. The numbers of children on the register on 31 March 1931 were 1,589 (boys 1,226 and girls, 1026) in the residential schools, a total of 3,841. The corresponding total in the previous year was 3,951.*

In the section *The Peak of Growth of Deaf Schools*, a minimum of 5,636 known deaf pupils can be counted for the 1933-1934 period. When it is taken into account that there were numbers of certain private schools that were not known to the authorities alongside the fact that there was a good number of known private schools for the deaf all over the country during the period of 1933-1934, it is becoming clear that large numbers of deaf children escaped notice and were not counted.

The Board of Education was only interested in counting deaf children in schools that were certified and recognised by that body, and outside of education there were many deaf adults in social, working and retirement lives who were yet to be counted.

The first comprehensive attempt to establish the exact numbers of the deaf population was undertaken by Dr. A. Eichholz on behalf of the Ministry of Health and the President of the Board of Education. Eichholz carried out a study of the Deaf in England and Wales only for the period between 1930 and 1932. Eichholz's study was far-reaching. He conducted surveys into the preceding years and threw light on the numbers of school-age deaf children as outlined below:

Year	Attending Certified Special Schools	Attending Public Elementary Schools	At Other Institutions	At no School or Institution	Total
1924	3,584	236	52	301	4,173
1925	3,551	319	37	247	4,154
1926	3,601	223	31	246	4,101
1927	3,544	196	41	257	4,038
1928	3,464	156	77	238	3,935
1929	3,334	166	66	203	3,769
1930	3,245	131	68	177	3,621

The drop in numbers between 1924 and 1930 was of little importance in that there was an unknown number of deaf children who did not attend schools at all for various reasons ranging from parents' objections to ill-health, travelling families and begging to education in private schools and so on.

Partially deaf children not included in the 1924-1930 figures as well as in figures for subsequent years were those for whom an education in local hearing schools was available. Only the partially deaf who were deemed "a bit too deaf" to receive an education in ordinary hearing schools were made to attend those schools for the deaf which had special classes for such pupils.

According to Eichholz, a return of partially deaf children was made annually to the Medical Department of the Board of Education by the School Medical Officer of each Local Education Authority in England and Wales. From the returns relating to the year 1930, the number of partially deaf children in England and Wales was ascertained to be 1,882. Of the 1,882 partially deaf children, 517 pupils were in special schools for the deaf whereas 1,243 pupils in ordinary public elementary schools, 19 in other institutions and 103 did not attend school.

Moving on from the school environment to the Deaf's adult life, Eichholz looked into various areas and his survey yielded interesting bits of information. Since the National Institute of the Deaf (NID) was formed in 1924, this body was collecting data on the numbers of the adult deaf in England and Wales and, as the years progressed, the authorities looked to the NID's figures as a "reliable source". Eichholz was to find that the NID's figures were some 40% short of "true " when he collected numbers of deaf people who were registered with or known to various regional and local Missions.

Eichholz found the Missions more of a reliable source of information on the number of the adult Deaf in Britain and during his research he recorded the following:

Sixty Missions in England and Wales were approached, and from the information returned by them, Eichholz concluded that there was a deaf-adult population of some 31,000, of which 18,268 were on the books of the missions. On top of that, there were some 11,000 Deaf persons who could not be traced; 882 in public assistance institutions; 827 in mental hospitals and 700 deafblind adults registered as blind persons in need of interpreters. Adding all together, the deaf adult figures came to 44,409. Adding the 3,621 deaf pupils in 1930 to that total, Eichholz arrived at a grand total of 48,030 deaf persons.

For all Eichholz's efforts and his prediction that the numbers of the Deaf were decreasing steadily due to improved hygiene and medical conditions, one year after his report was published, it was found that the numbers of deaf children in schools alone added to a minimum of 5,636, just over 2,000 more than in 1930. Eichholz's 1930 figures did not match these issued by the Board of Education – he was 330 short, and for the year ending 1931 he was 220 short and this denoted an increase in the number of deaf children when compared with his own figures. The difference can only mean that certain irregularities and miscalculations were made. Despite these, Eichholz's work was both admirable and pioneering and it set the ground for future surveys, but the surveys, alas, were not to materialise.

With the introduction of the "Classification Method" by the Board of Education and its adoption by subsequent education authorities under various titles, there were notorious attempts by the Oralists to reduce the true numbers of Deaf people by labelling some "partially deaf" or "hard of hearing" for propaganda purposes rather than educational purposes - figures were often manipulated and results therefore distorted.

Methods of counting the numbers of the deaf were conducted in accordance with Section 29 of the National Assistance Act 1948. Under this section, local authorities are required to compile and maintain classified registers of "persons who are blind, deaf or dumb and other persons who are substantially and permanently handicapped by illness, injury or congenital deformity." In the case of the Deaf, classification divides them into the following categories:

a) Deaf without speech, b) Deaf with Speech, c) Hard of Hearing

After 1989 the categories were:

a) Deaf, b) Hard of Hearing

Information on the numbers of the deaf on the registers of local authorities is recorded on Form SSDA910, which is submitted triennially. Registration of disablement with the Social Service Departments is voluntary and is not a condition for the provision of certain social services in the form of assistance with the supply of aids, equipment, etc. under Section 2 of the Chronically Sick and Disabled Persons Act 1970. Not all Deaf and hard of hearing persons are registered with their local Social Services Department, so the figures cannot be representative and must be taken as the minimum. After 1973 figures were taken annually until 1983 and from thence every three years. These figures shown here between 1973 and 2001 conform to Section 29 of the National Assistance Act 1948, counting only those registered with their local Social Services Departments and cover all age groups:

Year	Deaf With Speech	Deaf Without Speech	Hard of Hearing	
	Total	Total	Total	Total
1973	10,775	15,164	18,842	44,781
1974	11,110	14,683	20,143	45,936
1975	11,619	13,951	20,400	45,970
1976	13,101	14,371	25,531	53,003
1977	13,461	14,295	27,005	54,761
1978	14,149	14,752	31,125	60,342*
1979	14,250	14,825	32,449	61,524
1980	14,870	14,795	35,123	64,788
1983	16,113	15,722	47,179	79,014
1986	+	+	+	
	-	Deaf	Hard of Hearing	
1989	-	37,910	70,326	108,236
1992	-	41,821	95,323	137,144
1995	-	45,482	125,939	171,421
1998	-	50,111	139,467	189,578
2001	-	50,282	144,558	194,840

*Includes 316 persons for whom age breakdown not available   + Figures unavailable/unobtainable

Since the above figures do not include the Deaf who do not register with their local Social Services, no one will ever know for sure what are the true Deaf population figures or will be. The figures recorded so far for England and Wales only represent evidence by a long way that deafness is not on the wane, but most certainly on the increase despite modern scientific, technological and medical progress and innovations over the past 100 years.

The
EDINBURGH MESSENGER,

BEING A RECORD OF INTELLIGENCE REGARDING THE DEAF AND DUMB.

"Open thy mouth for the Dumb,"—Prov. xxxi. 3.

No. II.   TUESDAY, NOVEMBER 14th, 1843.   Price 1d. or 7s. per 100.

The Manual Alphabet
AS USED
IN THE INSTITUTION FOR DEAF-MUTES, EDINBURGH.

Deaf Magazines

Magazines for the Deaf most probably originated in Edinburgh. Robert Kinniburgh with his pupils began to produce them at the Edinburgh Institution for the Deaf and Dumb. There is an article in the *British Deaf Times* (1903, II) in which the editors stated that: -

> Yet earlier we have *The Tablet: and Record of Practical Instruction for the Deaf and Dumb No.2* dated May 25th, 1839, price 1d. The copy before us is pasted in a scrap book, so that we cannot detect the imprint. It is a cruder performance than *The Edinburgh Messenger*, but may well have been an earlier production from the same institution.

The same editors also wrote in an earlier paragraph in the same 1903 publication:

> Before us now is No. VII of *The Edinburgh Messenger*, dated Tuesday June 11th, 1844, price 1d. It consists of four pages, very well printed by the pupils of the Edinburgh Institution.

Unless new discoveries of older magazines are made, it is clear that the magazines published by deaf schoolboys in Edinburgh were the first recorded British magazines for the Deaf. The first issue was printed in October 1843. The magazine ceased after it reached issue number 12 dated January 1845. The Edinburgh Institution in 1847 relaunched the magazine under a different title, *A Voice for the Dumb*. This journal was issued three times annually for five years until it ceased publication in 1852.

In London, with the mission movement and the growth of the Association in Aid of the Deaf and Dumb (AADD), which later in 1873 became the Royal Association in aid of the Deaf and Dumb), the situation called for the need for Deaf people both to be in touch with each other and to be kept informed of meetings and the Association's activities. In 1855 *The Magazine of the Association in aid of the Deaf and Dumb* was first issued. This was in the year the Reverend Samuel Smith joined the Association, and he was most probably the editor. It is not known for how long the magazine ran for, but the RNID library has only three surviving copies for 1855 to 1857. There is a gap after that date until 1873 when, under the editorship of the Reverend Samuel Smith, *A Magazine Chiefly Intended for the Deaf and Dumb* first came out. It was published by the National Deaf and Dumb Society. It became a popular publication and sold well, besides being widely circulated although it was almost heavily laden with religious articles and leanings. In 1879 the title of the magazine was changed to *The Deaf and Dumb Magazine*. Samuel Smith retired as editor in 1881 and it was taken over by the Glaswegian Deaf, Alexander Fairley Strathern (1844-1890). Strathern edited and published the magazine

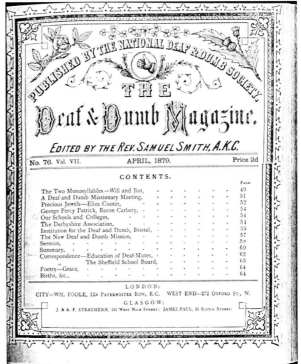

only for a short period before he resigned in June 1883, due to lack of support and also because of the National Deaf and Dumb Society's differences with the committee of the RADD. Under Strathern's editorship, articles of controversial nature aimed to generate discussions were introduced along with lively features, to the dismay of many priests associated with the RADD.

There was a gap of six months before the magazine was restored once more under the editorship of the famous Deaf Scot, James Paul (1848-1918, left) of Kilmarnock, in January 1884. The title changed slightly to *A Magazine for the Deaf and Dumb*. It ran for just over a year and came to an end in April 1885. This was practically the end of the RADD's nationwide connection with national Deaf societies and the organisation then concentrated on local mission work.

In the very last issue of the magazine James Paul recognised the fact that the need to keep in touch and maintain communication among members of the Deaf community was very strong and he introduced a new magazine, *The Deaf and Dumb World*, by a hearing man, Ernest J. D. Abraham. A stepson and pupil of John Jennings (1833-1884) at his South London Mission for the Deaf and Dumb in Ossery Road, off the Kent Road, Ernest Abraham launched the magazine soon after the RADD's own magazine folded. Its title changed to *Deaf-Mute World* in 1887. Although it was not as good as the previous magazines, it ran for two years until June 1887 before it ceased publication on account of heavy losses and ill-health of the editor. Abraham soon after moved north to Bolton, Lancashire, to take up mission work.

In July 1888 there appeared the first number of *The Deaf-Mute*, a monthly journal conducted by J. T. Maclean of Greenock. This was a 12-pages pamphlet in coloured cover. It was the organ of the ill-fated Deaf-Mute Association. This association was a national organisation established before the British Deaf and Dumb Association. Its president was Francis Maginn of Belfast and the committee consisted of John T. Maclean of Greenock, Ernest Abraham, missioner of London and Bolton, Alexander F. Strathern of Glasgow, Maurice Hewson, missioner of Dublin and Benjamin Payne, a Deaf teacher of the deaf in Swansea. An interesting and readable publication, it ran until August 1889. *The Deaf-Mute* had to cease publication after the Deaf-Mute Association folded. Another magazine had started to come into circulation, two months earlier, in June of the same year. This new magazine was fast gaining readership and popularity among the Deaf. The editor of the new magazine, *The Deaf and Dumb Times*, was Charles Gorham (1861-1922) of Leeds.

The Deaf and Dumb Times consisted of from 8 to 16 pages and was published monthly at 2d. a copy. Its contents surpassed those of the previous magazines in that it contained original, well-written articles, news, illustrations and correspondences on all topics concerning the Deaf. Charles Gorham retired in the autumn of 1891 and his magazine was taken over by Joseph Hepworth (1865-1921, left) and Henry Lund. The new editors changed the title to *The Deaf Chronicle*, which first appeared in November 1891.

Not long after its launch Ernest Abraham joined the staff and he later became the editor of the magazine with Joseph Hepworth moving aside to become manager, but still retaining the assistant editor role. Abraham later bought a significant share of *The Deaf Chronicle* and became part proprietor. At his suggestion the magazine was renamed *The British Deaf-Mute* in November 1892. With the advent of Ernest Abraham *The British Deaf-Mute* greatly improved in interest and attraction and became an independent publication. In October 1896 the name changed yet again to *British Deaf Monthly*. This magazine went from strength to strength and was described at that time as "the best known and most widely read publication for the deaf and their teachers in the world." This title was retained until December 1903 when the journal became the *British Deaf Times,* which continued until 1954.

Ernest Abraham left in 1902 to emigrate to Australia and Joseph Hepworth retook the reins of the editor until 1921. After Hepworth, the new editor of the *British Deaf Times* was Alfred Shankland, who assumed editorship in January 1922 and held the post until August 1925. He was succeeded by James Perkins, who took over in September 1925, and remained as editor until 1954.

Among the predecessors of the *British Deaf Times*, aspirants in the same field, were *The Herald*, edited by Ralph Clegg, and *The Advance*. *The Herald* was an interesting paper similar in size and character to *The Deaf and Dumb Magazine*. Their history, though, has not been preserved and no one knows much about these journals.

Other earlier publications include *Our Quarterly Paper*, which started as a local pamphlet published by the Rev. F. W. G. Gilby in London. The exact date of the origin of this publication is not known. It ran for a few years until in January 1884 it became a penny 16-pages monthly in coloured wrappers, entitled *Our Church Messenger to the Deaf*. It was conducted on strict Church lines, as was Samuel Smith's *Magazine*. Twelve years later in January 1896, this magazine was renamed *Ephphatha* and the literary editorship passed from the Rev. Gilby to A. M. Cuttell. The magazine came to an end in 1899 when it amalgamated with and became known as the *British Deaf Monthly*.

Rev. F. W. G. Gilby

Other magazines worthy of note that were published in the 19th century include:

The Quarterly Review of Deaf-Mute Education, which first appeared in January 1886. It ran until October 1896. This was the organ of the College of the Teachers of the Deaf and Dumb. It was first edited and issued under the direction of the following editorial committee: Thomas Arnold, Dr. David Buxton, Richard Elliott, John Howard, William Neill, William Sleight, William Stainer, J. Thomson, S. Schontheil and William van Praagh. The main work of editing fell to Dr. Buxton.

Our Silent People was the title of the Bolton, Bury and Rochdale Adult Deaf and Dumb Society's magazine. It was first published in September 1894 and the last issue was in June 1896. This was superseded by…

The Bolton Review, which began in September 1896 (vol.1 no.1) and ended in August 1897 (vol.1 no.12), after which its name changed to…

The Lancashire Review (vol.2 no.1). It was short-lived, ending in August 1898 (vol.2 no.12).

Our Little Messenger to the Deaf and Dumb, a four-page pamphlet selling for ½d, was begun by one Miss Tredennick in Ireland in January 1882. It ran for ten years until vol. 9 no.5 (May 1892) after then its title changed to…

Our Little Messenger, which started in June 1892 and ended in January 1895. There was a period of two months of silence before the magazine was revamped and relaunched under a new title…

The Silent Messenger (vol.1 no.1 – March 1895). This journal was edited by E. Harris and Francis Maginn. There was a change in series, and this journal ended in December 1898 (vol.1 no.12 of new series) when its name was changed to…

The Messenger in January 1899 (vol.2 no.1). The magazine continued uninterrupted until 1917, when another new series began and it ended around April 1918 (vol.1 no.7).

Early in the 20th century another publication came onto the scene, in 1905, the *Bolton, Bury, Rochdale and District Deaf and Dumb Society Quarterly News,* founded by Ernest Ayliffe, a former teacher of the deaf. The first issue came out in April 1905. Three years later the last issue (no.13) was printed in April 1908 before its name changed to…

The Quarterly News (no.14) in July 1908. With the change of title, the publication went national. In January 1909 the magazine (no.16) ceased publication under its title, which was changed to…

The Deaf Quarterly News (no.17) in April 1909. It continued until issue no.40 in January 1915. This journal achieved wide readership and became the most widely read periodical in the Deaf world. The title changed in wording to…

The Deaf Quarterly News, a Magazine to interest the Deaf and all who wish them well (no.41) in April 1915. The magazine was independent, and it was not until issue no. 157 in 1944 that the additional words *Under the Auspices of the British Deaf and Dumb Association* appeared on the title page. Two years later, in issue no. 164 (January-March 1946), the magazine became "The Official Organ of the British Deaf and Dumb Association".

Ernest Ayliffe remained the editor until he resigned in 1947 after completing issue no.168 (January-March). After 42 years of continuous editorship of the magazine, Ayliffe was succeeded by K. P. McDougall, who continued the journal until issue no. 183 in December 1950. The title once again changed to...

The Deaf News in January 1951. The series continued then uninterrupted under McDougall until issue no.203 in December 1954.

At the end of 1954 there were four major journals in circulation. Of these, two were very similar in nature and contents – *British Deaf Times* and *Deaf News*. Following discussions with members of the Deaf community, it was decided to merge the two periodicals into *The British Deaf News* (BDN) and the British Deaf and Dumb Association sponsored this merger. The first issue came out in January 1955 with K. P. McDougall as editor. There was a hiccup in the publication of the quarterly issues of the BDN around September-November 1961. The September issue came out very late and announced the "tragic death" of the editor. The December 1961 issue did not appear. Publication resumed with the March 1962 issue under the Rev. Mark C. Frame as editor. The Rev. Frame held the editorship until 1964, and there was a hiccup with the publication of the September 1964 issue being disrupted by Frame's suicide. After that tragedy, an Editorial Board produced further issues until 1966.

In 1966 the editorship was assumed by James F. Hudson, who remained in the post until his resignation in 1972. Between 1973 and 1983 an Editorial Board put out the BDN with no named editor and various people writing editorials. Sometime in 1980 Ralph Gee became the editor of BDN. Gee was also involved in other BDA work such as publicity and fundraising. In March 1981 Irene Hall joined Gee as assistant editor. Soon afterwards, in August 1981, Ralph Gee retired; and the BDN issues from September 1981 to February 1982 were published with Irene Hall as Acting Editor.

In March 1982 the BDA appointed Roger Brown, a hearing man from Tyne-Wear, as the new editor. He was then succeeded in 1984 by Bernard Quinn. In February 1989, when Bernard was moved to the post of Director of Information Services in the BDA, Irene Hall resumed the editorship of the BDN in March 1989. She became the first-ever Deaf female editor of ANY major British Deaf journals. She continued to edit the BDN until the June 1996 issue, after which the position of editor of *British Deaf News* was made redundant on 31 May 1996 due to BDA restructuring.

The BDA put the BDN out to tender. In July 1996, a team led by the former BDA Marketing Officer, Sheila Gregory, won the tender and produced the BDN for the next three years. The team included Sheila Gregory as Co-ordinator/Advertising Manager, Jenny Dodds, followed by Helga McGilp, as News Editor and Irene Hall as Features Editor. During this time there was also a change in the format of the BDN as the BDA had decided to implement a motion passed at a previous Annual General Meeting asking for a larger A3-size magazine with larger print and more photographs.

In July 1999 the BDN was put out to tender again. The contract was awarded to Red Lizard, a Deaf-owned company based in Redditch. Catya Nielson became the new editor and the BDN reverted to its A4 size. The title was yet again changed to *Signmatters* in 2003 when the BDA took back the responsibility of publishing its magazine.

The genealogical chart below shows the history of the development and mergers of the various magazines that eventually gave birth to *The British Deaf News* and then *Signmatters*.

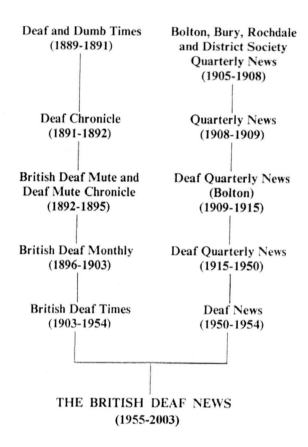

Deaf and Dumb Times
(1889-1891)

Deaf Chronicle
(1891-1892)

British Deaf Mute and
Deaf Mute Chronicle
(1892-1895)

British Deaf Monthly
(1896-1903)

British Deaf Times
(1903-1954)

Bolton, Bury, Rochdale
and District Society
Quarterly News
(1905-1908)

Quarterly News
(1908-1909)

Deaf Quarterly News
(Bolton)
(1909-1915)

Deaf Quarterly News
(1915-1950)

Deaf News
(1950-1954)

THE BRITISH DEAF NEWS
(1955-2003)

Among the plethora of magazines for the Deaf and hard of hearing available in Britain, there were two other journals that were regarded as major publications. One was the RADD's second series of *Ephphatha*, a quarterly magazine that began in March 1909 and ran for 50 years and 200 issues before it folded.

The other major journal was the National Institute of the Deaf's *The Silent World*, launched in June 1946 (vol.1 no.1). It continued to flourish until it reached vol.18 no.6 in June 1963. After that date, it became...

Hearing. This magazine was a continuance of *The Silent World*, taking vol.18 no.7 as its starting point. It ran for eighteen years until 1981 when it was closed down by the RNID. In 1984 the RNID relaunched its journal under a new title...

Soundbarrier. The journal became quite popular amongst the RNID's hearing readership. No.62 in 1992 was the final issue. The RNID then joined with BBC TV's See Hear team and to launch a new magazine...

See Hear, which came out in October 1992. It was a very glossy magazine and a vast improvement on the dull matt cover and bland format of *Soundbarrier*. Five years later in August 1997 *See Hear* came to an end, and a replacement took its place...

One in Seven came out in October 1997 and continues to the present.

Since the first known magazine for the Deaf was published by deaf schoolchildren in Edinburgh in 1839, there has been an incredible minimum count of 356 known journals for the Deaf published over a span of 164 years. There have been, and still exist, local and regional journals catering for various tastes and interests within the Deaf community of Britain. There were political magazines, the first being the *NUD Newsletter,* which ran between 1976 and 1984, and the present journal catering for the Deaf political movement is the Federation of Deaf People's official organ, *The Voice,* which was first published in 1998. The organisation serving the hard of hearing, Hearing Concern (formerly the British Association of the Hard of Hearing – BAHOH) issues its own journal, *Hearing Concern,* which is the continuance of the *Hark!* (1959-1992).

A list of all known journals can be found in the Appendices section.

Employment and the Deaf

Occupations taken by Deaf people in the past were not well chronicled until just before the end of the 18th century. Evidence exists to show that the pupils of Thomas Braidwood left school to take well-paid employment; a good number became artists of renown, one became an MP and Governor of Barbados, one reached the position of Auditor of Excise at the Scottish Excise Office, one became a famous astronomer; the list goes on, down to the pupil who became a rat catcher and became so successful that he was able to build his own tavern and run a successful business. There was also a profoundly deaf private pupil of Joseph Watson at the London Asylum, John William Lowe (1804-1876, right), who went on to become a barrister, having been called to the Bar of the Society of Middle Temple on 29 November 1829. Later, in Scotland, two Deaf brothers, Archibald (1831-1902) and Duncan (1836-1920) MacLellan, who were educated by Duncan Anderson at the Glasgow Institution for the Deaf and Dumb, went on to become lawyers after they emigrated to

Canada. There was also Arthur Henry Bather (1829-1892) who rose to become an Assistant Accountant-General of the Navy despite being profoundly deaf with a speech impediment.

With the creation of public schools for the deaf, employment opportunities for deaf pupils were made available by the schools and their connections with various members of their Boards of Governors. The headmaster of the London Asylum (founded 1792), Joseph Watson, created an early form of "6th Form" by establishing a manufactory in which pupils would learn the various trades that would put them in good stead in obtaining employment outside of the school. This move filled in a void between the day the pupils left school and the day they obtained employment, if ever they found one. Watson then went a step further than establishing a manufactory; he allocated the responsibility of obtaining employment for the pupils to the school itself. In other words, the school became the principal agency by which Deaf persons were assisted in obtaining employment. Subsequent schools, which opened all over Britain, took up this approach.

Following on from Watson's early efforts, a number of schools for the deaf established rapport with various local factories and companies that would offer deaf pupils apprenticeships in their chosen trades. Even so, opportunities were often limited and many deaf pupils had to be passed on to the Missions for assistance with job-seeking.

From all available sources unearthed during the research into British Deaf history, it turns out that the following trades were the most common with Deaf people during much of the 19th century, even though a good number were known to have held clerical positions and self-employed occupations such as journeymen carpenter, caulker and bricklayer: -

Males

Tailor, shoemaker, carpenter/joiner, general labourer, painter, French polisher, bookbinder, miner, blacksmith, agricultural labourer, upholsterer, cabinet-maker, assistant teacher of the deaf, domestic staff in schools for the deaf.

Females

Dressmaker, seamstress, domestic staff in schools for the deaf, domestic servants, tailoress, laundry/washer woman, cotton/textile worker, factory cleaners.

There were many thousands of Deaf people who were very often unemployed and who did not hold down regular jobs. Unemployment among the Deaf rose dramatically after the 1880 Congress at Milan when almost all Deaf people employed by schools for the deaf were removed from their jobs because their presence and their use of sign language might "contaminate" the deaf pupils, who were required to adhere to oralism.

Obtaining statistics on the state of employment of the Deaf in the 19th century is difficult, but there exists the *Report of the Royal Commission on the Blind, Deaf and Dumb* (1889, Appendix 18, p242), which provides statistics obtained from the 1881 census. This report gave the occupations of 5,607 Deaf people as follows:

MALES

Agricultural or general labourer	823
Boot, shoe, clog, pattern maker	530
Tailor	344
Textile manufacture	162
Carpenter, joiner	137
Mason, bricklayer	102
Painter, glazier, plumber	91
Cabinet maker, upholsterer, French polisher	96
Printer, bookbinder	95
Miner	89
Iron and steel manufacture	76
Blacksmith	55
Harness maker	43
All other occupations	1,188
Total employed	3,831

FEMALES

Domestic servant, charwoman	339
Dressmaker, seamstress	654
Washerwoman	158
Cotton manufacture	134
Tailoress	75
All other occupations	366
Total employed	1,776

The *Report* is interesting in one of its conclusions relating to the employment of the Deaf - that many of the occupations in which the Deaf were engaged tended to be those which could be followed independently and which did not require frequent communication with fellow workers. In addition to the table above, the *Report* gave much fuller information on the occupations of 7,101 males and 6,173 females returned as "deaf and dumb" in England, Scotland and Wales. Of these, 3,280 males and 4,408 females were returned as unemployed.

It was not only hearing people's ignorance of the Deaf that caused problems for the Deaf when seeking employment. There were times when the law turned out to be a major culprit, hindering rather than aiding Deaf people in obtaining employment. One of the earliest examples is *The Workmen's Compensation* Acts of 1897 and 1906, which required all employees to be insured by companies. A consequence of that law was that some unscrupulous companies seized on this opportunity to remove Deaf workers. A good number of companies refused to insure Deaf workers, claiming that the premiums were too high and this caused a furore; many Deaf people found themselves unemployed. In 1910 George F. Healey of the Liverpool Deaf and Dumb Benevolent Society had no choice but to get the Society to agree to pay employers the extra premiums demanded by the insurance companies for risks under the Workmen's Compensation and Employer's Liability Acts, if it wanted to prevent Deaf people from losing jobs. Missions for the Deaf followed Healey's example. Following investigations undertaken for his famous 1932 work, which was published in 1933 as *The Report of the Board of Education*, Dr. A. Eichholz wrote in page 183 of the *Report* that objections raised by employers were, in reality, excuses to veil their unwillingness to give work to Deaf persons.

There was a tendency in the 1920s-1950s to move Deaf people into what were often menial and monotonous jobs (though to be fair, some needed a degree of skill). This tendency was reinforced by many schools for the deaf which set up training centres such as the Laundry Training Centre, Woodwork Training Centre and Dressmaking Training Centre. Other trades that were taught by schools focused on bakery, boot making/repairing and (in one school in a ship-building area) welding/riveting. The situation was not helped by the publication and distribution of what came to be known as Circular 1337, issued to all local authorities, employers and schools by the Ministry of Health in 1934. This detailed the types of industrial work that were deemed suitable for Deaf people. The type of locality in which Deaf people lived was to be of importance in determining the suitability of local trades for them, so, for example, in Stoke-on-Trent it was the pottery industry that assumed great importance, whilst in parts of the Birmingham area work in Dunlop factories making rubber tyres was deemed very suitable for Deaf people.

The employment situation for the Deaf who had above normal and superior education was at best frustrating in the era before the 1960s in that the better jobs these Deaf people could hope for were in the clerical and administration posts provided by either the government or the local authorities; outside of that, many sought work such as draughtsmen, tracers, clerks and accountants. The range of available work for the Deaf was often extremely limited due to society's and the employers' insistence that certain occupations could not be offered to the Deaf. Such occupations involved direct contact with members of the public and, for example, barred the Deaf from driving public transport vehicles such as buses and trams and being employed as rent collectors, electric and gas meter readers, postmen, waiters, librarians and so on. The employment of Deaf people tended to become easier during the war years when many hearing people were called up to serve in the armed forces, but the Deaf often had to return to their previous tedious jobs once the wars were over.

The British government did little to improve the employment situation for the Deaf, who by the 1970s tended to apply for jobs under Deaf-friendly employers rather than to take bold steps to apply for jobs of their choosing. From the 1950s, deaf and partially deaf pupils, firstly from Mary Hare Grammar School in Newbury (Berks) and later from Burwood Park Technical Secondary School in Walton-on-Thames (Surrey) began to gain GCE successes; this both impressed and convinced prospective employers that they should not bypass the opportunity of employing such bright applicants. These Deaf and partially deaf people impressed in their work and that slowly changed the attitude of employers who once shunned the Deaf. The change, though, was not coming fast enough at that time for many deaf school leavers. The biggest obstacle was the attitude of hearing people towards the Deaf, and that attitude needed to be changed for the better.

The trades in which the Deaf showed proficiency in the past slowly depended on automation and technological changes created further obstacles for the Deaf such as the telephone. Business efficiency and turnover speed became important; both contracts and as well as material orders and financial decisions sales were made over the telephone. Both social and technological changes placed demands on and changes in the education of the deaf and the need for further education to both train the school leavers to obtain qualifications in their line of desired vocation and to provide them with the necessary skills to put them in good stead for employment.

The 1970s was a definitive era in modern Deaf history. It was the era when Deaf people decided to create changes, and to do that, they had to make themselves heard. Before change for the better could occur, one vital obstacle had to be overcome and that was the attitude of the hearing people, especially the authorities, the medical profession and the employers. While the British Deaf Association (BDA) was making early progress in its campaign to promote British Sign Language (although that title was yet to come for a year), forty-three Deaf activists met in a small upstairs room in the Wimbledon Ex-servicemen's Club on 13 March 1976 and formed the National Union of the Deaf (NUD). The NUD embarked on a campaign to change the attitudes of hearing people towards the Deaf, and by the end of 1986 many employment opportunities for the Deaf opened up, in particular within organisations of and for the Deaf; and the Deaf could now aim to be teachers in colleges and universities, lifeguards in local swimming pools, drivers of HGV vehicles, and could be employed by TV companies as researchers, presenters and producers, or could be actors in movies, theatre and TV, classroom assistants and teacher support for deaf pupils in mainstream schools and so on.

With the introduction of minicoms and the Typetalk Relay service established by both British Telecom and the Royal National Institute for the Deaf in 1989, the Deaf were now able to communicate using the telephone. This latter allowed access to certain occupations that relied on the telephone.

An area of major employment growth from the 1980s onwards for Deaf people was within Deaf organisations themselves, such as the BDA, which began to develop key services with Deaf people as managers and employees. The same was happening within other national Deaf organisations such as the Royal National Institute for the Deaf (RNID) and the National Deaf Children's Society (NDCS), even local ones such as Brent Deaf People's Limited (London) and Deaf Direct (Hereford & Worcester), which with dynamic Deaf managers at the helm began to provide a wide range of deaf-related services to their local communities.

It is also pertinent to record that a major "industry" was the growth in care homes and specialised residential services for Deaf people with learning difficulties and behavioural problems, and this growth called for the recruitment and training of deaf staff to provide specialised care in signing environments. Organisations like *SIGN*, and the RNID with its establishments like Poolemead (Bath) and Mulberry House (Walsall); Deafness Support Network in Cheshire with four care homes, and the Mayflower Hospitals NHS Trust (a semi-secure 42-bed custodial facility for deaf people in Bury, north Manchester) all recruited heavily and endeavoured to have a high ratio of Deaf-to-hearing staff with an emphasis on Deaf managers whenever possible. There was also the National Health Service provision for Deaf people. Three major hospitals began to focus on the development and delivery of psychiatric, counselling and other mental health services for Deaf people in London (National Deaf Services), Birmingham (National Deaf Mental Health Services) and Manchester (National Centre for Mental Health and Deafness). All put together teams that involved Deaf people as professional psychologists, psychiatrists, nurses, support team managers and counsellors. By the early 2000s the numbers of Deaf people being employed in various care establishments as nurses, care officers or assistants, and other medical/care-related specialists came to over 200 people.

Another major factor in the employment of Deaf people in the 1990s was the introduction of Access to Work through the Department of Employment, plus other business-related initiatives set up generally by the Government to encourage the growth of entrepreneurial activities across Britain. This led to the establishment of a large number of small Deaf-led and Deaf-owned companies specialising in providing services to select markets. These companies included film and multi-media companies such as *Remark!* and publishing companies such as Red Lizard, which briefly held a contract to publish the *British Deaf News*. Other Deaf-led or Deaf-owned businesses include the Common Ground Sign Dance Theatre, *The Deaf Internet Bookstore,* Deaf@x and Deafworks, to name a few.

There are no modern day statistics on the employment situation of the present day Deaf and without this a comparison with the past cannot be made. It is, even so, not difficult to see that there has been a radical change in the employment situation for the Deaf in the present day compared to what was available in the past. We can also be sure that in the future the situation will continue to improve, due to growing interest in BSL among members of the general public, supported by both the ongoing campaign by the BDA in promoting Deaf Awareness and the gradual elimination of discrimination against the Deaf after the coming of the Disability Discrimination Act 1995, plus continued government initiatives that support small businesses.

Deaf Awareness Movement - The Pioneers

Those who were deaf throughout history at times suffered terrible ridicule and their deafness was often looked upon as a "calamity" and a "terrible malady"; people tended to equate deafness with some terrible disease and even mental retardation.

Literature is rich with snippets of information on hearing people's attitude towards the Deaf throughout history. An example can be seen in the 1792 poem by the Rev. Thomas Beck entitled *The Cause of the Dumb Pleaded:*

> *But he, within himself, his world contains;*
> *The means of knowledge from his soul confin'd,*
> *Himself a riddle to himself remains,*
> *A grief to friends, a horror to mankind.*

The Rev. Beck reported that he had a friend whose only son was deaf; which deafness was supposed to have arisen from the impression made upon his mother's mind from seeing a miserable spectacle of this kind pass by her door!

Even more notorious were the lines written by one Rev. Rann Kennedy for a play staged to raise funds for the Edgbaston Institution for the Deaf and Dumb in August 1814:

> *Outcasts by birth that still wants in vain*
> *Rights dearer far than Julio's lost domain,*
> *That unacquainted with creation's plan,*
> *Might never feel the dignity of man,*
> *Yet wear his form, while sunk in mental death,*
> *They walk the earth mere vehicles of breath.*

The negative views and malign descriptions of deafness as put forward by hearing people had to be challenged and corrected. This meant mounting a sort of counter-attack by attempting to present the Deaf in their true light and to promote understanding among the general public. The first moves were in the form of manual alphabet charts that were initially handed out free to those who wished to learn how to communicate with the Deaf. The earliest known chart mass-issued to the public was that which featured in Daniel Defoe's *The History of the Life and Adventures of Mr Duncan Campbell* (1720). There were variations of this manual alphabet chart over the years, and some charts were sold in batches of certain numbers for half-penny each batch.

Promotion of the abilities of the Deaf to the public also came in other forms – art, science and literature. Deaf artists such as Charles Shireff, Walter Geikie and Thomas Arrowsmith found fame and renown for their works; John Goodricke and Francis Humberstone Mackenzie, both pupils of Thomas Braidwood, and who were both elected Fellows of the Royal Society; and John Philp Wood, the author of *The Antient and Modern State of the Parish of Cramond* and editor of *Douglas' Peerage of Scotland*. Deaf people such as these came to the notice of society, but their achievements were merely noted and applauded, rather than promoting the cause and understanding of the Deaf in general.

The great Braidwoodian artist Charles Shireff (1750-1831), announced in 1807 that he had completed his *Illustrations of Signs*, which was essentially a dictionary of signs. This work was to promote the sign language of the Deaf, but nothing came out of the announcement and the work has never been traced.

In 1809 a psuedonymous author, R.R., made one of the first known moves towards promotion of Deaf awareness when he published his delightful little book on fingerspelling, *The Invited Alphabet Or, Address from A to B; containing his Friendly Proposal for the Amusement and Instruction of Good Children*. This is probably the first book for hearing children to introduce them to the manual alphabet so to enable them to communicate with Deaf people. It has a charm radiating from its pages that no other books have and this charm most certainly comes from both the beautifully coloured illustrations and the wonderful rhyming text.

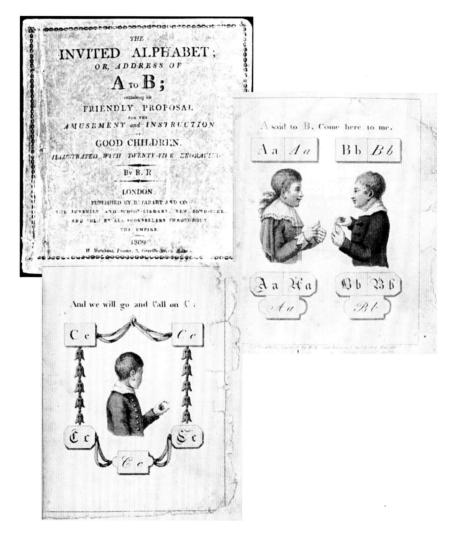

In 1855 George Hutton, a hearing Scottish teacher of the deaf, made what is probably the very first attempt to create a dictionary of signs. His *Specimen Dictionary of Signs* survives in the Volta Library (Washington DC, USA. No one knows why Hutton's project was not developed further into a proper dictionary, but it is possible that time and money was not available to him.

The earliest proponents of the Deaf Awareness movement were William Agnew (1846-1914) and Harry Ash (1863-1934).

William Agnew, a Glaswegian, had always been aware of the need for society to accept and understand the Deaf and he felt that the manual alphabet, rather than sign language itself, was the best step for a gentle start. Hearing people found it easier to learn the manual alphabet and communicate with the Deaf by forming words on their hands rather than trying to learn signs through time-consuming practice.

The period in which William Agnew lived as a young man was a very difficult one; it was at the height of the post-Milan era when both the movement and craze for pure oralism were in full swing. Anti-signs propaganda was being spread in all levels of society and deaf schoolchildren were banned from expressing themselves freely in sign and forced to learn to speak at all costs. Deaf adults were banned from visiting Deaf children in schools for fear they might contaminate them with signs.

William Agnew made contact not only with people of the nobility, but also with Royalty, including Queen Victoria who was very proficient in the use of the manual alphabet. Agnew saw the manual alphabet as the banner with which to attract society's interest in the Deaf and he hit decided to produce and distribute the chart on a mass scale never before attempted by any Deaf person. This distribution would serve a twofold purpose. The first was to spread the manual alphabet and therefore promote awareness and integration. The second was to raise funds to contribute towards the building fund of the Glasgow Institute for the Adult Deaf and Dumb. Using his contacts in the printing trade, Agnew produced and printed a great number of postcards that showed not only the manual alphabet chart but included information on the Deaf. These postcards sold extremely well and generated interest among many people in the Deaf, besides raising income for the building fund.

141

Postcard of the Yorkshire Institution for the Deaf and Dumb

Postcard promoting the Cornish Deaf and Dumb Mission

Postcard - The Deaf and Dumb Asylum, Margate

The initial steps to promote Deaf Awareness had begun and progress had to be given momentum. Although his postcards became popular, Agnew felt he had to do something more. The building fund for the new Glasgow Institute for the Adult Deaf and Dumb needed thousands of pounds for the purchase of land on which to build the Institute. Agnew hit on

142

another idea that again had a twofold purpose; to contribute to the building fund and to promote Deaf Awareness. He also wanted people to see and meet Deaf people and communicate with them. For these reasons Agnew organised the famous Grand Bazaar, which was held at St. Andrew's Hall between 19 and 21 November 1891. The Duchess of Montrose opened the event. During the three days of the Grand Bazaar, many people from all levels of society came and many visitors contributed over £6,000, a sum that staggered members of the Building Fund Committee, which son was able to purchase land and build the Deaf Institute in the centre of Glasgow.

Agnew (6th from left) with Deaf members during the building of the Glasgow Institute for the Adult Deaf and Dumb

The Glasgow Institute for the Adult Deaf and Dumb (circa 1965)

The public's interest in manual alphabet post-cards prompted a number of schools for the deaf and Deaf adults in various Deaf centres and Missions to produce and issue similar postcards, which both promoted awareness of the Deaf among the general public and generated income.

Harry Ash was in the mid-1890s working as a pen and ink artist in Chiswick, and he began to try finding ways to promote the sign language of the Deaf. The trend and passion for oralism was in full swing. Sign language was pushed into dark places. Like many Deaf people in Britain, Ash lived under conditions in which signing was both shunned and despised as anti-social and animalistic.

Ash hit on the idea of promoting signs, as opposed to manual alphabet, by creating his famous *Guide to Chirology* booklet. The initial print may have been first distributed in 1895, but no one is sure when. This guide sold for 2d a copy and was an instant success. Ash had a second edition printed, altering the signs and designs, and sold copies for 1d each. Again, all copies were successfully sold. In the end the *Guide to Chirology* ran into 14 known editions well into the early 1920s. Although the manual alphabet was featured in every edition, the main attractions were the different signs and their meanings conveyed in three different languages (German, Dutch and French) as well as English.

Ash felt that sign language was not the only thing society at large should know. Deaf people as individual human beings, Ash reasoned, were the equal of any hearing person and this had to be clearly put to the public. With that in mind, Ash created another publication, *The Illustrated Comic Graphic* (date unknown, probably early 1900s). It was in a slightly larger format than that of *Guide to Chirology* and contain sign illustrations, as well as added information on the Deaf, snippets from their history, ideas on how to solve some everyday problems connected with the Deaf and a variety of proposals for equipment to escape house fires and such like.

Ash's approach in combining the publicity of the manual alphabet, signs and intellectual capabilities of the Deaf in magazine formats was a pioneering attempt to promote Deaf Awareness. It was unfortunate that his venture was badly abused by the people he intended to help, the Deaf people themselves. Ash distributed batches of guides and magazines to various Deaf clubs for sale and distribution among members of the public, but some Deaf people sold these and pocketed the money either for themselves or for their clubs. This caused problems and financial hardship for Ash, who decided to halt the venture.

Ash also had plans to produce a dictionary of signs, but he was unable to find either sponsors or financial backing for the dictionary. With Ash retreating into his private life, the Deaf Awareness movement came to a halt.

If the general public are to be made aware of the existence and language of the Deaf, the best persons to do that are the Deaf themselves, not hearing people. Organisations for the Deaf have always been run by hearing people who know nothing or very little of the Deaf way, mentality, culture and language. Major organisations such as the RNID, BDDA and the RADD were more concerned about their own image and reputation in the eyes of hearing people. On top of that, they were very paternalistic. The

144

BDDA eventually changed its traditional stance to a campaign-led approach to further Deaf awareness among members of the general public as well as among the various local and national authorities. In 1971 the members of the BDDA voted to drop the word "Dumb" from its name and the organisation became known as the British Deaf Association (BDA).

In 1982 the BDA drew up its Manifesto, which for the benefit if the Deaf listed a number of demands for the Government; over 80,000 copies of the Manifesto were distributed around Britain.

The BDA also launched a National Deaf Awareness Week in 1982 between 4 and 9 October. The Week was actually launched on Saturday 3 October on the steps of St. Martin's-in-the-Fields, London, with the assistance of three showbiz personalities. This Deaf Awareness Week included Sign Language Marathons in which Deaf people from all over Britain participated in communicating and telling stories in BSL in public places. The Week's events attracted public attention and created awareness of both the Deaf and their language. The BDA Deaf Awareness Week continues to the present day and is held annually in October.

History of British Sign Language Research

The study of the *linguistics* of British Sign Language is a fairly recent development, and is not to be confused with the study of manual alphabets, which dates back many centuries and was popular amongst academics of the 16th-18th centuries, and is dealt with separately. It is pertinent to state here that there have been a number of attempts in history to set up studies of the use of various sign languages by Deaf people and the creation of dictionaries showing how signs are produced.

There have been references to monastic sign languages and the sign language of the Deaf has been linked with those used by the monks. No evidence exists to show that the Deaf actually adopted the signs of the monks, or even vice versa. For historical record purposes, connection between the monks' and the Deaf signs will be ignored until proof of connection presents itself.

However, it is noted that one of the earliest references to signs, though not strictly speaking a research study, is contained in a book entitled *Anngiers History of the Zion Monastery at Lisbon and Brentford*, which gives a list of words and an accompanying description of how they are produced in signs. Although the references in this book do not distinguish between gestures, which would be in general use among hearing and deaf people, and signs proper to a sign language, it is interesting to note that many of the signs described in this book are, with minor differences, still in current use. For example,

Hammer – make a signe with thyne hand up and down as thou did knocke.

The *Anngiers* book was published in 1450, and there is no other reference to the study of sign language until 1603 when King James I ascended to the throne. At that time the King was fascinated by the sign language used by a deaf woman that he met and he commissioned a study of sign language. Unfortunately, there are no records to indicate whether this commission was ever set up, or if it was, what happened to the study. The full text of the *Anngiers* book is given in the Appendices.

The first known attempt to produce a *dictionary* of signs was by the deaf artist and painter, Charles Shireff (variously spelt as Sherrif, Sheriff, Shirreff), the first pupil of Thomas Braidwood's Academy, who announced from Madras in India, where he was living and working at the time (1807), that his *Illustration of Signs* was nearly complete and would be available to subscribers as soon as possible. Again unfortunately, this work has never been traced and is presumed lost en route from India.

There are many independently documented and witnessed accounts of the use of sign language by Deaf people in Britain throughout the 16th-18th centuries, but there does not appear to have been any serious effort to undertake any research into this, most academicians preferring to concentrate on the development of the manual alphabet. John Bulwer's *Chirologia*, published in 1644, did make some attempt to illustrate how certain signs were produced but it was not an extensive study.

Apart from Charles Shireff's attempt, there was also an attempt by a Scotsman named George Hutton to create a dictionary of signs. In 1855 he produced the *Specimen Dictionary of Signs*, which was a basic outline for an ideal dictionary. Since Hutton emigrated to Nova Scotia, many of his sketches and explanations of signs refer mainly to those used in Canada and Scotland, and these signs were, and still are, completely different from present day British signs.

Hutton's attempt was truly remarkable as he saw the need to bring awareness and understanding of the Deaf's language to the public. His project was not further developed mainly due to both the pressure of work undertaken by him as headmaster of the school for the deaf in Nova Scotia and the lack of time. It appears that, as the years passed, his interest and enthusiasm waned. Two plates from his initial attempt are shown here on the next two pages.

No other known attempt to create a dictionary of signs appears to have been made until the late 1890s and early 1900s when Harry Ash, an illustrator educated at the London Asylum for the Deaf and Dumb, created a series of mini-sign dictionaries. Approximately between 1890 and 1910, he developed, designed and printed booklets entitled *Guide to Chirology* and *The Illustrated Comic Graphics*. These contained many photographed and drawn signs aimed at raising awareness of Deaf people's sign language, and 140 of these signs were reprinted in a special edition of the *British Deaf Times*. Ash could never obtain a financial backing for a complete dictionary of British signs.

Properly structured and academically recognised research into British Sign Language did not take off until well after the first study by William C. Stokoe, an American linguist, American Sign Language was published in 1960. This outlined the basis for an linguistic analysis. At that time Stokoe was almost alone in his assertion that American Sign Language was a proper language in its own right. Five years later, in 1965, Stokoe published his *Dictionary of American Sign Language*, the first to be based on linguistic principles through a notation system. It was a landmark in the study of signed languages and marked the start of sign linguistics as well as sign lexicography.

Stokoe followed this up with the publication of two further studies that advanced linguistic research into signed languages, *Semiotics and Human Signed Languages* (1972) and *Classifications and Descriptions of Signed Languages* (1974). By this time there were other American researchers also publishing papers, notably Klima and Bellugi.

In Britain, Allan B. Hayhurst, the Secretary-Treasurer of the British Deaf Association (BDA), had started in 1971 to compile a *Dictionary of B.S.L,* the first documented reference to the sign language as used in Britain as <u>British Sign Language.</u> The use of the word British was intended to distinguish it from other sign languages such as ASL (American Sign Language). However, as Hayhurst came to realise, the British version of a sign dictionary would be academically and linguistically incomplete without the inclusion of the notation system as used by William C. Stokoe, and which was now being accepted by linguists everywhere as crucial in the research of all grammatical aspects of signed languages. There was therefore a need to initiate proper linguistic research in Britain into BSL, as had now started in several other countries, notably Sweden with two projects under way during 1972 at the Institute of Linguistics, University of Stockholm, under the direction of Brita Bergman.

Progress in Britain was slow in coming. There were a number of reasons for this. The main one was that there was no centre in Britain adequately funded or staffed to undertake the research, although there was at Moray House College of Further Education, Edinburgh, a lecturer in linguistics, Mary Brennan, who was developing an interest in the subject.

Tenacious, a.

Toilsome, a.

Terrific, a.

Troublesome, a.

Thick, a. that measures much on the side.

True, a.

Thin, a. that measures little on the side.

U

For, prep.	*Of,* ad. belonging to.
From, prep.	*Off,* ad. away from.
In, prep.	*On,* ad. placed close to.
Instead of, prep. in the place of.	*Out of,* ad.

The BDA itself was chronically under-funded and any plans it had to develop research and to promote BSL as a language had to be put on hold until the organisation could come up with the necessary funding to implement its plans. Partial progress was made in 1977 with the award of a grant from the Department of Health and Social Security (DHSS) for a Communication Skills Programme that would focus both on the needs of Deaf people in Britain for an adequate BSL interpreting service and the training that individuals would need to attain the standards needed to become a competent interpreter. *[This Communication Skills Programme was later to evolve into what is now known as CACDP, the Council for the Advancement of Communication with Deaf People.]*

The BDA were fortunate to get on secondment from Gallaudet College, Washington DC, Willard J. Madsen, Director of Gallaudet's Sign Language Programmes from 1971-1977. Under his guidance, the BDA was able to issue a mini-dictionary entitled *Sign-It* and to initiate a number of programmes on sign language teaching, learning and interpreting. One outcome was an International Sign Language Seminar held at the Northern Counties School for the Deaf, Newcastle-upon-Tyne, in October 1977. This was the catalyst for the start of three other projects, some of which were already in the planning stages:

The Edinburgh British Sign Language Research Project, based at Moray House College of Education and funded by the Scottish Education Department (1979), headed by Mary Brennan.

The Sign Language Linguistics Research Group, set up at the University of Newcastle (1979) in partnership with the Northern Counties School for the Deaf and the BDA, directed by Dr. Lionel Evans, Principal at Northern Counties School.

Sign Language Learning and Use, a project at the University of Bristol under the direction of Dr. Jim Kyle, also supported by a DHSS grant. (1978). *[This project was eventually to lead to the formation of the Centre for Deaf Studies at the same university.]*

Whilst the larger organisations were searching for the necessary funds to establish their projects, a Ph.D student at Stanford University in California, Margaret Deuchar, was researching for a thesis on 'Diglossia in British Sign Language'. This focused upon the grammar of BSL. Her thesis, which involved nine months' research at Reading Deaf Club, filled a valuable gap in the knowledge of the grammatical make-up of BSL.

The Moray House project was to run for five years, and focussed mainly on the developing of the notation system of BSL, leading to a publication, *Words in Hand,* by the team consisting of Mary Brennan, Martin Colville and Lillian Lawson. Although this drew heavily on a coding system developed by the Bristol team and used in Deuchar's thesis, it was the first book in print to provide a structural analysis of the signs of British Sign Language and was to prove valuable to the BDA when the time came for its *Dictionary of BSL/English* project to be implemented.

The *Dictionary of BSL/English* project continued the work of A. B. Hayhurst's first dictionary of BSL and was a transition from the BDA's original dictionary of signs that advanced the use of signs in combination with spoken English (Sign Supported English) into one that demonstrated the signed language of the British Deaf community. The project lasted for over 10 years. The task for the compilation and completion of the project was handed to the University of Durham in 1982, supported by a generous grant from British Petroleum as well as the Department of Health and Social Security. It was a massive undertaking, bringing together on a voluntary, part-time basis, linguists, researchers and fluent native users of BSL.

The late 1970s and early 1980s not only saw an increasing need to study the characteristics of British Sign Language, but also a need to promote and increase the quality and sufficiency of sign language interpreting provision in Britain. In many instances, the scarcity of resources often meant that the need to promote interpreting provision was accorded funding priority over sign language research needs. In this connection, the BDA initiated a three-years pilot Interpreter/Tutor support project in Oxfordshire, Berkshire and Buckinghamshire in 1975. In Bristol the Sign Language Learning Project also devoted time into research into the qualities of interpreters.

Sign Language research received a much-needed boost from the International Symposium on Sign Language Research held in Stockholm in June 1981. There was also a NATO-funded conference the same year in Copenhagen, which was widely attended by both American and European researchers. These conferences directly led to the formation of the Deaf Studies Research Unit (DSRU) at the University of Durham in late 1982, with the consequent setting up of a number of sign language research projects. The DSRU was given the responsibility for the compilation and completion of the *Dictionary of BSL/English*. Amongst the most significant developments at the DSRU were the Allan B. Hayhurst Research Fellowship and the British Sign Language Training Agency (or Course as it was sometimes called). The BSLTA project revolutionised BSL teaching in Britain, leading to a standardisation of BSL teaching skills and the promotion of BSL as a thriving, living language to be taught as a subject in adult and further education classes, as well as in schools. Working in conjunction with the newly established CACDP project within the same university, the BSLTA project established the parameters for the successful teaching of BSL as a subject for learning at all levels; and trained well over a hundred Deaf BSL tutors in its 5-years existence. This in turn pushed forward the need for further linguistic research into BSL. The DSRU initiated a series of BSL research projects in the late 1980s.

Following the closure of the Moray House BSL Research Project in 1984, the universities of Durham and Bristol were the only centres devoted to BSL research in the late 1980s and early 1990s, although there was a three-years project on the acquisition of BSL by deaf children of deaf parents. This was undertaken by a research team led by Margaret Harris at Birbeck College, London, in 1986. It is not known what became of this project.

The Durham and Bristol research projects were developed with the help of a number of Deaf people as researchers, including Gloria Pullen, Lorna Allsop, Jennifer Ackerman, Frances Elton and Judith Collins. Bristol in particular between 1982 and 1991 undertook a considerable number of different projects that helped to widen knowledge on BSL variation, sign language development in deaf children and sign language interpreter training and provision.

Two other universities set up Deaf Studies programmes in the early 1990s: the University of Central Lancashire (Preston) and Wolverhampton University. Although they employed researchers as staff, these were not research programmes *per se*, but programmes designed to enable students to achieve degrees in Deaf Studies. These universities did not contribute significantly into the research of BSL linguistics.

In 1995 one of Britain's noted BSL linguists, Professor Bencie Woll, was appointed to the chair of Sign Language at City University, London. She had worked on the linguistics of BSL whilst working with Dr. Jim Kyle at the Centre of Deaf Studies, Bristol. At City University she was joined by Frances Elton whose contract at the Deaf Studies Unit, Durham University, had come to an end. Together, Bencie Woll and Frances Elton considerably advanced the study of BSL as a linguistic language and developed a course for Deaf people, who were tutors of BSL, that enabled them to acquire a better knowledge of linguistics to use in their teaching. At the same time, another noted BSL linguist Rachel Sutton-Spence commenced work in the Centre of Deaf Studies, Bristol, as a lecturer after completing her Ph.D on fingerspelling.

In the 1950s and 1960s a linguist named Charles Hockett wrote a series of papers exploring the 'essential characteristics' or 'design features' of human languages. The table below presents those characteristics and contrasts them with other forms of communication.

In 1999 Bencie Woll and Rachel Sutton-Spence collaborated on a book, *The Linguistics of British Sign Language* (Cambridge University Press), the first detailed explanation of the way BSL works. This book reviews in some detail Hockett's design and its applicability to signed as well as spoken languages. Apart from differences in articulation modality or 'channel' (visual, rather than auditory), sign languages and spoken languages are the only two communication systems which meet all the criteria Hockett proposed.

	Crickets	Gibbon calls	Apes taught to use signs from ASL	Gesture	Sign languages	Spoken language
Vocal-auditory channel	Auditory, not vocal	Yes	No	No	No	Yes
Interchangeability	Limited	Yes	No	Yes	Yes	Yes
Total feedback	Yes	Yes	Yes	Yes	Yes	Yes
Semanticity	No?	Yes	Yes	In part	Yes	Yes
Conventionality / arbitrariness	?	Yes	Yes	In part	Yes	Yes
Discreteness	Yes?	Yes	Debatable	Largely no	Yes	Yes
Displacement		No	Debatable	No	Yes, often	Yes, often
Productivity	No	No	Debatable	Yes	Yes	Yes
Traditional transmission	No?	?	Little evidence	Yes	Yes	Yes
Duality of patterning	?	No [Cotton-top tamarin: Yes]	No	No	Yes	Yes
Prevarication			Possibly		Yes	Yes
Reflexiveness			No		Yes	Yes
Learnability			Yes		Yes	Yes

"Design Features" of language and other communication systems

Recent research using functional imaging techniques to explore how the brain processes sign language has also revealed that, despite the surface differences between spoken and signed language, sign languages are processed in the same areas of the brain, on the left side, as spoken languages rather than in those areas of the brain used for visual-spatial cognition, gesture, face processing, etc.

The Linguistics of British Sign Language remains the most detailed and up-to-date book on the study of the linguistics of British Sign Language as these have evolved since Stokoe's study into the linguistics of American Sign Language in 1960 and has firmly knocked back the myth that sign language is simply a collection of gestures that represent objects. There will doubtlessly be other published studies into the linguistics of British Sign language but Sutton-Spence & Woll's work, as well as the BDA's Dictionary of BSL/English, will forever be the study that future linguists will have to improve upon, although Margaret Deuchar's 1984 book on BSL and the work on sign languages by Kyle & Woll in 1985 are still influential.

Movement for Legal Provisions for the Deaf

As can be seen in the chapter *The Status of the Deaf throughout Early History*, Deaf people were not favourably treated under the laws of many countries. Discrimination against the Deaf and all disabled people were perfectly legal in all countries of the world where no anti-discrimination laws existed. In recent history stretching over the last 25 years, the regulation of discrimination against the Deaf and disabled people in Britain relied on a combination of voluntary and self-regulatory measures.

It was estimated in 1994 that 69% of disabled persons were unemployed and they were 2½ times more likely to be unemployed than non-disabled persons, and they would stay unemployed for longer periods. This situation was equally true for the Deaf. Disregarding the Royal National Institute for the Deaf's wildly over-exaggerated claim that it represents something like between 7 and 9 million deaf and hard of hearing people in Britain, an Office of Population, Census and Surveys (OPCS) survey in 1988 stated that there were over 6 million disabled people in Britain and 14% of the adult population had at least one impairment which caused disability. The study estimated that there were 1 million blind people and a further 2 million partially sighted. There were 4 million people with mobility problems, of which half a million were wheelchair users.

It has been estimated that by the year 2031 in Britain the size of the disabled population will have grown to 8.2 million adults, representing an increase of 34% since 1986. Furthermore, 22% of adults of working age have a health problem or a disability, representing 10-15% of the general population. It is unfortunate that very little effort and research was made to discover the Deaf population numbers, but the statistics and figures given in the chapter *Deaf Population Figures* will suffice for this section.

Dr. A. Eichholz suggested from in famous 1932 survey that there should be a Deaf Persons Act that would create both legal protection and provisions for the Deaf of Britain. Protection would come in the form of anti-discrimination and provision would come in the form of access. Despite Eichholz's survey, various governments and authorities over the years resisted moves for such laws and regulations intended for the benefit of the Deaf. As the years passed and with new approaches to the labelling and administration of various groups of disabled people, it suited the authorities to place the Deaf under the "Disabled" category, even though the disability of deafness is clearly different from any of other disabilities: deafness creates a linguistic group with its own language, community and culture. The brief history outlined here on the movement for legislation on anti-discrimination and rights of the disabled will show the Deaf as a vital part of an alliance of various organisations of/for the disabled. The legal rights established for the disabled and subsequent legal developments can be seen in the following chronological order:

1944 Education Act

Local authorities were obliged to make specific provisions in special or mainstream schools for disabled children.

1944 Disabled Persons (Employment) Act

This Act required employers with 20 or more staff to employ disabled people making up 3% of their staff.

At a time when discrimination against the Deaf was still rife, the 3% quota at least offered employment to Deaf people in companies with 20 or more employees. It is known that, because of this quota, a good number of Deaf and disabled people could not be made redundant as long as the number of workers in any one firm did not fall below the figure of 20 employees.

1948 National Assistance Act

Local authorities were given the responsibility to provide accommodation and services to disabled people who were "substantially and permanently handicapped by illness, injury or congenital deformity."

1970 Chronically Sick and Disabled Persons Act

The local authorities were required to improve services to disabled people and keep registers of local disabled people.

This Act, pioneered by Alf Morris MP, made it possible for the Deaf to request a wide range of aids such as flashing light doorbells and baby alarms, flashing light/vibrating alarm clocks and flashing light responders to telephone rings from local social services departments. Masny provided these for the needs of the Deaf.

1970 Education (Handicapped Children) Act

The responsibility for the education services of children with learning difficulties was transferred from health to local authorities. This was a wide-ranging piece of legislation with implications for many aspects of disabled people's lives.

1979 Warnock Report

This Report recommended a greater integration of 'special needs' children into mainstream schools.

1981 Education Act

This Act provided the legislative framework for the integration of children with 'special needs', including the deaf into ordinary schools. The statementing process was introduced, and the Act encouraged the involvement of parents in determining their children's educational needs.

1986 Disabled Persons (Services, Consultation and Representation) Act

This Act enabled disabled people and their representatives to have full assessments of their needs done by local authorities.

1988 Education Reform Act

Under this Act every pupil, whether with special needs or not, is entitled to a broad and balanced curriculum.

1989 Children Act

This Act provided a comprehensive legal framework for the protection and promotion of the interest and the welfare of children.

1990 National Health Service and Community Care Act

This required local authorities to assess needs and then put together a package of care which can be purchases from a range of agencies and suppliers.

1993 Education Act

This Act required the Local Education Authorities to assist schools in identifying any child who may have special educational needs and to give additional support where needed.

1995 Disability Discrimination Act

This important Act gave disabled people certain rights in the areas of employment, access to goods and services, and buying or renting land or property.

It is the 1995 Disability Discrimination Act that this section is more concerned about because the Act much more than any other completely changes the course and quality of life for all disabled people and the Deaf benefited enormously from this Act.

In the battle against discrimination, the first move for an anti-discrimination bill for disabled people was made by Jack Ashley MP following the recommendations of a parliamentary committee on restrictions against disabled people. This was followed by a succession of bills from backbench MPs over the next ten years with increasing support of MPs from all parties. In order to reinforce strength to achieve anti-discrimination legislation, many voluntary organisations grouped together and formed the Rights Now Campaign. The British Deaf Association played a major part within that group and its Deaf members turned up in large numbers each time the Rights Now group lobbied Parliament – numbers of Deaf people varied between 300 and 600 at each lobby.

The formation of the Rights Now Campaign pushed the issue of anti-discrimination legislation up the political agenda to a stage where the Government could no longer ignore it. The history of attempts to introduce anti-discrimination legislation for the Deaf and disabled people is littered with tales of obstruction by MPs for various reasons throughout different Parliamentary sessions. The Civil Rights (Disabled People) Bill introduced as a Private Members Bill by the Labour MP Harry Barnes in 1994 was the 17th attempt to introduce anti-discrimination legislation for disabled people. This Bill was talked out of time by the conservatives who also demanded last-minute amendments despite it having previously received all-party support. The defeat of this particular Bill became a catalyst for change. Backbench Conservatives who supported the anti-discrimination legislation threatened to overturn the Government's frail majority in other voting issues and they were therefore able to force the Government to announce its own proposals to counter disability discrimination. In July 1994 the Government published a White Paper setting out its alternative to the Civil Rights (Disabled People) Bill.

Six months later the Disability Discrimination Bill was introduced and was sped through parliamentary reading stages. It received the Royal Assent on 8 November 1995.

The involvement of the BDA, its members and other deaf supporters in this campaign cannot be underestimated, for their numbers added strength to every gathering disabled and Deaf people lobbying outside Parliament. Many Deaf people were able-bodied and were able to travel from far and to add their support and numbers. Some examples of the activities undertaken by the Deaf in the early days of campaigning for anti-discrimination legislation are given below:

February 1983.

Donald Stewart MP failed to get the required 100 MPs to vote to send on his anti-discrimination Bill. The lobby outside the House of Commons was made up by a large crowd of disabled people organised by the Liberation Network of People with Disabilities (LIBNET). The Deaf were present in large numbers, supported by the Birmingham members of the BDA.

November 1983.

Deaf people from every corner of Britain descended on Parliament on Friday 18 November to stand up and be counted. On that day Robert Wareing MP presented his anti-discrimination Bill, which unfortunately was rejected by 210 to 164 votes. The BDA had just over 500 Deaf members firstly outside the House of Commons, and then in Westminster Hall to argue for the Bill. The photo below shows a small part of the large Deaf group lobbying on the day.

April 1986.

On Wednesday 9 April a much smaller group of around 100 disabled people, of which the Deaf formed the majority, gathered at the House of Commons to put pressure on MPs by lobbying them to support Tom Clarke's Disabled Persons Bill that was to be read in the House on the following Friday 11 April. The lobby was successful in that on that Friday the Conservative Minister at the Department of Health, Barney Hayhoe accepted the proposals made in Tom Clarke's Bill.

April 1987

Over 600 Deaf people attended another lobby organised by the BDA to persuade the Conservative Government of the day to implement the Disabled Persons Act, which had

Deaf participants at the BDA lobby on 11 April 1986

BDA members as part of the April 1987 lobby outside Parliament

been made law in the summer of 1986. It is ironic that the only organisation (BDA) that cannot use the telephone system to contact its members could turn out the largest contingent for the lobby with only two days' notice.

The active participation of the Deaf in association with other non-deaf disabled groups went a long way to create an achievement that was largely theirs by right. The Disability Discrimination Act is slowly changing society's attitude towards the Deaf and the quality of life is beginning to improve for the Deaf. There is still a long way to go, however, in eliminating discrimination against the Deaf, particularly on the part of some major companies Easyjet that refused to carry 11 Deaf passengers in October 2003 on the grounds that these passengers had no carers and were therefore a danger in the event that the aeroplane had to be evacuated within 90 seconds. The company later apologised but it had already caused inconvenience and distress to the Deaf passengers.

The final part of the DDA came into force on 1 October 2004.

Campaign for BSL Recognition

The initial campaign for recognition of the sign language of the Deaf in Britain actually started with the Deaf Awareness movement of William Agnew and Harry Ash, although this was not recognised until around 1999 by the British Deaf History Society (BDHS). The use of "language" as paired with the word "sign" did not actually come into being until 1960 in the USA, and was first used in Britain in 1971 as "British Sign Language" (BSL).

Signs were not generally shunned by society in Britain until the advent of the oralists and the Milan Congress of 1880, when a frenzied worldwide campaign by the anti-signs oralists led to the seizure and monopolisation of the education of the deaf and the mass expulsions of all employees, Deaf and hearing alike, who used signs in teaching deaf children. For over 95 years after Milan, signs were banned in schools for the deaf in Britain and sign language barely survived in the world outside of school. It was kept going by those who found oralism to be of no use to them.

The BDA was in the forefront on the battle to promote and defend sign language throughout its existence, but, as the years dragged on, the organisation seemed to either waver or weaken in its resolve to act effectively in promoting sign language among members of the public. By 1975 the BDA was old, weary and inefficient. The organisation included a committee of "Yes" Deaf people who kow-towed to the hearing people who effectively ran the BDA and who were seemingly cosy with their lofty positions and with the fame and reputation their status commanded from society. The RNID was labelled as the "Oralist's Advertising Agency" whilst the National Deaf Children's Society (NDCS), founded in 1944, were giving largely oralist advice to parents of deaf children. The RADD, on the other hand, kept to its mission work and spoke out against the suppression of sign language. Its missioners were appalled at the deaf school leavers who turned up at the Deaf clubs, unable to speak properly and even worse, unable to sign. These Deaf youngsters had to be re-educated and needed counselling, care and guidance. This angered a number of Deaf people who felt that these school leavers were deprived of their right to an education and quality of life as a Deaf person using sign language.

The anger and the bitterness that Deaf people experienced after having to undergo the oralist method during what was supposed to be the "happiest days of their lives" was taken on board by a small number of Deaf people who were not afraid to put their reputations on the executioner's block; these people felt

VIGILANTIA GNARUS ET AUXILIOR

that the time was right to make changes, and that the only way to bring around changes was to demand, not to beg. The National Union of the Deaf (NUD) was established in March 1976 as the first ever Deaf pressure group and its aim was to fight for the rights of the Deaf. The focus of the initial move in the battle against the oralists had to be on none other than an attack on them. Instead of guns and bombs, the NUD had only words and a battered old typewriter with the irritating jumping 'i', which always positioned itself higher out of line with other letters. The first attack was on the RNID Conference in Harrogate, where not only all the oralists would attend, but one Dr. Reuben Conrad was to present a paper on his research into deaf schoolchildren. The first "Epistle to the Teacher of the Deaf" was typed

Paddy Ladd - NUD

Maggie Woolley - NUD

Arthur F. Dimmock - NUD

Raymond Lee - NUD

Stan Woodhouse, MBE
(1920-83) - NUD President

and printed and distributed among all those who attended the conference and thus the seeds of change were sown. The chronology of events in the campaign for recognition of BSL is as follows:

1977

The NUD allied itself with the both National Council for Civil Liberties and the Disability Alliance and commenced active campaigning for the recognition and acceptance of BSL, attacking other methods of signing like the Paget-Gorman systematic method. The NUD supported both Total Communication and BSL. The second "Epistle to the Teacher of the Deaf" was issued and slowly a good number of teachers became confident enough to get in touch. They raised doubts about the oralist system they were obliged to use in teaching Deaf children. The NUD gave support to the Registry of Interpreters programme which was being established – this project later became the Council for the Advancement of Communication with Deaf People (CACDP).

1979

In an effort to promote both BSL and greater access to TV and the media, the NUD created, scripted and produced "Signs of Life" with the assistance of the BBC's Open Door Community TV team. The programme was broadcast on 10 May and was a success, bringing BSL to the nation. Oralism was, nevertheless, still a tough nut to crack and the NUD felt that there were other ways of attacking it. The British Government was simply not interested in BSL and was of no help at all – the Government was more interested in chucking the Deaf into the "Disabled" category and letting matters rest there.

1981

The NUD looked to the United Nations' "Declaration of the Rights of the Child" and "Convention on the Prevention and Punishment of the Crime of Genocide" in an assessment of the position of the BSL-using members of the Deaf community and began its work on *The Charter of Rights of the Deaf – Part One: The Rights of the Deaf Child*.

1982

The Charter of Rights of the Deaf – Part One: The Rights of the Deaf Child was published in 1982, and a copy was handed to the UN Human Rights Commission in Geneva. At the NUD's third Convention in Kenilworth members voted on a motion recognising Deaf people as members of a linguistic minority group with BSL as their first and preferred language.

1984

At a time when schools for the deaf were closing down and deaf children herded into mainstream schools following the Local Education Authorities' (LEA) over-enthusiastic response to the 1982 Education Act, the NUD brought in Harlan Lane from the USA to present a paper at its 4th Convention at St. Joseph's Centre for the Deaf, Manchester, "Why the Deaf Are Angry", which was a prelude to his monumental work, *When the Mind Hears*. The NUD, continued to work hard on many individuals and convinced them that many deaf children's' education would have been better, had BSL been used. These individuals became allies and went on to make noises to change the thinking of many people at grass-roots level. Furthermore, this influence worked its way up…

1985

The International Congress on the Education of the Deaf was held in August 1985 – 105 years after the Milan Congress. The BDA refused to work with the NUD on campaigning issues during the Congress week and, as a consequence, the NUD worked with the more active and militant branch of the BDA, the North West Region Branch. On the first day of the Congress week, Deaf people gathered at Manchester Airport with banners urging oralists to reconsider their positions. And there were street demonstrations in favour of sign language which attracted national TV News. The Congress was boycotted and an alternative congress was held at Manchester Deaf Centre, the highlight there being Harlan Lane presenting a paper entitled *Language, Power and the Deaf*, and which generated an electric atmosphere in the Deaf centre. On the evening before the final day NUD members decided not to attend the Mayor's dinner and concentrated on drawing up 10 proposed resolutions on behalf of the Deaf of the world, as well as one of NUD's own, which were presented to the committee of the International Congress. The committee evaded discussing the resolutions, citing lack of time, but that week will always be recorded in history as the week that the Deaf came out of their shell and BSL came into its own.

The BDA jumped on the bandwagon following the success of the NUD campaign in Manchester and took up the battle for the recognition of BSL The course and nature of campaigning for the recognition of BSL in the following two years after Manchester 1985 were not effective. The major organisations of

National Union of the Deaf begins the battle for British Sign Language

Thousands of profoundly deaf people leave school almost illiterate, with unintelligible speech and lipreading no better than most hearing people, claims the Nation Union of the Deaf, a pressure group of abou... ...'s

people being taught by deaf people but a teacher should be able to provide an oral model in school.

"The NUD plan certainly seems to go on...

the Deaf, in particular the BDA, were not organising events that would make an impact on the public and the Establishment, despite the BDA promoting BSL during its annual Deaf Awareness week. Wearily, the NUD mustered together for one final campaign. It issued a seminal report entitled *The Future Training of the Teachers of the Deaf*, in which making teachers competent in BSL was one of a number of vital points made in the report. A copy was handed to the Department of Education and Science (DES). With this report out and copies mailed to national newspapers and TV, Monday April 6th 1987 was earmarked for a lobby and demonstration outside the DES headquarters in Waterloo, London. A small group of no more than 12 NUD members gave up their time and pay from work to set up a larger than life lobby, attracting a large number of members of both the press and the public. Two

They describe as disastrous the reactions to the discovery a century ago that deaf children could be taught to speak.

The Victorians decided, it was best for the children and everybody else that the children be immersed in the speaking world. Alexander Graham Bell was one who maintained that if deaf people were allowed to use sign language rather than speaking and to marry, the entire population of the world would eventually become deaf. A virtual ban on the use of sign language was imposed and is only now beginning to disappear.

In 1979 the most recent study showed deaf school leavers possessing an average reading age of eight and three-quarters — just about high enough to read a tabloid paper headline. Many have such low scores they cannot be measured.

Dr John Kyle, of the Centre for Deaf Studies at Bristol University, is among those convinced of the importance of deaf children being allowed to communicate in whatever way they can—through speech or through sign language.

Those not allowed to use sign language learn to smile and nod their heads a great deal in lessons, but no assessment is made of their understanding. The National Union of the Deaf says that the speech of nine in 10 deaf children is, anyhow, virtually unintelligible.

Deaf push for sign language in schools

The NUD claims that profoundly deaf school leavers have an average reading age of 8¾, can barely lip read and are unintelligible. Yesterday's lobby launched a campaign for courses which insist that teachers of the deaf are skilled in sign language.

Mr Raymond Lee, secretary of the union, said: "We have up to now been attacking individual schools for banning sign language but now we are putting the blame where it belongs, with the DES".

Monday April 6 1987

Progress for deaf lost in welter of words

Ministry to be warned that sign language is the way forward, reports Sarah Boseley

Experts turn deaf ear to signs

JUDITH JUDD
■ Education Correspondent

GOVERNMENT hostility towards sign language is consigning thousands of deaf people to a life of illiteracy, according to a campaign that begins tomorrow.

The National Union of the Deaf will lobby the Department of Education and Science to encourage officials to increase the use of sign language in schools.

The NUD blames education policy for 'alarming' levels of literacy among Britain's 50,000 profoundly deaf people. They have an average reading age of eight and a half and 90 per cent of them cannot speak intelligibly.

Many deeply resent the way that their desire to learn through sign language has been frustrated by their teachers.

RETURN TO VICTORIAN VALUES IN DEAF EDUCATION! BRING BACK SIGN LANGUAGE AND DEAF TEACHERS!

TV appearances by a NUD associate member, Rikki Kittel, on TV-AM and BBC's Newsround, added to the impact of the day. Newspapers carried articles on the day of the demonstration and again on the following day.

Harlan Lane, the author of *When The Mind Hears*, joined in with the group along with two TV producers and a director, Nigel Evans.

Harlan Lane in an interview with The Times reporter

The consequence of that demonstration was that the NUD had two meetings with the DES to thrash out numerous thorny issues relating to education for the deaf and BSL, but the DES made it clear it was not interested and was more concerned about implementing integration of deaf children into hearing schools...

Having given about 12 years of their youthful lives to battling for BSL and Deaf rights, members of the NUD, weary and in need of a break, decided that they could not do any more campaigning on a shoestring budget, having spent most of their well-earned money on many of the NUD's ventures since its inception. The NUD went into hibernation, waiting for fresh developments.

In the meantime, the BDA was slowly developing its approach and plans for promoting BSL. Its work involved the development of the Registry of Interpreters, which later was to become the Council for the Advancement of Communication with Deaf People (CACDP). Alongside that, the BDA created another project, the British Sign Language Training Agency (BSLTA), which took off in January 1985 with Clark Denmark as the first BSLTA Research Fellow at Durham University. This was a two-years project to establish a training programme that would enable native Deaf users of BSL to become teachers of BSL. From that small beginning, there are at present many Deaf BSL tutors in various colleges and universities scattered all over Britain.

The BDA was working in a much wider field than that of academia; it promoted BSL in its *British Deaf News*, through all available TV programmes and at major live events, at which

the BDA always demanded interpreters. The BDA broke new ground and made history when on Thursday 20 October 1984 Christine Reeves, a BDA Executive Councillor, gave a speech in sign language at the Liberal Party Assembly. Not only that was an achievement, her signed speech was broadcast nationally on TV. Although Christine Reeves' performance captured the attention of millions of people, a fact little known was that another Deaf lady, Lilian Lawson, the BDA Administrative Officer, gave a signed speech at a fringe meeting earlier in the day at the same Assembly. These two seemingly small incidents at one political party conference effectively removed the barrier that hindered Deaf people's participation in politics and defeated the oralist dictum that 'if deaf people were to participate effectively in the hearing world, they must learn to speak like the hearing.' The BDA had always recognised the impossibility of trying to lipread speakers for hours, with eye-dazzling background light badly interfering with the eyes. On top of that, not one hearing person had clear mouth and lip movement that would make him or her easy to lipread. Sign language was, and still is, the way to close participation with all levels of society and that was the BDA's approach.

The BDA had a powerful tool in its quest for BSL recognition – the appointment of Diana, Princess of Wales, (left) as its Patron in 1983. This much-loved Princess took a keen interest in sign language and made an effort to find time to learn BSL. She signed on practically every public occasion organised by the BDA so that Britain could see her signing. In a slow but sure way, interest in BSL grew and demand for BSL courses and classes followed.

The BDA played an important role in Europe and liaised with some MEPs in discussions on the position and recognition of sign languages. This liaison with a small band of MEPs led to a campaign for the European Parliament to recognise the sign languages of every member country, including Britain. In September 1987 Eileen Lemass MEP opened her report on Irish Sign Language in the European Parliament and ended her report by urging Parliament "to take the initiative and recognise the rights of Deaf people, and to ensure their rightful participation in the future development of the

*L to R:Knut Sondergaard (Director of the Danish Association of the Deaf), Eileen Lemass MEP
and A. Murray Holmes, Vice-Chairman of the BDA at the presentation of the BDA's report,
"BSL - Britain's Fourth Language", at the beginning of the Deaf Awareness Week in November 1987.*

European community." She was warmly applauded by all MEPs present at the packed Parliament and the debate that ensued was very involved and passionate. One MEP from West Germany asked, "Why hasn't this Resolution been put before Parliament years before now – it's a right of Deaf people." At the end of the debate the European Parliament took a vote on the motion and the resolution. All MEPs present voted in favour of the motion and the resolution – not one MEP abstained.

In November 1987 the BDA's 6th annual Deaf Awareness Week launched a report entitled *BSL - Britain's Fourth Language,* and in it the BDA demanded official recognition for BSL by the British Government. Both Eileen Lemass MEP and Malcolm Bruce MP, the father of a deaf daughter, threw in their support for the demand. The British Government stayed silent. The following year in June 1988 history was made when the European Parliament officially recognised sign languages and gave its support. The British Government still remained silent.

New ground was broken by the BDA in April 1995 when Jeff McWhinney was appointed its Chief Executive Officer. Being a Deaf person and educated at Mary Hare Grammar School, Jeff McWhinney was in a good position to push the BDA forward because he had the right Deaf views, attitude and approach.

Despite these advances, there were impatient grassroot Deaf people who wanted BSL recognition immediately, not later. The problem, they felt, was the British Government, and they felt that they had to do something about it.

In 1997 a group of Deaf people formed an organisation named the Federation of Deaf People (FDP) and its principal aim was to achieve BSL recognition as soon as possible. The FDP produced a magazine, *The Voice,* which sold fairly well. Membership of the FDP rose and the organisation began to organise marches in central London in support of BSL recognition. The massively popular and very well-attended FDP marches are significant in that:

1. They were the first regularly organised marches to campaign for BSL recognition.
2. These marches attracted the largest ever numbers of Deaf people at any time in history.
3. These marches generated greater publicity than any events organised by the Deaf or their organisations.

Although the FDP's marches were peaceful and often good-humoured, there was a small group of Deaf people who wanted to make some noise and impact. They felt that causing

The four pictures show scenes from a FDP march for BSL recognition.
This march took place in London on 7 July 2001.

disruption would achieve some publicity about the passion for the battle for BSL recognition. This group of people formed the Deaf Liberation Front (DLF). Its members climbed on roofs, up street lamp posts, telephone poles and such-like and set up posters demanding BSL recognition. Very often the police could not do much except to wait for the protesters to come down quietly.

This two-pronged attack in the battle for BSL recognition fast gained attention and both the FDP and BDA's efforts were rewarded when an announcement was made by the Labour Government through the Department of Work and Pensions (DWP) on 18 March 2003 recognising BSL as a language.

Many Deaf people, though, see this recognition as a kind of "tokenism" rather than as a full and unequivocal recognition of a language along the lines of English and Welsh languages. The campaign continues…

One of the Deaf Liberation Front's demonstrations
- Manchester, March 2001

Books and Publications

Books written and published by Deaf people were relatively few in the early years of Deaf history. The earliest known published work by a deaf person is that of John Audelay who wrote *Alia Cantalena de Sancta Maria* in the 15th century, possibly around 1440. Audelay's work was later published in a limited edition of 450 copies in 1926 by The Seven Acres Press.

Digiti Lingua was published in 1698 and was written by an anonymous deafened person.

A Deaf man from Monaghan in Ireland named John Burns compiled and published *An Historical and Chronological Remembrancer of All Remarkable Occurrences, From the Creation to this Present Year of Our Lord, 1775.*

John Audelay's work published in 1926 - number 12 of 450 copies is in the Raymond Lee Collection.

John Burns' 1775 book

John Philp Wood (1762-1838), one of the early Braidwoodian pupils, was a very exceptional Deaf person. He was appointed Scotland's Auditor of Excise by the Prime Minister, Spencer Percival, in 1809. Wood's talents did not end there. Due to the excellent education he received from Thomas Braidwood, Wood became masterful in the English language, thanks to the use of manualism (fingerspelling) in his education, and he went on to write two books of great importance before becoming the editor of a renowned publication, *The Peerage of Scotland.*

In 1791 Wood published an acclaimed work entitled *A Sketch on the Life of John Law of Lauriston, Comptroller General of the Finances of France.* This was followed by another now famous publication in 1794 entitled *The Antient and Modern State of the Parish of Cramond.* This work, a survey which spanned a period from 1790 to 1793, singled out Wood as Scotland's first ever person to write a parochial history. The book was a precursor of the technique later employed by Sir John Sinclair in connection with his monumental work entitled *The Statistical Account of Scotland*, published in volumes between 1791 and 1799. In 1813 Wood was persuaded to prepare the second edition of *The Peerage of Scotland*. Wood was a proficient genealogist and he used his knowledge and writing skills to improve vastly the second edition.

There is a list of illustrious deaf authors whose writings greatly contributed towards the advancement of not only literature in general, but the history of the Deaf in particular, besides showing that deaf people are capable of writing books should they be given the opportunity to do so.

Charlotte Elizabeth Tonna (1790-1846, below) and Harriet Martineau (1802-1876, below left) were two of the earliest deaf writers to gain universal renown for their works.

Wood's edition of The Peerage of Scotland.
Note the middle name spelt Philip.
It was a printer's error as the name was actually Philp.

These two women were courageously outspoken in their views and they were not afraid to write them down. Tonna spoke out for those who were suffering under terrible employment conditions in her time. Her writings went a long way to influence the introduction of the Factory Act 1850, which brought in the reforms that Tonna sought. Martineau on the other hand made it known that she was against slavery and campaigned for its abolition through both voicing her opinions and in her writings. When she visited the United States, Martineau did not shirk from making known her opinions despite receiving threats of personal injury during her travels in the States. She was, even so, forced to abandon several journeys and had to return to England.

Another deaf person who became a writer, and who went on to achieve fame and renown in a particular field, was John Kitto (1804-1854, right). Born in abject poverty to alcoholic parents, Kitto was taken away from his parents by his grandmother and had a happy time with her until he had to return to his parents. Kitto was 13 years old when he fell from a ladder while helping his father with building work and this resulted in his deafness. After this, Kitto was put into a workhouse, where he learned to read and write. He wrote *Workhouse Journal* around 1820/21.

In 1825 Kitto published his next book, *Essays and Letters*, and it was very successful. Kitto involved himself with the Church Missionary Society and was based in Malta for nearly three years before returning home. His works include *The Deaf Traveller* (1833-35), *The Pictorial Bible* (1835-38) through to the *Cyclopaedia of Biblical Literature* (1845), *The Lost Senses: Deafness and Blindness* (1845) and *Daily Biblical Illustrations* (1849-1851). Kitto was acknowledged as an authority on the Bible and his commentaries were highly valued. Almost always in ill health, Kitto moved to Canstätt in Germany where he later died. Kitto's name is now immortally associated with biblical study and literature.

Alexander Atkinson (1806-1879) of Newcastle was born deaf and attended the Edinburgh Institution for the Deaf and Dumb under the headmastership of Robert Kinniburgh. Nothing would have been known of what a Deaf person's schooldays would have been like but for Atkinson's only and truly important work, *Memoirs of My Youth* which was published in 1865. Atkinson's recall of his schooldays was awesome and his work was the first account of life in a residential school for the deaf to be written by an British Deaf person. There is no other published work describing the schooldays of a Deaf person that is both very detailed and of great surdohistorical importance. This work was re-published by the British Deaf History Society in 2001.

Another deaf pupil at the Edinburgh Institution, John Carmichael (1803-1857), emigrated to Australia, arriving at Sydney in October 1825. He became an artist of renown and was credited with the design of the first Australian postage stamp and the engraving of the first Australian maps. He published a little known but highly valued book entitled *Select Views of Sydney, New South Wales* in 1829.

Another Scottish Deaf man, who was also a former pupil at the Edinburgh Institution, emigrated to Nova Scotia in Canada in 1851 by way of America. This man, George Tait (1828-1904), went on to co-found a school for the Deaf in Halifax, Nova Scotia. This school was opened on 4th August 1856. He founded the school with another former pupil of the same Edinburgh Institution, William Gray. In 1877 George Tait published his autobiography, the *Autobiography of George Tait, A Deaf Mute Who First Gave Instructions to the Deaf and Dumb in the City of Halifax*. This work ran into 14 editions between 1877 and 1896.

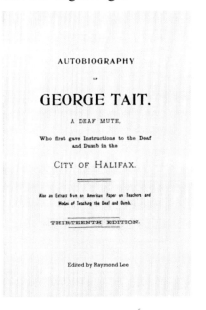

AUTOBIOGRAPHY

OF

GEORGE TAIT.

A DEAF MUTE,

Who first gave Instructions to the Deaf and Dumb in the

CITY OF HALIFAX.

Also an Extract from an American Paper on Teachers and Modes of Teaching the Deaf and Dumb.

THIRTEENTH EDITION.

Edited by Raymond Lee

There is a myth surrounding Abraham Farrar (1861-1944) in that many thought he wrote numerous books. The fact is that Farrar wrote no book about Deaf history; he edited the Rev. Thomas Arnold's *Manual for Teachers* and wrote an introduction for Neville Dixon's 1890 translation of Pablo Bonet's *Simplification of the Letters of the Alphabet and Method of Teaching Deaf-Mutes to Speak.*

Other deaf writers in the 20th century are the romantic novelist Kate Oxley (1896-1978) who wrote under the name of Kate Whitehead, and Jack Clemo (1916-1994) who concentrated mainly on poetry. David Wright (1920-1994), a former pupil of Spring Hill School, Northampton, wrote two autobiographies — *Monologues of a Deaf Man* and *Deafness*. Wright also had a number of poetical works published, the first entitled *Poems* was published in 1949 and he went on to win several awards for his poetry. Wright co-authored three books about Portugal and was an editor on several literary projects. Several Deaf professionals have written on subjects deriving from their work, such as Iain Poplett on physics and Richard Goulden on bibliography.

There was still a void, in that of Deaf-related literature, in the world of publication as the 1970s dawned on the British Deaf community. Deaf people were second class citizens at that time and their history was both being ignored and largely unknown. Young deaf children had no role models to look up to and they were being taught about the great hearing people who shaped the world, and who yet did nothing for Deaf people. The seventies began to see great changes as Deaf people began to form new organisations. The Scottish Workshop with the Deaf (SWD) was founded in 1976 by a group of deaf and hearing friends. Among the Deaf activists associated with the SWD were Jock Young, Lilian Lawson, Murray Holmes and John Hay and among the hearing were George W. G. Montgomery, the Rev. Stuart Lochrie, Martin Colville, Susan Turfus and Liz Scott-Gibson. The SWD began to see the importance of publications, and over the years from its inception the organisation published over 18 major books and numerous booklets, papers and articles.

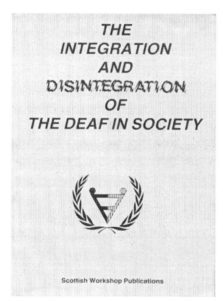

THE INTEGRATION AND DISINTEGRATION OF THE DEAF IN SOCIETY

Scottish Workshop Publications

The first publication was *Deafness, Personality and Mental Health* in 1978 (reprinted in 1979). The SWD's most famous and influential book was *The Integration and Disintegration of the Deaf in Society* (1981) and it sold out very quickly. Arthur F. Dimmock became more involved in SWD publications and his association with G. W. G. Montgomery led to the publication of the marvellous biography of the renowned Deaf artist, A. R. Thomson - *Tommy* (1991). The SWD continued to turn out books such as *Cruel Legacy* (1993), *The Venerable Legacy* (1998) and this work was re-titled *The Hand of Time* (2000) when it was revised. Other books include *Deaf Workers are Good Workers, Beyond Hobson's Choice, Silent Destiny, No Lesser God* and *Language for the Eye*. The importance of the SWD's contribution in the field of Deaf-related literature cannot be underestimated; its impact has led to changes for both better lives and respect for the Deaf as human beings.

The National Union of the Deaf (NUD) was also founded in the same year as the SWD, but it did not publish books until 1982 when it published *Charter of Rights of the Deaf: Part One - The Rights of the Deaf Child,* and ten years later it published *Deaf Liberation*, a collection of NUD papers. This book was edited by Raymond Lee.

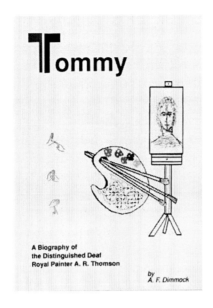

In 1983 a former pupil of Mary Hare Grammar School, Jessica Rees, published her autobiography, *Sing a Song of Silence,* and there has been a growth of books written by Deaf people about their own lives (and some were privately published), notably that of Raymond Banks Thorpe's *Torpy* (1995), Barrie Curtis' *Chasing A Dream* (1998) and Hamish Rosie's *My Island* (1999).

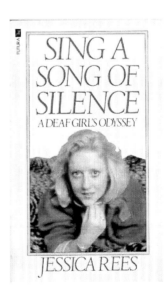

The late 1980s and the 1990s saw an explosion of books on BSL, including Dorothy Miles' *British Sign Language: A Beginners Guide* (1988) and Cath Smith's *Signs Make Sense* (1990) - and from that a growth in videos and DVDs on storytelling and sign language courses followed. These were mainly produced by the CACDP and Chase Video, which is an unit of Royal School for the Deaf, Derby.

There was all the same a need to record the history of the Deaf in Britain and the BDA signalled the importance of this when it commissioned Peter Jackson to work that subject. The result of his work was a book entitled *Britain's Deaf Heritage* (1990). This book became an instant bestseller. It was later revised and updated and published by the same author in 2001 under the new title of *A Pictorial History of Deaf Britain*.

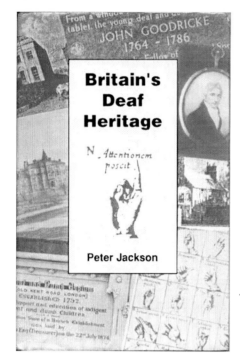

There were histories of schools for the deaf published from time to time. Such books are Robin Herdman's *History of the Northern Counties School for the Deaf, Newcastle 1838-1988* (1988), Anthony J. Boyce's *The History of the Yorkshire Residential School for the Deaf 1829-1979* (1996) and Doreen E. Woodford's *A Man and His School: The Story of the Llandaff School for the Deaf and Dumb* (1996). These books were published on a small scale but they were all vital contributions to the building up of the history of the Deaf. Books on the Deaf community and its clubs are rare, but Joyce Paull's *Our Deaf Club - 40 Years of Surbiton Deaf Social Club (*1998) and Peter and Maureen Jackson's privately published *A History of the Deaf Community In Northwich and Winsford 1880-2000* (2001) are among the few books around that record the histories and activities of local Deaf communities. A. F. Dimmock's *Sporting Heritage* (1991) charted the history of the Southern Deaf Sports Association (SDASA).

Deaf History became an increasingly important issue, and after the founding of the British Deaf History Society by Raymond Lee and John A. Hay in 1993, the BDHS's first book, *Bermondsey 1792* (1993), was published by the National Union of the Deaf (NUD) and this kick-started a run of publications that is unequalled in British Deaf history. With Raymond Lee running the Publications department of the BDHS, the Society published 27 more books in the next 10 years to 2004, and all these books relate to Deaf history. Books on subjects ranging from the lives of individual Deaf persons such in Peter R. Brown's *Banton* (1994)

Raymond Lee - BDHS

to records on Deaf people in Peter W. Jackson's magnificent *The Gawdy Manuscripts* (2004) have become collectors' items due to the low volume of numbers published. The BDHS's second book, *A Pictorial History of the Evolution of the British Manual Alphabet* (1994) changed hands for £85 as recently as 2001.

The BDHS's contribution to the Millennium was *Deaf Lives* (2001), which continued short biographies and noted the achievements of 144 Deaf persons throughout British history. Reproductions of earlier books are also undertaken by the BDHS from time to time and such books include the 1698 classic *Digiti Lingua* (1999), the 1809 book *The Invited Alphabet* (2000), Alexander Atkinson's 1865 autobiography, *Memoirs of My Youth* (2001), and the 1894 *Autobiography of George Tait* (2002). The BDHS continues to research and publish works on Deaf history.

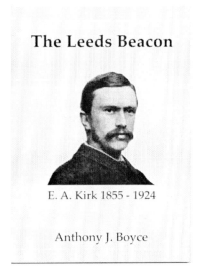

The Leeds Beacon

E. A. Kirk 1855 - 1924

Anthony J. Boyce

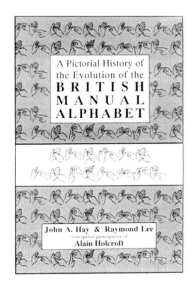

A Pictorial History of the Evolution of the **BRITISH MANUAL ALPHABET**

John A. Hay & Raymond Lee
with special participation of
Alain Holcroft

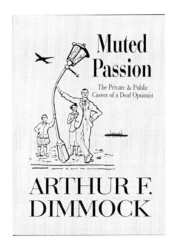

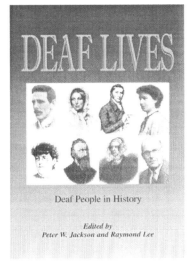

Samples of BDHS books

Another contribution to Deaf literature and history is Peter W. Jackson's series on Deaf murders and Deaf crimes. Although not all stories in his books are confined to Britain alone, the extensive research put into the work by the author resulted in a series of books that stand out in criminological literature as well as being of surdohistorical value. His books on Deaf crime are not without controversy and they have evoked ill feelings within a small section of the British Deaf community.

Peter W. Jackson - BDHS

The first book, *Deaf Crime Casebook,* was published in 1997 and it immediately caused a storm. Despite that, the book sold well and the second book, *Deaf to Evidence,* came out in 1998; *Deaf Murder Casebook* in 2000; *Deaf Target* in 2002 and the most recent about the Gallaudet University-linked murders, *Death Around the Green,* was published in 2003. There are more books in the series to be published.

177

It is envisaged that Deaf literature and publications will continue to grow in the future as long as the BDHS continues to exist and its Research and Publications Department be allowed to thrive and become an independent section concentrating on books.

The Present Era

Time has marched on and sweeping changes have taken place. These changes should have been of great benefit to the Deaf in all areas and levels of society, employment, education, technology, politics and culture. In the main the Deaf benefited from the changes, but there are still areas where improvement needs to be made. Deaf people's lifestyles have improved by leaps and bounds; they are leading their lives in a vastly different way to those in the past. Outlined here are the major changes that have arrived since the late 1970s

1. Television

The development of subtitles on both BBC's Ceefax and ITV's Oracle text pages in the late 1970s (around 1978) led to the creation of a subtitling system that benefited the Deaf. The '888' sign became the standard slang for TV subtitles.

Subtitles opened a new world to the Deaf, who were able to follow what was being said on TV programmes and films; and who were introduced to a world of how hearing people speak and think, which certainly was very different to their own Deaf world. They woke up to the fact that hearing people were not superior to them despite the traditional oralist policy making out the inferiority of the Deaf – and this realisation led Deaf people to believe that they were and are the equals of hearing people, not inferior to them.

From 1980 to the present day subtitled TV programmes grew in numbers. These caused many Deaf people to go out less often, preferring to stay home and watch TV. The negative aspect of this trend was that fewer people attended Deaf clubs and as a consequence, along with emerging technological innovations such as the fax machine and the minicom, a good number of Deaf clubs began to close for good. Those clubs that survived struggled to get by, and they were mainly propped up by Deaf people who came to socialise by playing snooker, darts and having a pint at the club's bar. Sign Language on television is another step forward for the Deaf, but signed programmes are very few, reflecting the domination and monopoly of TV by hearing people: there is not a channel dedicated to the Deaf even on an obscure digital cable or satellite channel. Whilst subtitles satisfy the great majority of Deaf people, there are Deaf people who nevertheless need programmes in BSL. The battle for such programmes shall continue until this need is met.

The work of the Deaf Broadcasting Campaign (DBC) cannot go unmentioned here, for this organisation had the aim of television programmes made accessible to Deaf viewers via subtitles and sign. The DBC, formed in 1980 following the success of the NUD's *Signs of Life*, not only mounted public campaigns and petitioned from time to time but slowly built rapport with TV companies and executives, winning their trust and from there they were able to discuss and press for the needs of the Deaf at executive levels. Even film and TV stars threw in their support and sided with the DBC at its public demonstrations and campaigns. The rest is history. The timeline of TV programmes for the Deaf is given in the Appendices.

Right: DBC demonstration at Covent Garden Market, December 1980.

179

2. Telecommunications for the Deaf

In the late 1960s the Deaf community made an important breakthrough in the world of telecommunications with the introduction of teletypewriters (TTYs with acoustic couplers). This TTY technology helped the Deaf gain access to the regular telephone network some ninety years after Alexander Graham Bell invented the voice telephone. Despite the obstacles faced within a monopolistic telecommunications environment, TTYs were obtained from telephone companies and volunteer organisations, enabling deaf people to communicate with each other on the telephone infrastructure. The resulting telecommunications movement initially endured a time of scepticism, reluctance and, oddly, fear from some members of the Deaf community. But that changed as experience over the first few years led the Deaf community to accept the TTY with enthusiasm, and scores of consumers and professionals began contributing substantially to the marketing of the technology, development of new products, and improvement access.

Little did Deaf people realise then how significant this development would be to the world's deaf and hard of hearing populations in the areas of empowerment, cohesiveness and cultural enlightenment. Equally the development of telecommunications for the Deaf has been the foundation for major initiatives in innovation, design, and policy for today's accessible products and services for all deaf people, not only in telecommunications, but also in education, employment, recreation, and other life activities.

From this small beginning, telecommunications for the Deaf has come on by leaps and bounds, sometimes so quickly that many people find it difficult to keep up with new technology.

For many Deaf people the early teletypewriters or phonetypes were marvellous but cumbersome. They could only be used in set locations as the machines were not mobile.

This situation did not last for long, as firstly computers and then mobile phones with text facilities were widely used and soon gave all Deaf people equality of access.

A Concise History of Telecommunications, with special reference to Deaf use

1837   Samuel F. B. Morse demonstrates the telegraph, the first electrically operated machine for distance communication.

1874   Thomas Alva Edison patents the duplex telegraph, which allows two messages to be transmitted simultaneously over the same wire. Emile Baudot develops a five-level telegraphic coding system.

1876   Alexander Graham Bell demonstrates his voice telephone at the Centennial Exhibition in Philadelphia.

1893   Elisha Gray's Telautograph, an electric writing machine for use with the telephone, is demonstrated at the World's Fair in Chicago.

1912   William E. Shaw demonstrates the "Talkless Telephone".

1920s   Bell Telephone Laboratories established.

Bell System creates the *"Deaf Set"* for hard of hearing persons.

Bell System demonstrates transmission of pictures over telephone lines.

1934   Congress passes the Communications Act, which includes a provision requiring the recently established Federal Communication Commission to ensure "universal services... so far as possible to all the people of the United States".

1946   The first mobile phone system established by the Southwestern Bell Telephone Co. These phones are installed in cars for two different people to communicate with each other.

1957   Bell Laboratories demonstrates a TV-Telephone.

1964   Visual Speech Indicators are developed. These hand-held devices are equipped with a moving needle that indicates whether or not someone is speaking on the other end of the telephone.

The first long-distance call by deaf persons using electric writing machines occurs between the Vocational Administration Office in Washington D.C., and the San Fernando Valley State College Leadership Training Programs in California.

James C. Marsters recommends TTY communication over regular telephone lines.

Robert H. Weitbrecht develops an acoustic telephone coupler for use with teletype-writers by deaf people.

The annual American National Association of the Deaf Convention in New York City includes exhibits of telephone devices.

First public demonstration of a TTY call between deaf persons takes place in a hotel at the Alexander Graham Bell Association for the Deaf convention in Salt Lake City, Utah.

AT & T demonstrates the Picturephone at the World's Fair in New York City.

The Victor-Comptometer Corporation Electrowriter is used at the World Games for the Deaf in Washington D.C.

Robert H. Weitbrecht in Redwood City, California, places the first long-distance TTY call to James C. Marsters in Pasadena, California.

1965   First transcontinental TTY call takes place between Robert H. Weitbrecht in New York and James C. Marsters in California.

Andrew Saks suggests the relay telephone service concept.

1966   Andrew Saks establishes the first telephone relay service in Redwood City, California.

James C. Marsters establishes the second telephone relay service in Pasadena.

1968   First mobile phone is developed for use outside the car.

174 TTYs are in use by end of the year in the USA.

1972   First phonetype transatlantic call is made between Jack Ashley, M. P., and Robert H. Weitbrecht in California.

1973   The first telephone call made in the U.K. between two deaf men using a Phonetype, one in Birmingham and the other in Bromley, Kent.

The first local network established in Sheffield with seven Phonetype users.

1975   The first "Link-Up" service between deaf and hearing persons opened at the Cheshire Home, Ampthill, Beds.

1978   Phonetype network totals 165 units with five Link-up bureaux.

1979   Development in conjunction with Kegwain Ltd of a new portable electronic terminal named "Vistel".

1981   Distribution of "Vistel" terminals begun.

1982   Grant received from the D.H.S.S. for the replacement of all Phonetypes by Vistel.

The first "999" call service for Vistel users inaugurated with the help of the Nottinghamshire Constabulary.

The first electronic mail network established for use by deaf people.

Development of the first teletext recording system incorporating a TV/video selector facility for extra reliability.

1983   Coordination of "HASICOM" project to develop communications for deaf-blind people.

The first directory of Vistel users published with 500 names and numbers.

The first of the present day mobile phone networks was started in Chicago.

1984   Publication of the second directory of Vistel users with 700 names and numbers.

1985   Development of new Vistel model initiated by T.C.S. Ltd. in conjunction with the Breakthrough Trust's technical team.

1986   The first public sector Vistel terminals installed in 32 libraries, 18 hospitals and an airport.

The first international electronic mail links set up between the U.K., Eire and

Holland, followed later by Portugal.

1989   British Telecom and the RNID join up to set up a national relay service for deaf people

1991   RNID Typetalk opens Pauline Ashley House, Speke, South Liverpool, with 50 Operating positions, taking the first live call on 1 July. 300 calls were taken on the first day.

RNID Typetalk employs 7 full time operators and 15 part time operators. The Mayor and Mayoress of Knowsley and the Mayoress of Liverpool attend the official launch.

1992   Operator numbers increase to 52.

1993   Operator numbers increase to 117.

1994   OFTEL places a requirement into the BT licence to provide a relay service for people with communication difficulties.

1995   Nokia and the RNID develop a hand-held textphone with fax facilities for deaf people.

1998   Mobile phone technology develops text messaging facilities, allowing deaf people to achieve equality.

Videophones allowing Deaf people to "sign" over telephone networks are developed.

2000   Louise Ellman MP awards RNID Typetalk the Charter Mark. RNID Typetalk introduces RNID Typetalk Assist. In February Typetalk relays its 10 millionth call. Typetalk now relays on average 6,400 calls a day with 536 Operators. Since opening they have relayed 11,651,089 calls.

2001   BT TextDirect is launched at the BT Centre in London. The first official call was made by the RNID chief executive, James Strachan, from the BT Centre to Maria Eagle, Minister for Disabilities at Whitehall.

2002   Mobile hand-held videophones are developed.

Many Deaf people now own a mobile phone and use it for texting messages, not only among each other, but to hearing people. The use of SMS replaced the pager system of a few years ago. It is ironic that the telephone that usually prevented the Deaf from either communicating with each other or from obtaining well-paid jobs is now no longer a problem and that many Deaf people cannot do without the phone nowadays!

It is the mobile and satellite technology that Deaf people are looking to for improvements, especially on the videophone side. This would enable them to communicate with other Deaf people using signs rather than to rely entirely on text at present.

3. Further and Higher Education

Few Deaf people in the past attended colleges and universities as a part of their apprentice-ships with their companies. Sitting through courses such as ONC and HNC was in many ways an ordeal due to the impossibility of lipreading the tutor who was forever talking to either the blackboard or the Bunsen burner. Very few Deaf people succeeded in gaining doctorates such as Ph.D – in particular Bernard Pitcher (1909-2002), who was the first Deaf person in Britain to be awarded a Ph.D. Even then, he had to bring along carbon paper into lectures and place it under each page of fellow student's notebook so that he could have a copy of the notes!

On the other hand, aspiring Deaf people seeking degree courses such as a BA in English Language or a degree in Art and Industrial Design were often turned away in the late 1960s and early 1970s on account of their deafness, in that they would not be able to follow the course tutors. The disappointment and bitterness felt by Deaf people at that time led them to rebel and demand greater access to higher education through the use of interpreters and note-takers. This concern and bitterness was shared by parents and by educationists who knew the unfulfilled and unused potential of young Deaf students.

In 1962 there were 44 universities in Britain. Following the Robbins Report on Higher Education (1961-1963), the numbers expanded by 1976 to 81 universities, 30 polytechnics, 27 colleges of education and 44 higher education colleges. There were, even so, no provisions or facilities available to meet the needs of aspiring Deaf students.

In 1971 the Open University was launched. It offered deaf adults a path to higher education courses. Its main advantages were that it had an open access admission policy and home-based teaching, known as distance-learning. While the educated and highly talented Deaf people found Open University and its courses beneficial, there were problems for many deaf participants where technical language was concerned. It required tuition and devotion by staff to enable Deaf students acquire self-study discipline. This problem was further compounded by the lack of subtitles of televised Open University courses and Deaf students were frustrated by the state of affairs.

The National Study Group on Further and Higher Education (later NATED) was set up in 1975. It produced guidelines for all colleges and HE institutions and their lecturers on the problems facing the Deaf students. The National Bureau of Handicapped Students (NBHS) followed, and short-term bridging courses were devised to help Deaf students wishing to enter HE institutions. As a result of these two pressure groups, the number of Open University deaf students was in excess of 200 by 1984 and only 50 deaf students were studying in the non-university sector of higher education.

Schools also took in the vision given in the new Education Acts and plans, which aimed firstly to expand the work of school-seniors by appointing teachers in particular subjects rather than all-purpose teachers, and then secondly to expand the sixth-form departments at, among others, Burwood Park College (1973-1996), Doncaster College for the Deaf, Mary Hare sixth form college, Tewin Water and Derby and also by using local colleges. Some of these departments such as Doncaster and Derby were to become colleges for Deaf people in their own right. Many of these developments were by nature residential. Meanwhile, some local authorities were trying out a variety of local arrangements to meet the needs of post-school education and some developed greatly like Bulmershe College of

Higher Education (now merged with Reading University), Sheffield Polytechnic, Bradford and Ilkley Community College, Nene College (Northampton), Brixton College and the City of London Literary Institute (The City Lit.).

The trials and experiences of all these initiatives opened up the way for the longed-for entry to Higher Education, at first for one or two Deaf persons, but later for many. Eyes had always been cast on the USA and its dedicated Gallaudet University. This totally overlooked the relative sizes and populations of that country and the UK. Eventually England and Wales found its own path and great progress was made, some universities both providing for and meeting the communication needs of Deaf students, in ones and twos, in groups, and eventually in large numbers. Pioneering universities included Bristol, Durham, Wolverhampton and University of Central Lancashire.

A parallel and important development, largely thrust forward at rapid speed by the place of sign language and culture studies, was the use of Deaf staff at all levels, so that, for these staff members, there was a growth of acceptance by other staff members, and of opportunity to be fully involved as professionals, able to, and expected to, write, research and lecture.

Wolverhampton University

These new provisions were helped along by rapid improvements in Information Technology (IT), in the form of new computers and systems, by improved school education for many deaf children and by the various acts and decisions that led to the support offered by some universities through their Disabled Students Services. Wolverhampton University, as an example, has residential rooms equipped according to need for handicapped or disabled students, unlike the non-disabled, to remain for the full duration of the course and offers good support to them in many other ways.

The developments in higher and further education have been rapid and continue, but do not yet cover the whole country, nor meet all the needs. Some progress is being made in extending further and higher education to young Deaf people with additional disabilities.

4. Psychiatric Services for Deaf People

In the past doctors' failure to comprehend fully the nature and state of deafness often created terrible consequences for Deaf patients – a one-way ticket to the mental asylum. Many deaf people, who suffered from even minor or temporary mental illnesses, were often either thought to need longer periods in mental hospitals or condemned to a lifetime locked up. This shocking state of affairs was primarily and solely the fault of the medical profession and the oralists in that they were unable to communicate with Deaf patients using signs. Doctors, of all people, should and ought to know better about deafness and its offshoot, sign language, but they are the worst persons to consult about deafness. The medical profession is interested only in the medical and clinical sides of the ears, and nothing else. That is the limit of their knowledge about deafness.

Hearing doctors' failure to understand that their own problems in communicating with the Deaf led to even greater frustrations in the Deaf patients – some Deaf persons of renown such as Charles Gawen, the artist brother of the prominent Deaf sculptor Joseph Gawen (1825-1901), were completely misdiagnosed as "mad". Charles Gawen, who was employed as an illustrator by the *London Illustrated News*, was dumped into the Middlesex Asylum where he ended his days. Another example is of Doug Old, who was born in Portsmouth in 1923. When he became deaf in 1934, doctors committed him to a mental hospital where he had to mix with the adult insane because there was no children's ward there. Doug's shocked parents had to fight for over two years to get him released. Doug was admitted to the Brighton School for the Deaf where he was introduced to sign language… and he later developed to become a fine sportsman and master carpenter. Doug represented Great Britain in table tennis in two World Games for the Deaf, in Milan in 1957 and in the USA in 1965. There was a study carried out in 1989 by L. Timmermans that found that the average stay of a Deaf person in a mental hospital was 19.5 years compared with 148 days for a hearing person, and it also confirmed that many patients had been incorrectly diagnosed.

Oralism contributed a large part towards triggering the emotional and psychological problems of the Deaf with its inhumane policy of banning sign and prohibiting promotion of "Deaf identity" in education. After receiving oralist education, deaf children were actively discouraged from joining the Deaf community. They were told that they must live in a

hearing world and speak like hearing people in order to survive. As a consequence of the oralists' uncaring attitude and deliberately malicious advice, Deaf people who found they could not manage as "hearing persons" in the world outside of school developed psychological as well as emotional problems. They felt tricked and put under intolerable pressure by the oralists - and yet all these measures of the oralists were perfectly legal and the British government did nothing to remedy the terrible situation.

Not one hearing person thought of establishing psychiatric services to help Deaf people and such provisions were shockingly non-existent until 1964 when a small department of Psychiatry Services for the Deaf was opened in Manchester as an outpatient facility.

In 1968 Dr. John Clifford Denmark (1924-1998, left), the son of the principal of a school for the deaf, established the first specialised psychiatric service for the Deaf at Whittingham Hospital in   Preston, Lancashire. Dr. Denmark recognised that Deaf people of all ages were prone   to psychological and emotional problems, mainly because of communication difficulties with the hearing, their hearing parents and teachers. From this small beginning, other   specialised units were opened in London (Springfield) and Birmingham, along with   the small outpatient facility in Manchester. Dr. Denmark and his staff visited a number of mental hospitals and took away Deaf inmates to Whittingham for the treatment that they deserved. A good number were released into the world outside to lead normal lives. Where Deaf persons had either recovered from their mental illness or had been diagnosed as not being mentally ill but in need of rehabilitation, they would be sent to centres such as the RNID's Grange Court in Devon and Richardson House in Blackburn. In the north of Britain there is also the Hays Rehabilitation Unit in Scotland.

The provisions of psychiatric services for the Deaf have expanded since 1968. Since the second unit was established in Springfield Hospital in 1974, new ideas and developments in the referral, diagnosis and treatment of Deaf patients were brought in and these improved the service. The introduction of Deaf professionals trained as counsellors and therapists was a wonderful step forward and the future of the psychiatric services can only improve.

5. Mainstreaming and the Closure of Schools for the deaf.

At present the policy of implementing the mainstreaming of the disabled is in full force with the backing of the present Government, the local authorities and many organisations of and for the hearing disabled. Despite taking over 25 years in trying to inform the hearing people that the needs of the Deaf were, and still are, different to that of the hearing disabled, the Deaf's pleas are still being ignored by the authorities.

The main reason for mainstreaming is both political and financial. It is a money-saving measure for many local authorities who are under increasing pressure to seek funding to finance their pet projects outside of education. They see the policy of mainstreaming a blessing in that it saves a minimum of some £9,000 per person, a figure quoted by one education officer from the Borough of Brent in 1986, or even £18,000 as recently suggested (2002), by not sending them to a specialised school for the deaf. These savings by the local education authorities (LEAs) do not find their way back into the education of the Deaf and therefore Deaf education is both at a loss and at a disadvantage.

Not all Deaf persons succeed in the mainstreamed educational environment on their own, and a good number of deaf pupils still needed communication help and support and Deaf role models to see them through. Not all LEAs provide these in every school in their boroughs, but there is a slow but growing number of Deaf people employed to work as assistants with Deaf children in mainstreamed schools, and they use signs to communicate. This may be seen as some sort of cheap compensation to make up for depriving the deaf child of his or her rightful education in a language that he or she uses. Children of various ethnic minorities have teachers who use their respective languages but not Deaf children who are members of a linguistic minority in their own right. Mainstream schools do not employ permanent qualified teachers of the deaf, either Deaf or hearing, to teach their deaf pupils. They employ peripatetic teachers who visit mainstream schools where deaf children are placed. This is the measure of the extent of hearing authorities' ignorant, deliberate or otherwise, and uncaring attitude towards the needs of the deaf child.

The policy of integration has caused harm to a good number of deaf children in that they are being put into surroundings that are both unsuited to and inappropriate for their needs. There have been reports of some deaf children having been teased and mocked by hearing pupils and consequently suffered psychological and emotional problems due to communication difficulties and hidden fear. Not only that, deprivation of their Deaf identity and sign language has led to problems in the world outside of school. The anger and bitterness of mainstreamed deaf pupils led to the establishing of the Deaf Ex-Mainstreamers Group (DEX) in 1994. This group believes that bilingualism should be adopted in mainstream surroundings and classes.

To illustrate an example of the problems of integration, an abridged version of a note from one caseworker reads:

> *A young deaf boy was taught in a good primary school. Due to his parents splitting up, he moved to another part of the UK to be near to his mum's parents' home. He attended a local school with no support. (I questioned him thoroughly). Apparently he was assessed and the LEA decided he could cope because he could "speak" and the LEA paid no regard to his actual listening skills and personal development needs.*

Consequently he misbehaved and was suspended from school several times. Now he attends college in a deaf course in order to "catch up." But the damage due to the lack of appropriate support was done and the college has to be like the Red Cross in dealing with his attitude and so on.

The schooling happened during the last 7 years, not 30 years ago.

On the other hand, there are talented deaf people and hard of hearing people who are able to survive in mainstream conditions with the additional assistance of the teachers during and after class. Their speech is not impaired and they are able to communicate with ordinary children although they have to make extra efforts to hear or lipread what was being said.

Integration should be a two-way process if it is to be both workable and a success. The sad fact remains that hearing children are not required to learn sign language as a part of their curriculum whereas Deaf children are required to learn to hear and to speak - and this places the burden on the Deaf child to "become normal like hearing children around him." This is seen by the Deaf community as "untrue integration" because there is no effort to place some responsibility on hearing children to play their part in the other half of the "two-way process" that is required to make integration work.

Even hearing teachers in mainstream schools have various reservations about the situation concerning the Deaf. Below is an article reprinted from one newspaper - South Tyneside Today dated 27 February 2004:

DEAF PUPILS NEED SPECIAL TEACHING

DEAF children will be failed by the education system if they are forced into mainstream education, a borough teacher has warned. A change in Government policy means local education authorities (LEAs) are now encouraged to send deaf children to regular schools.

The decision has caused outrage among parents at Northern Counties School in Newcastle, which caters for children with hearing and other disabilities. The unique school, which caters for about 100 children from across the north-east, is facing closure due to falling rolls - a direct result of pupils being sent elsewhere. But this policy is not in the best interests of children who need specialist education, according to a teacher from South Shields.

The secondary school teacher, who did not want to be named, claims mainstream schools lack the training, support and resources to cope with children with severe difficulties.

She said: "The Government seems to think it is a good idea for children to suddenly start attending mainstream schools. But they have failed to provide mainstream schools, such as the one where I teach, with any additional support or resources to help children with severe difficulties. Neither have I had any training, since the first day I entered school, in the teaching of deaf children."

She added that while teaching in Sunderland, she watched a bright, determined girl leave school with no GCSEs because she was partially sighted and the school was incapable of providing for her needs.

She added: "Mainstream schools are not to blame. It's a money-saving scheme that ministers are throwing their weight behind, but not a single penny of funding."

The term "mainstreaming" is used here as the present term "inclusion" is a deliberately dishonest name to cover up what is de facto exclusion for deaf children. The Deaf have been persuaded that sign is all that matters. Delighted that their beloved sign is getting some kind of recognition, they have stood by and hardly noticed the destruction of the educational infrastructure of their community and culture.

The issue of the integration of the deaf is a sensitive issue that is too clouded in political furore to enable an accurate history to be written at present. Very little factual information and statistics can be obtained from the current government departments in order to paint a fair and unbiased picture of the situation that would enable one to judge the success or failure of the scheme. Until the British government is prepared to fund research into the situation, the true history of present day educational situation of the Deaf cannot be written.

A small section of pupils of a hearing school - where are the deaf pupils?

Pupils of a school for the deaf - all pupils are deaf.

6. Deaf Theatre, Drama and Cabaret

In recent history Deaf drama has always been held at Deaf clubs on special occasions and at Christmas periods. The BDA began to hold drama competitions at its annual Congress Week and this became a popular event up to the present.

Even so, forming a group of professional actors employed solely in Deaf drama had been quite difficult until 1961 when the RNID Mime group was formed in that year. The choice of mime was basically both to avoid the need to speak to the audience and to attract theatre-goers to the visual beauty of mime. The Mime Group consisted of Deaf and hard of hearing actors giving shows via mime, movements, dance and signs. As the group progressed it added acting and expressions that were more typical of theatre than mime. Eventually in 1969 the RNID Mime Group changed its name to National Theatre of the Deaf (NTD). The NTD established the first national summer school, a ten-day course run by professional (hearing) tutors in mime, movement, dance and sign-mime. This course was run annually until 1978.

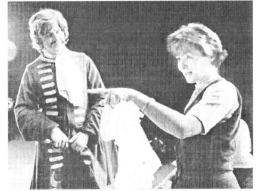

The NTD travelled all over Britain giving performances to the general public in local theatres. The late Sir Laurence Olivier was so impressed by the Deaf that he agreed to become the patron of the NTD. A row then developed between the US and UK Deaf over the title NTD as there existed a NTD in the US. The American Deaf resented the clash of similar titles and a two-years argument ensued. The row was settled when the British group changed its title from NTD to British Theatre of the Deaf (BTD).

Pat Keysell, right.

The quality of performances and shows presented by the BTD received critical acclaim as the years went by. In 1971 the BTD performed at the World Deaf Congress in Paris and

in 1974 the BTD broke new ground when it was invited to put on a fringe show at the Edinburgh Festival. The success of the Edinburgh event, which ran for 2 weeks, brought confidence to the Deaf actors, who decided to go professional in September 1974 and staged its first professional performance with the play *Hassan*. A hearing person, Pat Keysell, who joined the BTD in 1968, was to become its guiding influence. She directed the BTD's second play, *Boy in Darkness*. She went on to organise voice-over facilities to accompany the Deaf's performances, and later ran the National Deaf Children's Society (NDCS) Festival of Mime for 12 years.

Masquerade

191

The BTD's Deaf actors included Jean St. Clair, Ian Stewart, Michael Hanrahan, Elsie Whitby, Mira O'Reilly, Susan Alexander, Chris Harrowell, Lydia Handscombe, Herbert Marvin and Issy Schlisselman. Over the years the BTD went on to present notable plays such as *Under the Sun* and *Masquerade*, both of which received rave reviews in the press.

The BTD came to an end after its last play, *The Most Dangerous Animal of All,* in 1977. The end came when the BTD's biggest sponsor, the RNID, stopped its grants when the BTD became professional. The BTD turned to the Arts Council as well as box office sales for income. The Arts Council later cut down funding to the BTD and from that point the BTD lost money and closed down a year later.

The BDA Drama shows continued annually, but new generations of Deaf people developed different tastes and approaches and this led to the staging of Deaf Cabaret events with Deaf performers signing songs, jokes, poetry and suchlike. Popular events with the present day Deaf people are the Deaf Idol and Deaf Cabaret events. These events are relatively new and may remain popular in time.

In the week during the 1985 International Congress on the Education of the Deaf event in Manchester, a new group emerged: the Deaf Comedians. This group, led by Doug Alker, performed on the stage for the very first time at the "Alternative Congress" organised by the NUD and the NW Regional Council of the BDA and it had the whole audience in constant laughter with its witty series of scenes taking the mickey out of the hearing world. From that day on, the Deaf Comedians toured Britain and is still going on at present.

Another group that sprang up is the Common Ground Sign Dance Theatre, formed in 1986. It was inspired by a vision of integrated Deaf and hearing cultures. The Theatre comes to many towns and cities in Britain.

Yet another group, the London Deaf Drama Group, is a long-running group that is continuing at present. A good number of well known Deaf actors worked with this group before graduating to TV; two being Mark Arbuthnot and Fifi Garfield, who later appeared in the BBC series, *Switch*.

At present, the Deafinitely Theatre company is the only professional Deaf drama group in Britain and its work has been both well noted and acclaimed. Its hits include *Two Chairs*, *Motherland*, *Loss* and *Dysfunction*. Deafinitely Theatre was set up in January 2002 by Paula Garfield, Steven Webb and Kate Furby to produce performance written by Deaf people. In the two short years since its foundation its reputation grew, not only within the Deaf community but in the London theatre community in general. The work of Deafinitely Theatre is Deaf-led but the company is accessible to hearing people as well. It also runs projects and workshops for youth theatres, community groups, colleges and schools.

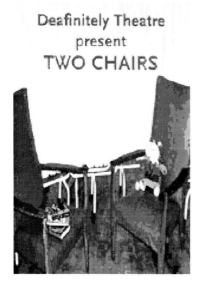

Deafinitely Theatre present
TWO CHAIRS

There were in the past several smaller groups such as the Sixty-Six Club's Deaf Drama Group, Birmingham Deaf and Hearing Drama Theatre and Deaf Adult Players Group. Many more theatre groups will certainly spring up and Deaf drama should continue to flourish.

Access to mainstream theatres had always been a problem for the Deaf until the emergence of signed performances. At first there were a few performances for which theatre managers would engage sign language interpreters and these performances were well attended, even though the numbers of Deaf theatregoers were proportionally lower than expected.

In the early days of Sign Language interpreted performances, such events were seemingly limited to venues such as the National Theatre, the Royal Shakespeare Company and The Almeida in London, with very few venues in the provinces thrown in. The most popular West End shows were hardly accessible to the Deaf. As a result of this, a company called Signaway was established by Terry Ruane, a former member of the British Theatre of the Deaf, and his interpreter wife Donna. Signaway approached the Society of London Theatre, and, with funding from the Arts Council, established a project in 2000 that saw a wide range of interpreters engaged in a variety of shows at venues ranging from the Barbican to the London Palladium. This project was successful. Signaway later in 2004 changed its name to Theatresign in 2004 continues to provide sign interpreting services of the highest quality.

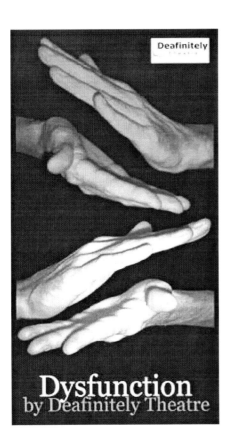

Deafinitely Theatre's two productions:

Motherland (above)

Dysfunction (left)

7. Modern Deaf Sports

There have been many developments in modern sports over the recent years. Many Deaf competitors participate in hearing competitions nowadays unlike in the past when they took part in Deaf competitions. All the same, Deaf sportsmen still struggle to achieve Olympic standards on both track and athletic events and this is mainly due to deafness as most races need a starter's gun, but the standard of Deaf sportsmen has improved dramatically in the recent past.

The newly formed UK Deaf Sports oversees Deaf sports in the UK and has taken over the role of the British Deaf Sports Council (BDSC). While the BDSC retains its autonomy as the sole representative of Great Britain in events organised under the auspices of the CISS (Comité International des Sports des Sourds), UK Deaf Sports established itself as the best body for seeking funds to cover expenses for international tournaments. Local Deaf clubs took part in Club Tournaments in Europe throughout the year 2003, especially in the football section. The expenses are usually paid by either the participants or their clubs.

There are various sports in which the Deaf partake and these are:

1. Athletics

There were great improvements in British athletics in recent years in World Games for the Deaf (WGD) events (known as Deaflympics), and many athletics were bringing home a growing number of medals. The Great Britain athletic team regularly participates in both the Winter and Summer Deaflympics as well as in the European Athletics Championship competitions. There were amazing achievements by Britain's two young female individuals who both ran against each other in two races (Women's 800m and 1,500m) in the European Deaf Championship 2003 at Tallinn, Estonia. They both came first and second respectively in both events. One of them, Lauren Peffers from Scotland, broke two European Junior records when she ran in two senior level races.

Lauren Peffers on left.

2. Basketball

Deaf Basketball was mainly played in deaf schools during the 1950s and 1960s. The basketball team of Donaldson's School, Edinburgh, under the guidance of its teacher, T B Hignett, made its mark by winning the local league run by the Scottish Association of Boys' Clubs in 1959/60.

The CISS included basketball as one of its sports in the World Games for the Deaf quite recently. In preparation to compete in the 2001 Deaflympics in Rome, the Great Britain Ladies team used Doncaster College's sports facilities for coaching and training purposes. With little competitive basketball experience at international level, the Great Britain Ladies team was hammered by "cricket scores" in every match throughout the opening stages. Great Britain Ladies team still showed true British grit by continually practising and playing international friendlies in an attempt to match the standards of other Deaf international teams. There are growing opportunities of achieving higher standards and enrolling new players through trials and training courses all over England, with an increase of potential players drawn from all over the UK, in contrast to the Rome squad that practically consisted of Doncaster College girls. There is, though, no sign of Great Britain putting together and training men's teams in this sport.

Badminton

Badminton has been the mainstay of British Deaf sports for many years, being regularly played in many Deaf centres with large halls. Many Deaf competitors are achieving high standards in this game, equalling hearing players, by competing in their local leagues, representing either deaf or hearing clubs.

As for international competitions, British badminton players always bring back bagfulls of medals. Fiona Wilson of Glasgow, Martin Bogard of Essex and Andrea Hardwick of Glasgow and Leeds are amongst the few individuals who carried the torch for Deaf badminton. Bogard actually won at least one medal in every WGD that he competed in with the Rome Deaflympics as his swansong.

Chess

There are two Deaf chess associations in the United Kingdom, namely the Scottish Deaf Chess and Draughts Association, which is the oldest of its kind in the world as it was established in 1902, and the English Deaf Chess Association, which was established in 1972. Although both continue to run annual championships and club events, the number of Deaf participants has declined since Internet chess was introduced in the mid 1990s. The Chess associations are at present surviving rather difficult times, because the younger generation seems to have taken little or no interest in the game. Chess is nowadays hardly played in schools for the deaf which are in a decline. Many outstanding chess players came from two schools, Burwood Park School, which has since closed, and Mary Hare Grammar School, which still runs a Chess Club. The younger Deaf generation spends much more time on the Internet than on chess, but a few individuals do play chess.

Both the Deaf Chess associations are members of the International Committee of Silent Chess (ICSC), which was established in 1949, and continue to participate with some success in world chess championships. Philip K. Gardner (EDCA) and Ian Carmichael (SCDAD) are the current champions in their associations.

Cricket

Cricket is a quintessentially English game. Cricket was popular in Deaf residential schools in their heydays with teams competing against local hearing schools or cricket clubs. Deaf clubs had teams taking part in local leagues in addition to inter-club matches. Even the West London cricket team pitted their skills against the Deaf team from Australia. English national teams under the auspices of the BDSC had tours in Denmark and the West Indies before the first Deaf Test matches were held in Australia in 1990. Until recently the England Deaf cricket team took a trip to Australia and such arrangements present opportunities for younger generation of Deaf cricketers to play for England.

Football

Football is the oldest and most popular sport in Deaf history. There are many accounts of Britain winning Gold medals five times in the Deaflympics. Throughout the years Deaf clubs participated in local hearing leagues. Some of the finest Deaf players went on to play as semi-professionals. Currently there is a player, Daniel Ailey, who plays for Doncaster Reserves. Numerous international friendlies as well as matches against local semi-professional clubs were played by Deaf football teams. This was likewise for the Great Britain team in preparation for its qualifying games for Deaflympics, European Championships and the World Cup tournaments. There is an annual British Deaf Cup tournament. In addition, Deaf football clubs travel often to various European countries to take part in tournaments with European clubs in 11, 7 or 5-a-side matches.

The Great Britain Football squad

Deaf Ladies football matches have been growing in numbers and have generated interest. A Great Britain Ladies Football team has been formed recently and the team qualified for their first major tournament - the Melbourne Deaflympics, which is being held in 2005. A league for Deaf Ladies football clubs for the 2003 season has also been established. Currently there are four teams, with several clubs showing interest in joining the league in the 2004 season.

The Great Britain Ladies Football squad

Golf

The Deaf community recently organised many golf tournaments, both competitive and as fundraising events. Currently there are several golf matches organised in order to raise funds for the Great Britain Football Team for its trip to the 2005 Melbourne Deaflympics.

In Scotland there are annual golf tournaments between West and East Scotland Deaf Golf teams.

.

Indoor Games

Indoor games has been with the Deaf since the earliest days of Deaf history. Deaf Clubs are always holding indoor games competitions. These include darts, card games, snooker, pool, dominoes and Scrabble. In the past Deaf Clubs met each other annually to compete in various games. At present the closure of many Deaf Clubs has led to a decline in the annual indoor games activities. The surviving clubs at present still continue the tradition, albeit with fewer prizes. In recent times annual national individual pool competitions have been organised with many entries from all over the UK.

Lawn Bowls

Deaf Lawn Bowls are popular, especially in Northwest England, Scotland and Wales. Inter-club matches are often played in Scotland. The Scottish Deaf Bowls Association organises annual tournaments where clubs from Edinburgh, Glasgow, Dundee, St. Vincent's, Ayrshire, Aberdeen, West Lothian and so on, play singles, pairs, triples and fours in three different categories: men, ladies and mixed. Liverpool Fairfield has a team playing in the hearing league. On the international level, the World Deaf Lawn Bowls Championships is held every four years, the recent one in New Zealand in 2002 when Scotland led the medals table. The BDSC also organises national bowl tournaments, the last event held at Gloucester during the August Bank Holiday weekend of 2003.

Netball

There were plenty of organised netball tournaments within the UK recently, with regional teams visiting each other. There has been a development on moves to establish netball training in West Midlands in order to promote Deaf netball. It is slowly growing, and there is work afoot to create a good quality British team to compete in the 2005 Melbourne Deaflympics and other international matches.

Rugby

Rugby is one of the newest and rapidly growing sports, with Wales winning the Deaf Rugby World Championship in 2002 in New Zealand. All British countries regularly meet for training, using proper rugby facilities. Wales won the opportunity to host the next Rugby World Cup in 2005.

On 6th March 2004 the English Deaf rugby team played against the World Champions, the Welsh Deaf rugby team, at Newbury RFC as a part of their Four Nations Tournament and won the match 14-11 after a thrilling and hard fought game. The event was attended by a crowd of nearly 700, which indicates a growing interest in the sport.

Swimming

When schools for the deaf were in their heydays, there were many swimming tournaments in which deaf swimmers competed with their hearing counterparts. Mary Hare Grammar School regularly enters tournaments and its swimmers often joined their local clubs. Some swimming events, both domestic and international, are held at intervals, but with deaf children in mainstream schools and the closure of schools for the deaf, it is increasingly hard for these children to get in touch with those interested in swimming as a sport and thus form local and regional teams and events. There is a slow but steady growth of interest in swimming by the younger generation of Deaf people .

Wales' victory against New Zealand in the 2002 World Championship final.

Table Tennis

Although Deaf people play table tennis in their local Deaf clubs, there is no nationally or regionally established tournament in this sport, even though Britain somehow always managed to send a team to the Deaflympics. Few local Deaf clubs, mainly part of the Federation of London Deaf Clubs Sports (FLDC), organise annual table tennis tournaments during the winter periods. With the closure of a good number of Deaf clubs over the years, there is nowhere for the Deaf to play table tennis; some joined the hearing clubs but got nowhere from there.

Tennis

British tennis players have improved and achieved higher standards nowadays than in the past. There are currently plenty of funds for competitions and Deaf tennis players are guaranteed the best services in training and coaching. There are numerous competitions ranging from Juniors to Over 35's. Two of the current finest young Deaf players, Peter Wilcox (pictured right) and Anthony Sinclair, played in international competitions and achieved pleasing results. They have a good many years ahead of them; and it is anticipated that they will bring medals home very soon from the various tournaments, especially the Deaflympics.

Snooker

This game is popular among the Deaf of Britain and where there are snooker tables in Deaf clubs, they are regularly used. Annual national and regional tournaments arranged by the BDSC are features of the Deaf community calendar. With the closure of Deaf clubs, the competition is dwindling due to lack of tables and consequently practice. Whether this game will recapture its former glory and status remains to be seen.

8. Then and Now: The Evolution of the British Deaf Community

Society is always changing, and the British Deaf community as a cultural group is no different. Sometimes these cultural groups can keep up with the changes; sometimes the changes for these cultural groups are unique to themselves. Sometimes changes are forced onto the communities. We have shown comparisons throughout this book how changes have affected Deaf people in education, in employment, in home life. This section endeavours through a selection of pictures to show how some other changes have affected Deaf people over a period of time.

Assistive Hearing Devices

Horn (18/19th Century)

Body-worn aid (1960s)

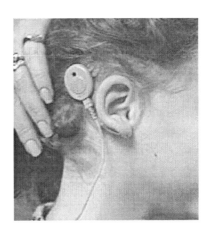

Cochlear Implant (21st century)

The Multiphone (1930s)

Classroom Aids (1970s)

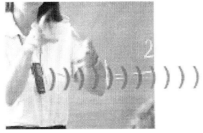

Infrared radio aids (21st century)

British Deaf & Dumb Association Congress Dinner, 1903
formal evening wear — all men

BDA Congress, 1998 — informal evening wear

Deaf Entertainment

Syllabus—1888-89.

The Lectures, Essays, and Debates begin at EIGHT o'clock.

November 5. *Lecture—"The Bronze Pot."
Mr. Alexander Walker.
November 12. Essay—"Lord Nelson."
Mr. William Smith.
November 19. *Lecture—"Little Wealth, Much Health, and a Life of Stealth."
Rev. Gordon J. Murray, B.D.
November 26. Discussion—"What to Read."
December 3. *Lecture.
Rev. James A. M'Clymont, B.D.
December 10. Essay—"Earl Godwin."
Mr. John T. Lyon.
December 17. Essay—"Tales."
Mr. Charles M'Hardy.
December 24. Discussion—"How to Improve Ourselves."
December 29. Social Meeting.
January 1. Re-Union.
January 7. Discussion—"Signing *versus* Spelling."
January 14. Lecture.
Mr. George Strachan.
January 21. *Lecture—"Electricity"—with experiments.
Mr. James C. Barnett.
January 28. Essay—"The Famous French Deaf Mute."
Mr. James M'Hardy.
February 4. Discussion—"Education — Combined *versus* Oral."

Left: Part of a programme from the Aberdeen Deaf Mute Association, 1888-1889

Below: A Deaf Drama Group during the 1970s

Left: A Deaf television audience,1987

Below: Deaf Idol, 2003

Formal signing - 1900s. Dr. Elliott, head of the London Asylum for the Deaf and Dumb, Margate, with two old pupils

Formal signing - 1995. David Pilkington signing the names of those who died from AIDS. World Aids Day.

Informal signing - 1998. Children at Heathlands School.

Deaf Art: Changing styles by Deaf Artists

Benjamin Ferrers, c.1690

Richard Crosse, c.1780

William Agnew, 1893

Melissa Martyn, 2003

Transport

Charabancs outings were very popular just after World War I. The above photographs show (left) Reading Deaf Club members and (right) Leeds Deaf Club members on outings, both in 1919.

Cycling was a key means of transport for many Deaf people in the 1900s-1920s. The gentleman on the left is on the seafront at Brighton in 1900; the two ladies on the right are at the top of a hill in Preston in 1923.

Moving forward 80-100 years, we find that Deaf people love to ride powerful motorcycles or take part in moto-cross events.

Leisure (Outings & Recreational Activities)

Outdoor recreational activities by Deaf people have changed beyond all recognition in 100 years. In the top pictures, we have a picnic and a day out to the seaside by members of the Clapham St. Bede's Deaf Club, whilst in the middle picture, we have a group from Southampton all dressed up for a day out in the country in 1919. Indeed, dressing up seemed to be the order of the day. Nowadays, Deaf people are more adventurous and dress casually and appropriately for the activity, as in the pictures of the Deaf Mountaineering Club and hang-gliding.

9. The Changing Demographical Map of the British Deaf Community

One of the biggest impacts on the British Deaf Community over the last half of the 20th century has been the influx of people whose ethnic origin came from countries outside the British Isles. This influx has come in waves very similar to the population of Britain as a whole, starting in the late 19th century with seamen from China deserting their ships in (mainly) Liverpool and forming a Chinese community that later came to be called Chinatown. They were followed by Lascars, a name given to seamen from East Africa, who settled in the Tiger Bay area of Cardiff.

Consequently, for many years, Liverpool had a small number of Deaf Chinese who were descendants of those seamen, whilst Cardiff had a few Deaf people who were the result of relationships between some of the Lascars and local Welsh women.

Around the same time, and up to the 1930s, some well-to-do Indian families were rewarded for their services to the British Raj with permission to emigrate to Britain and the odd-brown face then began to appear in a few Deaf circles. One now elderly Indian woman informed the BDHS that when she started school in the 1940s, she remembered being the only one of Asian origin in her school right up to the time she left school and stated that it was a strange feeling because many of the native British children had never seen an Asian child at that time.

All these people, however, were the exception – the vast majority of Deaf British people were white. In photographs of deaf schoolchildren in the first half of the 20th century, right up even to the 1960s, it would be very rare to find a face that was not white.

The Second World War was the catalyst. The US forces that came to Britain had many regiments that were composed almost entirely of Black Americans. It was not just the US forces – many Commonwealth countries fought on the side of the Allies and many of them sent troops to Britain, especially from Caribbean countries. When they went home after the war, they found there was nothing for them in their own countries whereas Britain, even in the days of post-war austerity, offered prosperity. Starting with the arrival of the *Empire Windrush* in 1948, many thousands of men and women from Caribbean countries migrated to Britain.

In the ten years between 1951 and 1961, nearly quarter of a million people from Caribbean countries came to Britain and the government had to bring in an Immigration Act in 1962 that placed restrictions on the numbers that could be admitted into the UK. A second Immigration Act of 1968 was brought in to limit the numbers of people coming into Britain from India, Pakistan and Bangladesh. By the 1970s, however, the demographical map of the British Deaf community was changing as more and more deaf children were born to the descendants of these immigrants. These children are usually called second or third generation British descendants of Caribbean origin.

The first impact of the demographical change was seen in the schools but in 1972, over 70,000 Ugandan Asians were kicked out of Uganda, where they had their homes, by the then president, Idi Amin, and because many of these people had British passports, they immigrated to Britain. A large percentage of these Asians, who were mostly Indian, included Deaf people who soon became assimilated into the British Deaf community. In the main, these were older people in their 20s-40s and these immigrants gave the Deaf community a better age range balance.

It was not until the 1980s and the 1990s that there were sufficient numbers of second and third generation Deaf people from various ethnic minorities to make a significant impact on the adult British Deaf community. More and more football, cricket and other Deaf sports clubs now boasted participants from various ethnic minority groups; more and more ethnic minority people, particularly young Asians, were starting to take an effective part in British Deaf political activities or in Deaf television projects.

The demographical map of Deaf Britain was subjected to more changes since 2000 with the influx of asylum seekers and refugees from countries such as Somalia, Sudan, Afghanistan, Iran and Iraq. Other refugees came from Sri Lanka, Zimbabwe and Palestine. Also, with the expansion of the European Union to 25 countries and freedom of movement of all citizens from one country to another, there have been immigrants other countries within the EU.

The result has been that a very different Deaf Britain has developed in the 2000s compared to the 1900s.

A class in 1900.
All children are "White" British

A class in 1993.
This class is multi-ethnic with a mixture of
Asian, Middle-East and Chinese children

George Scott
"White" British Deaf World
Games Winner, 1928

Candy Perkins
"Black" British World Deaf
Games Winner, 1997

The Appendices

APPENDIX 1

Gesture in the Middle Ages

(Taken from *British Deaf Times* XXXI: March/April 1934 & May/June 1934)
by Kate and Selwyn Oxley

The list below is of very real interest to all interested in the Deaf or deafness, as it represents the first list (which we have seen or even heard of) that in any way indicates methods of manual signing in use in places where it was the custom for silence to be observed. This list occurs in the appendix, pages 405-409, of *Anngiers History of the Zion Monastery at Lisbon and Brentford.*

Though it is not, we gather, quite accurate to the original one which we note is signed by a certain Thomas Betson, no doubt one of the Monks or Lay Brethren in residence, it is no doubt a very good copy of the old manuscript. There does not seem to be any exact indication of the date when the list was drawn up.

The symbolism herein noted is, as one would surmise, confined to a narrow sphere, namely, things of necessity pertaining to a religious house. They seem to conform in many cases to many of the signs at present used by the Deaf, but we think they will be of value to our experts on account of the splendid foundation they afford for further research in this most interesting field of our language, and we have therefore copied the list exactly as it was printed, save for the occasional elucidation of some more than usually difficult words. Of course, we cannot vouch for or guarantee the genuineness or the reverse of this list, but we bring it to the notice of *British Deaf Times* readers and others interested for what it is worth and accept no responsibility in the matter whatever.

A TABLE OF SIGNS

Used during the hours of silence by the sisters and brethren
in the Monastery of Zion (Isleworth, Middlesex)

Abbas	– make the signe for age and also for woman.
Aftirwards	– meve *(move)* thy fore fyngere of thy right hande undir the litle finger of the lefte hande.
Aged	– drawe down thy righte hande streght overe thy heer *(hair)* and overe thy righte eer *(ear)*.
Ale	– make the sygne of drynk and drawe thy hande displayed afor thy eer dunwarde.
Anone	– close thy righte hande and holde up thy little fyngere.
Appull	– put thy thombes in thy fiste and close thy hande and meve afore the(e) to and fro.
Awtere (altar?)	– rysse *(raise)* the bak of the righte hande and make after a blissynge *(blessing)*.
Basyn or Chargeon (dish)	– turne thy fore fyngere of thy righte hande in the palm of thy lefte hande.

Bedde (bed)	– make the signe of a house and put thy righte hande under thy cheke and close thine eer
Bedes (beads)	– fomell (fumble) with thy righte thombe upon thy fore fyngere in a manere of departygne of Bedes in Praiere (*prayer*).
Belles (bells)	– make a sygne with both thy hands closed liftying (*lifting*) up and downe in a manere of rynging.
Blissing (blessing)	– make a signe of Blissing as the Bisshope doth.
Boke (book)	– wagge and meve thy righte hande in manere as thou shulde turne the leves of a boke.
Brede (bread)	– make with thy two thombes and two forefyngeres a round compass, and if thou wole (*would*) have white, make the sygne thereof, and if brown toche (*touch*) thy cowtte sleve (*sleeve*).
Brome (broom)	– swepe with thy open hande to and fro on thy left cowtte sleve.
Broder (brother)	– join togidere sidelygnes (*join together sidewise?*) thy two fore-fyngeres.
Butter or other Fatties	– draw thy two righte uphere fyngeres to and fro on thy left palme.
Bisshope (Bishop)	– holde thy righte haund (*hand*) streght overe thy fround (*forehead or front?*) and hede (head).
Candel (candle)	– make the sygne for butter with the sygne for day.
Candelstyke	– join thy eithere fiste and holde the right overe the lefte.
Chalice	– holde up thy righte thombe with thy fyngeres in manere of beving of a cuppe.
Chapter House	– make the sygne of a hows with the sygne of discipline.
Chaunter (chanter)	– make the sygne of a preste (*priest*) with the synge aftir syngyng (*singing*).
Chese	– holde thy righte hande flatwyse in the palm of thy lefte.
Chirch (church)	– make the synge of a hows and aftir make a Benediccioune.
Chmyng (chiming)	– make a sygne as if ye smote with a hammer.
Cloister	– make a rounde circle with thy righte forefyngere towards the erthe.
Clothe	– rubbe up and downe the endes of all thy fyngeres upon thy lefte.
Colde	– make the sygne of water trembling with thy hande, or blow on thy forefyngere.
Collector	– make the sygne of a boke and drawe thy fyngeres to the warde in manere of gadering (*gathering*).
Confession	– make the synge of herying and aftir ley thy hande upon thy breste.
Cuppe	– holde up thy thombe and fyngeres rounde as bevyng coffe.
Day, or Light	– put thy righte forefyngere streght upon thy eghe (*eye?*)
Dekone (deacon)	– make the sygne of a brothyre (*brother*) and aftir a crosse in thy froant (*front*), i.e. cross yourself in the front.
Dissh	– make a circle with thy righte forefyngere in the myddes (*midst*) of thy lefte palme.
Dortour (bedrooms)	– the sygne of a hows with the sygne for slypyng (*sleeping*).
Drynk (drink)	– bowe (*bend*) thy ryte forefyngere and put it on thy nedere lyppe (*lip*).
Egges	– make a token with thy righte forefyngeres upon thy lefte thombe to and fro, as though thou should pill egges.
Etying (eating)	– putte thy right thombe with two forefyngeres joined to thy mouth.
Epistolary	– make the sygne of a boke with a crosse on thy breste.
Encence (incense?)	– putte thy two fyngeres unto thy two nose thirles (*nostrils*).
Fader (father)	– joyne thy righte thombe with thy forfyngere togidere openly.

Fysshe (fish)	– wagge thy hande displaid sydelynges (*sidewise*) in a manere of fish taill.
Flesshe (flesh)	– ryse up with thy rizt fyngeres the skyne (*skin*) of thy lefte hande.
Girdell (girdle)	– drawe thy forefyngeres of eithere hande rounde aboute thy myddell (*middle or waist*).
Gode (goad)	– putte thy righte thombe streght under thy chynne.
Gospeler	– the synge of a boke with a crosse on youre foreheade with youre thombe.
Glasse	– make the sygne of a cuppe with the sygne of red wyne (*red wine*).
Grayll (grille?)	– make the sygne of a boke, bendying thy fyngeres up and downe in manere of gratying (greeting).
Hammer	– make a sygne with thyn hande up and downe as thou dide knockke.
Hard	– putte thy righte fiste oupere (over) thy righte ere.
Hevyng (heaving)	– putte thy righte forefyngere, all the other closed, streght on thine ere.
Hote (hot)	– holde the side of thy righte forefyngere fast unto thy mouth closed.
House	– close thy fyngeres endes to gidere upward and sprede them abrode dunwarde in manere of sparres.
I, myself	– putte thy righte forefyngeres endes to thy breste.
Inke (ink)	– make a sygne with thombe and two fyngeres closed as thou shulde write.
Inough (enough)	– close thy fiste to gidere and holde up thy thombe and this may serve for "I know it well."
Kepying (keeping)	– putte thy righte hande under thy lefte.
Kerchy (handkerchief)	– make the sygne for clothe with thy handes over thy hede.
Kyng (king)	– putte all thy fyngerees endes closed to gidere on thy forehede.
Knyfe (knife)	– drawe thy righte hande sidelynyes to and fro through thy lefte hande.
Lay Broder	– make the sygne of a broder and drawe thy thombe and two fyngeres downe overe thy heere and ere.
Lessone (lesson)	– drawe thy forefyngere on length overe thy breste and seruethe also for long.
Licence	– lifte up thy hande displaied afore thy face in esy manere.
Litle (little)	– bowe all thy fyngeres and holde up thy little finger.
Locutory (eloquent?)	– make the sygne of a howse and the sygne of a spech.
Man	– putte and holde thy hede in thy righte hande.
Masse	– make the sygne of a blyssing.
Masboke (Mass Book)	– make the sygne for a boke of a blyssing.
Milke (milk)	– drawe thy lefte little finger in manere of mylking.
Mustard	– holde thy nose in the upper parte of thy righte fiste and rubbe it.
Pere (pearl)	– joyne all thy fyngeres in length of thy righte hande and wagge dunwardes.
Potengere (soup plate)	– make a circle in the balle of thy lefte hande with the forefyngeree of thy righte hande.
Potage (i.e. stew)	– make a circle with thy righte forefyngere of thy righte hande in the palme of thy lefte hande.
Preste (priest)	– make the sygne of a broder and put thy forefyngere to thyn ere and breste, or els make a circle therewith upon thy hede.

Prynay, or Rereclorteur	– make the sygne of a howse and stryke downe thy righte hande by thy clothes.
Procession	– make a circle with thy forefyngeree towards the grounde.
Quene (queen)	– make the sygne of a woman with the sygne of a crowne on thy forehede.
Rede (red)	– putte thy forefyngeree to the rede place of thy cheke.
Ryngyng	– make a token with thy fiste up and downe as thou shulde rynge.
Salte (salt)	– phillipe with thy rizt thombe (*flip with your right thumb*) and thy forefyngeree overe the lefte thombe.
Sawser (saucer)	– make a rounde circle in thy lefte palme with thy righte little fyngeree.
Sensyng (censing)	– meve thy righte hande to and fro as thought thou shulde cense.
Sextteyn (sexton)	– make the sygne of a broder with the sygne for ryngyng.
Silence	– putte thy forefyngeree sydelynges to thy mouthe and drawe it up and downe.
Sight-kepyng	– make the sygne of light with the sygne for kepyng.
Slepyng (sleeping)	– putte thy righte hande under thy cheke and therewith close thy eere.
Spekyng (speaking)	– putte thy two forefyngeres endes flatly upon thy mouth.
Spone (spoon)	– lifte sydlynges up and downe thy thombe and if fyngerees joined in forme of takyng potage.
Standyng	– meve thy hande esely upwarde.
Sudary	– rubbe thy fyngeree ends of thy righte hande upon the endes of the lefte.
Sustor (sister)	– make the sygne of a woman with the sygne of a broder.
Texte or Pax	– kiss the bak of the lefte hande, with a crosse in thy breste with thy righte thombe.
Vergeous (virtuous?)	– drawe thy lefte fyngeres joyned with thy righte fyngeres.
Vyneacre (vinegar)	– make the sygne of wyne (wine) and drawe thy forefyngeree from thyne ere to thy throte (throat).
Warme	– putte thy forefyngeree faste upon thy mouthe.
Wasshyng	– rubbe thy righte hande flatlynges upon the bak of thy lefte hande.
Water	– joyne thy fyngeres of thy righte hande and meve them dunwarde droppingly.
White	– drawe thy two righte fyngeres by thy cheke dunwardes
Wyne	– meve thy forefyngeree up and downe upon the ende of thy thombe afore thy eghe (eye).
Writyng	– make a sygne with thy thre righte fyngeres as though ye wrote.

Deo gratias,
    Pray for youre,

      THOMAS BETSON
      (approx. 1450 A.D.)

Timeline of the Development of TV and Deaf TV Programmes

(An article contributed by Clark Denmark)

1896:	First moving pictures
1910:	Movie pictures (Silents)
1925:	Sound in movies
1936:	BBC formed (broadcasting in black and white)
1950:	Colour in movies
1955:	ITV formed
1964:	First programme for the deaf (News review for the Deaf)
1967:	Colour in television
1979:	Signs of Life (NUD – Open Door. BBC)
1981:	See Hear! (BBC)
1986:	Listening Eye
1992:	Sign On
1997:	Vibes
2000:	Vee TV

Brief History of Deaf Broadcasting

First Deaf Programmes

In 1955, the BBC produced a television programme for deaf children. This was followed by the highly successful *Vision On*, which catered for hearing and deaf children. The presenter was Tony Hart, a well-known artist and his co-presenter was Pat Keysell, a hearing person whose parents were deaf. The programme was very popular amongst deaf and hearing children. There were times when a deaf person was involved in the programme. He was Cyril Robbins MBE, a mime artist.

In 1964 BBC2 launched a new programme called *News Review for the Deaf*. Bill Northwood was the presenter and the programme was shown regularly every Sunday at teatime, and there were occasions when deaf issues were shown at the end of the programme.

In 1979, the National Union of the Deaf (NUD) fought for regular TV programmes for the deaf and applied to the BBC for a place in its Open Door Community Programmes Unit slot. The NUD submitted an idea and a script, which the BBC accepted, and this led to a one-off programme called *Signs Of Life*. The team that created the programme is well known - Paddy Ladd, Maggie Woolley, Raymond Lee and Arthur Dimmock, amongst others. The programme was written, produced and performed by Deaf people only while all the TV crew members were hearing. *Signs of Life* was a success and it led to the BBC seriously considering the Deaf's demand for a weekly TV programme for the Deaf.

See Hear!

Two years later, in 1981, a new programme for deaf and hard of hearing people called *See*

Hear! was launched. The co-presenters were Maggie Woolley who had been involved in the production of *Signs of Life* and Martin Colville, a hearing son of deaf parents. The programme was shown regularly on Sunday mornings and repeated on the following Monday or Tuesday.

The TV production team was hearing but it advertised for a deaf researcher and appointed Paddy Ladd. He was then working as a BDA administrator, and was also involved with the NUD. The BDA felt that it was important for him to move to the BBC so as to have a strong influence on the contents of deaf programmes. It was not easy to represent the deaf person's view in the programmes and therefore the team agreed that the presenter should be a deaf person. Again Paddy Ladd was chosen and the programmes continued. Soon after, other deaf presenters became involved in future *See Hear* programmes.

During 1979-81 ITV launched a programme for the Deaf called **Breakthrough**, which was shown weekly in two regions: Plymouth South West (TSW) and Aberdeen (STV). There were four presenters, of whom two were hearing and two deaf - Maureen Denmark, Peter Jones, Rachell Bastikar and Peter Collins. The style and content of the programme was based on magazine format.

Listening Eye

During 1984-1991 Tyne Tees Television based in Newcastle made a bid for a deaf programme for Channel Four. The producer was Bob Duncan, a hearing man, and eight deaf programmes were agreed, the series called **Listening Eye**. The programmes were documentaries on deaf issues. 16mm film was used for *Listening Eye*.

A deaf researcher was employed, Rachell Bastikar who is the first deaf woman to work in ITV. She also worked as a presenter along with Clark Denmark for some series. The programme continued for six series.

Another deaf programme for children was called **Hand In Hand**, made by hearing people based in Bristol (HTV). Also there was **Storywheel** broadcasted by Channel Four.

In 1991 Sue Shephard from Channel Four, who was the commission editor for education programmes, felt she needed to refresh programmes for deaf people. She decided to axe *Listening Eye*, which had a great impact on the Deaf community because there was then only a half-hour programme for deaf people each week, *See Hear!* on BBC.

Sign On

The producer of *Listening Eye*, Bob Duncan, tried to introduce a new proposal for a deaf programme in partnership with **Deaf Owl**, which had been training in the North East Media Training Centre in Gateshead, near Newcastle. Sue Shepherd from Channel Four accepted the proposal and commissioned Tyne Tees Television to produce the deaf programme as it has experience through its *Listening* Eye work. Bob Duncan was appointed as Executive Producer with Rachell Bastikar as researcher. Six new presenters were employed for the programme called **Sign On**.

Thirty programmes were made with four different areas covered:

1. Newswatch
2. Deaf World
3. Deaf View
4. At Leisure

In the following years Channel Four had to reduce the number of programmes because of the cost of production. In 1995 the format of *Sign On* changed from one topic covered in a half hour story to various topics shown in short clips. The audience viewing figures for *See Hear* and *Sign On* were as follows:

-       See Hear 250,000 - 375,000
-       Sign On   72,000 - 200,000

In 1991, Deaf Owl Production Limited was formed as the first all-deaf production company in Britain. It had contracted with Tyne Tees Television (*Sign On*) to receive 5% of the income received from Channel Four for 5 to 7 minutes of inserts for *Sign On* for ten programmes. Deaf Owl made several programmes for *Sign On* over two years but, unfortunately, due to lack of money, was forced to close. *Sign On* continued to make programmes in the following years. Two Deaf Owl employees joined the *Sign On* team and other employees went on to do various work in the media.

Subtitling on Analogue TV is covered by the Broadcasting Act 1990

Channel 3

The *Broadcasting Act 1990* required Channel 3 licensees, as a licence condition, to provide a minimum amount of subtitling for the deaf, and specified that in 1998 at least 50% of the channel's output per week must be subtitled; after 1998 the greatest number of hours that the ITC considers practicable must be subtitled. The ITC recently announced new requirements from 1999. These provide for annual increases up to 80% in 2004. In 1997 50% of output was subtitled on Channel 3.

Channel 4

The subtitling provision in the Act does not cover Channel 4 but the Channel agreed to work towards the 50% target in 1998 and this has been incorporated into the Channel 4 licence. The Channel also agreed to match the increases in Channel 3 from 1999 so that at least 80% of programme hours were subtitled from 2004. In 1997 56% of output was subtitled by Channel 4.

Channel 5

Channel 5 Broadcasting is required, as a licence condition, to implement proposals contained in its application in relation to subtitling. From the start of the service in 1997 23% of programmes were to be subtitled, and the channel achieved this aim in its first nine months of service. Thereafter C5 increased the number of hours at least in line with specifications set out annually by the ITC. From year six Channel 5 will be subtitling at least 50% of broadcasting hours.

Subtitling, Sign Language and Audio Description on Digital Terrestrial Television are covered by the Broadcasting Act 1996

The ITC Code On Subtitling, Sign Language and Audio Description on Digital Terrestrial Television, issued on 14 February 1997, also specified interim targets as follows:

i) at least one per cent of programmes should be signed by the start of the second year,

ii) at least two per cent of programmes should be signed by the start of the fourth year,

iii) at least three per cent of programmes should be signed by the start of the sixth year, and

iv) at least four per cent of programmes should be signed by the start of the eighth year of broadcasting by the DTT programme service in question.

Quotas

The Act requires specific minimum amounts of certain programming in digital services to be subtitled, to be accompanied by audio description or translated into or presented in sign language (subject to an Order by the Secretary of State). The minimum amounts, which will apply from the tenth anniversary of the service, are:

Subtitling:	50%
Audio description:	10%
Signing:	5%

MEDIA RELEASE FROM THE LIAISON GROUP FOR SIGN LANGUAGE ON DIGITAL TERRESTRIAL TV (BDA, RNID, NDCS and DBC)

Leading charities representing deaf people in the UK today welcomed new ITC regulations for signed programmes on digital terrestrial television channels (DTT).

The regulations are set out in the Broadcasting Act 1996 and come into force on Monday 15 May 2000. This is the first time that there has been a legal obligation on broadcasters to provide access to programmes for deaf people who use sign language. The digital terrestrial channels are initially required to sign one per cent of their output each week, rising to five per cent by 2008.

The charities would now like to see these requirements extended to cable and satellite channels who currently have no legal obligations to either subtitle or sign programmes for deaf and hard of hearing audiences.

Concern was raised that broadcasters ensure both a high quality of signing and a range of signed programmes for their viewers. Signed programmes should be broadcast at different times in the day, and not confined to middle of the night slots. Deaf viewers would also like to see signed programmes advertised in listings magazines and on the channels themselves.

Broadcasters are urged to consult with deaf people and the organisations that represent them for advice and assistance in helping them deliver quality signed programmes.

Austin Reeves (Deaf Broadcasting Campaign), chairman of the liaison group, said:

"The ITC targets are modest, but a step in the right direction for deaf viewers. We are keen to work with broadcasters to ensure that they reach – or even exceed - their targets. Equally important, however, is that a high quality of signing is maintained, as well as decent scheduling, and a wide range of programmes – especially programmes presented by deaf people themselves."

The liaison group is made up of representatives from the British Deaf Association (BDA), Royal National Institute for Deaf People (RNID), National Deaf Children's Society (NDCS), and the Deaf Broadcasting Council (DBC).

"'One BBC' for hearing people. Another for deaf and hard of hearing people.

"Greg Dyke's 'One BBC' will have two audiences - hearing people, and deaf and hard of hearing people - unless millions of subtitle users are provided with a full service for a full licence fee," said RNID. "The new Director General gives his first public address on "One BBC" at the Voice of the Listener and Viewer conference today. RNID hopes this will extend beyond changes to management structures. 'One BBC' will be welcomed by licence fee-payers only if it is inclusive in reaching out to all its licence fee-paying audience, including millions of deaf and hard of hearing people who use subtitles.

"Subtitles are essential for deaf and hard of hearing people to follow television programmes.

- One million people depend on subtitles to watch television.
- Four million use subtitles regularly.
- 20% of licence-fee paying households contain a deaf or hard of hearing person.

"Yet despite this, the BBC continues to trail its commercial rivals on analogue subtitling output. In 1999 57% of programmes across BBC1 and BBC2 are subtitled compared to 61% on Channel 4 and 64% on ITV. And only 4% of the BBC's videos were subtitled, compared to more than 90% of Disney's.

"RNID would like the BBC to commit to a policy of exceeding ITC targets by 10% by the end of 2001 as the UK's publicly-funded broadcaster. "

Joe Saxton, Director of Communications, RNID, said:

"It seems astonishing that the BBC, as the public service broadcaster, should be trailing behind ITV and Channel 4, in its subtitling output. Millions of deaf and hard of hearing people are still not getting a full service for a full, and recently increased, licence fee. For them, the suggestion of one, inclusive BBC is a welcome, but distant dream. They look to the BBC to set the pace, as 'One BBC' for all its licence-fee payers".

Journals, periodicals and newsletters associated with the Deaf held in the RNID Library.

Name of Journal	Date
A Magazine Intended Chiefly for the Deaf and Dumb	1873-1884
A Voice for the Dumb	1847-1852
Aberdeen Deaf and Dumb Visitor	1918
Aberdeen and the North Deaf News	1957-1958
Ability Unlimited	198-
Anglo-Celtic News	1961-1962
Argonaut	1962
Audiology Digest	1961
Aural News	1946-1998
Aural Venture	1950-1954
Ayrshire Deaf and Dumb Mission	1925
Beds and Herts Deaf News	1970-1972
Berean Deaf	2002
Bexley Deaf News	1983-1986
Bi-Monthly Notices	1962-1966
Birmingham and District Social Club for the Hard of Hearing News Sheet	1951-?
Birmingham and Midlands Adult Deaf and Dumb Mission	1919-1920
Blake Lodge Magazine for the Deaf in the South West	1963-1975
Books and Topics which may Interest the Missioner to the Deaf	1947-1955
Bournemouth and District Hard of Hearing Club Magazine	1944-1949
Bristol Club for the Hard of Hearing News Sheet	
British Association for the Hard of Hearing News Letter	
British Association of the Hard of Hearing Quarterly News Letter	1950-1954
Bucks Centre Committee for the Deaf Bi-Monthly Notices	
Bucks-Oxon-Berks Deaf News	1954
Bulletin (Deaf Ex-Mainstreamers' Group)	1999-2000
Bulletin (London Lipreading and Social Club)	1948
Bulletin (National Deaf Children's Society, Technology Information Centre)	1988-1997
Bulletin (UK Council on Deafness)	2000
Bulletin (Voice Bureau, RNID)	1980
CACDP Standard	1992
Calypso	1974-1982
CBS News	1970-1973
Centenary Year Newsletter	1989-1990
Central Deaf Club Newsletter	1989
Centre Point	1974-1976
Cheerful Earful	2003
Communication	1971-1980
Communication Works Bulletin	1989-1990
Communique	1993-1997
Connect	1990-2000
Connections	1984
Contact	1979-1996
Contact News	1996

Courier	1964-1967
Court Grange News	1969-1971
CRI Pack for the Deaf	1988
Customer Newsletter (Deafworks)	1999
Cutting Edge	2000
D & D	1903-1908
DACTY	1902-1921
DBC Newsletter/News	1983-1987
DBC Review	1992-1993
Deaf Action Project Bulletin UK	2000-2001
Deaf and Dumb Society Record	1912
Deaf Arts UK	
Deaf Chatter	1961-1963
Deaf Church Conference Report	1967-1975
Deaf Concern	1996-1998
Deaf Footballer	2001-
Deaf History Journal	1997-
Deaf Link	2000-
Deaf News	1980-1981
Deaf News for Wilts and Dorset	1982-1983
Deaf News Magazine	1975-1983
Deaf News Report	1987-1989
Deaf Voice	1994
Deaf Welfare	1955
Deafness Matters	1997
Dene Hollow Association Magazine	1930-1946
DEX News	1994-1998
D-Info	2003
Eastbourne and District Hard of Hearing Association News Letter	1954
Ephphatha	1896-1899
"Everybody"	1960-1963
Eye Say	1979-1995
Fact Sheet - See Hear!	1985-1986
Favour	1987-1991
Glasgow Deaf and Dumb Institution School Magazine	1900-1920
Go Ahead	1992-1995
Grapevine	1993-1997
HAD News	1999/2000-
Hamilton Lodge School Chronicle	1967
Hamilton Lodge School Magazine	1948
Hands Up	1983-1984
Handshake	1956-1959
Hark	1959-1992
HCIG Newsletter	2001-
Hear and Now	2000
Hear Here	1938-1960
Hear We Go	1996
Hear Here	1992-1998
Hearing	1963-1981
Hearing Concern	1993-

Hearsay	1990-1996
Hearsay!	1987-1998
Hearsay (Parents' Association)	1968
Here and There	1964-1994
Hertfordshire League for the Hard of Hearing News Bulletin	1949
Hertfordshire League for the Hard of Hearing Quarterly News Bulletin	1947-1949
Herts and Beds Deaf News	1957-1962
High Wycombe and District for the Hard of Hearing	
Hull and East Yorkshire Institution for the Deaf News Letter	
Hush	2001
INFO	1979-1980
Information Bulletin	1998
Institute of Laryngology and Otology Library Bulletin	1957
Irish Deaf Journal	1988-1993
Islanders	1988-1990
It's Life	1978
Jewish Deaf Association News Letter	
Journal of Laryngology and Otology	1921-1939
Journal of the Glasgow League for the Hard of Hearing	1928
Joy for the Deaf	1976-1985
Joy Unspeakable	1960-1975
Kingston Calling	1949-1954
Language and Speech	1958
Lewisham Deaf News	1955-1975
Lincolnshire Deaf Magazine	1969-1970
Lincolnshire Deaf Newsletter	1967-1968
Lincolnshire Deaf Quarterly News	1931-1933
Link	1968-1993
Linkup	1998
Lipreader	1958-1990
Lipreading	1983
Listen	1970-1985
Liverpool Deaf Announcer	1948-1955
LIWRS News	1963
London Calling	1980-1991
London Lipreading and Social Club Bulletin	1948
London Wavelength	1978-1980
Look Hear	1985-1994
Look Listen	1964
Mach Plus One	1972-1975
MAG	1964-1965
Magazine	1949
Magazine (Dene Hollow)	1927-1946
Magazine (Hearing Dogs for the Deaf)	1995/1996
Magazine (Royal School for Deaf Children, Margate)	1976-1996
Magazine (Young Usher Group)	1994-1995
Magazine for the Deaf of Plymouth and in Devon and Cornwall	1951-1952
Magazine for the Scottish Deaf	1929-1936
Magazine of Mission to Deaf and Dumb for Glasgow and West of Scotland	1927-1929
Magazine of the Ayrshire Deaf and Dumb Mission	1926-1927

Mailshot	1989-
Middlesex and Surrey League for the Hard of Hearing Youth Section News Letter	1962
Midland Regional Association for the Deaf News Sheet	
Modern Hearing	1957-1960
Network	1985-1993
News and Notes	1984
News and Views	1984
News Bulletin (Deaf Welfare Examination Board)	1976
News Bulletin (Spurs Club for the Deaf)	1985
News Letter of the Deaf Children's Society	1954-1956
Newsahead	
Newscode	1968
Newsleaf	1996
Northumbria	1915
Northumbria New Series	1920-1929
Notes and News for the Deaf of Manchester and District	1956
Nottingham and District Social Club for the Hard of Hearing News Letter	1956
Nutfield News	1955
Oak Lodge School Magazine	1963
Occasional Paper (NUD)	1977
Oldham Deaf Mute Gazette	
One in Seven	1997-
Online	1994-2002
Our Deaf and Dumb	1892-1898
Our Little Messenger	1892-1895
Our Little Messenger to the Deaf and Dumb	1882-1892
Our Magazine	1957
Our Mission Chronicle for the Deaf and Dumb and Those Interested in Them	1915
Our Monthly Church Messenger to the Deaf	1894-1895
Our Monthly Friend	1895-1912
Our Notice Board	1901-1920
Our Quarterly Friend	1913-1928
Our Quarterly Paper	1892-1893
Plymouth, Devon and Cornwall Magazine for the Deaf	1947-1962
Quack!	1961/62
Quality Times	1995
Quarterly Report	1964-1981
Quarterly Review	1952-1970
Quarterly Review of Deaf-Mute Education	1886-1898
Quiet	1992-1995
R.S.D.C. News	1996
Reaching Out	1999-
Resound	2000
Review	1962-1970
Royal Deaf Asylum Magazine	1908
Royal Deaf School Magazine	1908
Rubella Children Parents Group Newsletter	1955-1960
S.E.E.D. News	

School Magazine (Glasgow Deaf Dumb Institution)	1912-1920
School Magazine (Yorkshire Residential School for Deaf Children)	1946-1985
Scottish Deaf Sportsman	1948
See Hear!	1992-1997
Sefton Deaf News	1978
Sequel	1999-
Sharrow Magazine	1958
Sheffield Deaf News	1986-1988
Signmatters	2003-
Sign On	1991-1994
Signpost	1989-
Sign-Post	1974-1977
Signs of Joy	1988
Society of Hearing Aid Technicians Monthly Newsletter	1950
Sound Sense	1998-2001
Sound Waves	1997-
Soundbarrier	1984-1992
Soundbreaker	1978
Sounds Positive	1996-1997
South East England Deaf News	1981
South East Regional Association for the Deaf Quarterly News	1963
South Somerset Deaf Herald	1977-1978
Speech	1935-1957
Speech Pathology and Therapy	1958
SPIN	1994-1999
Spit News	
Spring Hill School Magazine	1930-1945
St Joseph's Magazine	1922-1984
St Vincent's Club for the Deaf News Bulletin	
Suffolk Deaf Journal	1949-1951
Suffolk Deaf Mission News	1946-1949
Suffolk Sun	1954-1961
Sussex Deaf Post	1978
Sussex Deaf Quarterly News	1934
Switch On!	1970-1971
Switch On!	1997
Talk	1956-
Talk About!	1987-1995
Talking Sense	1984-
Talks About Jesus to our Silent Ones	189-?
Tewin Water School Magazine	1953-1964
Tewin Water Times	1964-1965
The Albany	1917-1967
The Albany Magazine	1894-1897
The Albion Magazine	1907-1915
The Anerley Residential School Magazine	1906-1938
The Best of Both Worlds	1967-1975
The Bluebird	1948-1987
The Boar	1959-1976
The Bolton, Bury, Rochdale and District Deaf and Dumb	

The Bolton Review	1886-1897
Society Quarterly News	1905-1909
The Brief	1998
The British Deaf Monthly	1896-1903
The British Deaf News	1955-2003
The British Deaf Sportsman	1934-1935
The British Deaf Times	1903-1954
The British Deaf-Mute and Deaf Chronicle	1892-1895
The British Deaf-Mute and Deaf-Mute Review of Reviews	1895-1896
The Bucks Deaf News	1978-1988
The Central Advisory Council for the Spiritual Care of the Deaf and Dumb Letter	
The Class Magazine	1940
The Club News	1964
The Compass	1986-1989
The Corsican Chronicles	1953-1959
The Cross School Magazine	1895-1897
The Deaf and Dumb Herald and Public Intelligencer	1876-1877
The Deaf and Dumb Institution, Margate Pamphlet	1883-1904
The Deaf and Dumb Magazine	1883-1897
The Deaf and Dumb Times	1889-1891
The Deaf and Dumb World	1886
The Deaf Children's Society Newsletter	1953-1954
The Deaf Chronicle	1891-1892
The Deaf Chronicle (Southsea)	1925-1926
The Deaf Mountaineering Club Journal	1966-1968
The Deaf News	1951-1954
The Deaf Quarterly News (Bolton)	1909-1922
The Deaf Quarterly News (Liverpool; Carlisle)	1915-1950
The Deaf Scot	1934
The Deaf World	1933
The Deaf-Mute	1888-1889
The Deaf-Mute World	1886-1887
The Dirty Earmould	1993
The Edinburgh Messenger	1843-1845
The Floreat	1947-1952
The Friendship Magazine	1969-1976
The Hampshire Deaf Chronicle	1924
The Herald	1885-1887
The HI Reporter	1989-1990
The Independent Courier	1953-1954
The Irish Deaf-Mute Advocate and Juvenile Instructor	1886-1890
The Journal of the Society of Audiology Technicians	1960-1961
The Journal of the Society of Hearing Aid Audiologists	1956
The Lancashire Review	1897-1898
The Langside School for the Deaf News Bulletin	1938-1939
The Leicester Deaf Chronicle for the Deaf and Dumb and Those Interested in Them	1916-1920
The London League News	1948-1950
The Magazine for the Deaf and Dumb (Kilmarnock)	1884-1885

The Magazine for the Deaf and Dumb (London)	1855-1857
The Magazine of the Ayrshire Deaf and Dumb Mission	1925-1927
The Magazine of the Sir Winston Churchill Schools for the Deaf	1980-1981
The Mancunian Watchword	1947-1948
The Margate Royal Asylum Magazine	1907
The Merseyside Social Club for Hard of Hearing People Magazine	
The Messenger (Belfast)	1899-1918
The Messenger (Devon Deaf Church)	1996-
The Middlesex Hospital Club for the Hard of Hearing Newsheet	1950
The Midland Deaf Magazine	1923-1929
The Mountonian	1913
The Needwood Phoenix	1987-1988
The New Leaf	1995
The Northern Deaf News	1945-1946
The Page	1930/31
The Phoenix	1954-1988
The Quarterly News	1908-1909
The Rainbow	1974-1978
The Raven Newsletter	1975/76
The Royal Cross School Magazine	1897-1976
The Royal Magazine	1909-1910
The Royal School Magazine	1907-1975
The Rubella Group for Deaf Blind Children Newsletter	1960-
The Seagull	1949
The Silent Friend	1890-1892
The Silent Mancunian	1930-1935
The Silent Messenger	1895-1898
The Silent Missionary	1951-1960
The Silent Northerner	1946-1964
The Silent World (Birmingham)	1909-1910
The Silent World (London)	1924-1984
The Silver Lining	1954-1963
The Slough Deaf Social Club "Club News"	1950-1956
The Society of Audiology Technicians Newsletter	1951
The Southend on Sea and District Hard of Hearing Group News	
The Spurs Club Chronicle	1938-1984
The Sun	1969
The Sussex Deaf and Dumb Association Gazette	1935-1947
The Teacher of the Deaf	1903
The Voice (Federation of Deaf People)	1998-
The Voice (South Wales Parents)	1959-1961
The Wigan Window Box	1960-1965
The Word	1982
The Yorkshire Residential School for Deaf Children School Magazine	1946-
TIC Bulletin	
Tinnitis Helpline Newsletter	1992-1993
Tottenham and District Group Newsletter	
Typetalk Update	1999
Ulster Institute for the Deaf Newsletter	1958
Update	1992-1996

US Families	1994-2001
Usher UK	1995-1999
Venture	1983-1985
Voice of the Deaf	1981
Voices	1979
Volunteer Newsletter	1990-1992
Wales Hi!	1994
Watch	1979-1993
West Ham School Magazine	1959-1965
Western Deaf News	1975-1976
What, Why, Where and When?	1978-1980
Wilts and Dorset Deaf News	1949-1979
Young Sense	1984-1986

APPENDIX 4

List of books published by the British Deaf History Society.

Bermondsey 1792
Raymond Lee & John A. Hay   1993   (Publisher: NUD)

A Pictorial History of the Evolution of the British Manual Alphabet
Raymond Lee & John A. Hay   1994

Banton
Peter R. Brown   1994

Muted Passion
A. F. Dimmock   1995

Walter Geikie 1795-1837
Raymond Lee   1996

John William Lowe 1804-1876
Raymond Lee   1996

Arthur James Wilson 1858-1945
A. F. Dimmock   1996

The Leeds Beacon
Anthony J. Boyce   1996

Notice Biographique sur L'Abbé de L'Épée
Patrick W. Seamans (translator)   1997

Early Photographs of a London School for the Deaf: Homerton 1900-1921
Doreen E. Woodford   1998

A Short Account of a London School for the Deaf: Homerton 1900-1921
Doreen E. Woodford   1998

Bright Memory
Dorothy Miles (Anthony J. Boyce - editor.)   1998

Ackmar Road
Geoffrey J. Eagling   1998

Digiti Lingua 1698
Raymond Lee (editor.)   1999

The Lady in Green
Anthony J. Boyce & Elaine Lavery   1999

Touch, Touch and Touch Again
Doreen E. Woodford   2000

R. R.'s The Invited Alphabet 1809
Raymond Lee (editor)   2000

Deaf Lives
Peter W. Jackson & Raymond Lee (editors)   2001

Manchester Memoirs
David Woolley   2001

Braidwoodian Buildings and Locations
Raymond Lee   2001

Alexander Atkinson's Memoirs of My Youth
Raymond Lee (editor)   2001

Arthur Henry Bather 1829-1892
Doreen E. Woodford   2002

Autobiography of George Tait
Raymond Lee (editor)   2002

Gems From The Gentleman's Magazine
Raymond Lee (editor)   2003

Language of the Silent World
Raymond Lee (editor)   2003

The Gawdy Manuscripts
Peter W. Jackson   2004

Preston Pride
Peter W. & Maureen Jackson   2004

APPENDIX 5

TIMELINE OF EVENTS CONNECTED WITH BRITISH DEAF HISTORY

469-399BC	Socrates mentioned the existence of sign language.
427-347BC	Plato declared that deaf people are not capable of ideas or language.
384-322BC	Aristotle declared that the deaf are to be classed with idiots and those incapable of thought.
23-79AD	Pliny the Elder mentioned the name of a deaf painter, Quintus Pedius.
354-430AD	St. Augustine declared that the deaf were incapable of religious faith and education.
482-565AD	Emperor Justinian defined grades of deafness and applied law in accordance with grades of deafness.
673-735AD	The Venerable Bede published his *De temporum ratione*, in which he wrote a chapter entitled *De computo vel loquela digitorum* (Of counting and speaking with the fingers) which introduced the first known manual alphabet.
1426-1486	Princess Joanna, the deaf daughter of James I of Scotland, reported to have had an interpreter.
c1440	John Audelay wrote *Alia Cantalena de Sancta Maria*.
1450	*Anngiers History of the Zion Monastery at Lisbon and Brentford* published. The book gave descriptions of signs used by monks.
1522	Johannes Aventinus' *Abacus atque vetustissima verterum latinorum per digitos manusque numerandi* published in Nuremberg. This work depicted the one-handed manual alphabet following from Bede's work.
1528	Rudolph Agricola (1443-1485) had his *De inventione dialecta* published posthumously.
1576	The marriage of Thomas Tilsye (deaf) and Ursual Russel and their use of signs in wedding vows were written down in the parish register of St. Martin's Church, Leicester.
c1570	The Spaniard Pedro Ponce de Leon taught two deaf brothers to speak at the monastery of San Salvador near Oña.
c1580	The Spaniard Melchor de Yebra (1526-1586) wrote a small pamphlet, *Refugium Informorum* depicting an improvised version of a one handed manual alphabet system.
1579	Cosma Rossellio's *Thesaurus artificiosae memoriae,* containing a description of the one-handed manual alphabet published in Venice.
1595	A deaf manservant named Edward Bone was observed by Richard Carew in his *Survey of Cornwall* to have used three different methods of communication: lipreading, sign-supported English and an early form of British Sign Language.

1620	Juan Pablo Bonet's *Reduccion de las Letras y Arte para enseñar á habla los Mudos* published in Madrid; it used Yebra's handshapes in demonstrating the single-handed manual alphabet.
1622	Girolamo Cardano (1501-1576) had his *Paralipomenon* published posthumously in Basle. In this work Cardano referred to Agricola's work and declared that the deaf were capable of communication, education and intelligence.
1625-29	The Spaniard Ramirez de Carrion taught two deaf men to speak. Carrion used the manual alphabet before proceeding to teach speech.
1637	John Hacket, Archdeacon of Bedford, wrote of a deaf gentleman who was both intelligent and fluent in sign language, Sir Edward Gostwicke (1620-1671). Sir Edward also had a younger deaf brother William, who was also fluent in signs.
1641	John Wilkins (1617-1672) had his *Mercury, Or the Secret and Swift Messenger* published. This book made the first known mention of the two-handed manual alphabet system.
1644	John Bulwer (1614-1684) wrote two books: *The Natural Language of the Hand* and *The Art of Manual Rhetoric*. Members of the Royal Society dabble in the Arthrological Method in search of an ideal manual alphabet system for the next 50 years.
1648	Bulwer saw his the famous *Philocophus: Or, the Deafe and Dumbe Mans Friend*. Published. This was the first English book explaining the subject of deafness and its accompanying language problems, but had no bearing on the actual teaching of deaf persons.
1662	Dr John Wallis (1616-1703) presented two deaf men, Alexander Popham (aged 11) and Daniel Whalley (aged 25), to King Charles II as evidence of his successful teaching. Wallis was labelled a fraud by Dr William Holder (1616-1698), who claimed to have a few years earlier taught Whalley to speak.
1672	The first Will authenticated as being written by a Deaf person was made by Framlingham Gaudy (1641-1673), who was the brother of another Deaf person, Sir John Gaudy (1639-1709).
1680	George Dalgarno's *Didascalocophus, Or the Deaf and Dumb Man's Tutor* published.
1692	Jonathan Lambert became the first deaf and dumb person to settle on Martha's Vineyard in America. Over the next 200 years this island would be home to dozens of deaf people, who communicated using Kentish signs, or a variant of it, brought over by new settlers from Kent. Monsieur La Fin wrote *Sermo Mirabilis, Or the Silent Language* extolling the Paduan system.
1698	A remarkable little book, *Digiti Lingua*, was written by an unknown deaf person. It contained a manual alphabet chart that, with a few modifications, is still in use in Britain in the 21st century.

1715   Thomas Braidwood, founder of the first school for deaf children, was born at Hillhead Farm, Hillhead, in Lanarkshire.

Henry Baker (1698-1774) was teaching a select group of deaf children in a private capacity.

1720   Daniel Defoe's *The History of the Life and Adventures of Mr Duncan Campbell, Deaf and Dumb* was published. The work contained a modern manual alphabet chart.

1729   Samuel Heinecke, the father of oralism, born.

1750   Charles Shireff born. He went on to become Thomas Braidwood's first pupil. From then on, Shireff became a miniaturist of renown; and travelled to India and back. He also mixed with members of the high society circle that was especially connected with the arts.

1754   Francis Humberstone Mackenzie (Lord Seaforth) born. After an education under Thomas Braidwood, Mackenzie went on to become Britain's first-ever Deaf MP and Governor of Barbados. He also became the second Braidwoodian-educated Deaf person to become a Member of the Royal Society.

1760   Thomas Braidwood opened his school for the deaf in Edinburgh with 10 year-old Charles Shireff as his pupil.

1762   John Philp Wood born. A Braidwoodian pupil, he went on to become Auditor of Excise in the Scottish Excise Office, wrote two books and edited *The Peerage of Scotland*.

1764   John Goodricke born. After education at Braidwood's Academy and then Warrington College, Goodricke became an astrologer of renown, discovering stars. He became the first Braidwoodian deaf person to become a Member of the Royal Society at the age of 21, a few weeks before his tragic death.

1765   Joseph Watson, a nephew of Thomas Braidwood, born. Watson went on to become a teacher of the deaf under Braidwood and then the headmaster of the first public school for the deaf.

1769   Thomas Braidwood offered to turn his private school into a public school funded by charitable contributions, but the public did not respond enthusiastically to the offer. Braidwood continued to run his Academy as a private enterprise.

1774   John Creasy born. Another Braidwoodian pupil, he went on to become a teacher of the deaf and inspired the events that led to the foundation of the first ever public school for the deaf in England. Creasy also trained Deaf people to become teachers of the deaf.

1775   John Burns wrote *A Historical and Chronological Remembrance of All Remarkable Occurrences, From the Creation to this Present Year of the Lord, 1775*.

1781   Jane Poole born. A Braidwoodian pupil at Hackney, she later went blind in her old age and made a will that was to become a cause celebre in that a high court battle was fought over her eligibility as a Deafblind to make out her own Will. The jury found in her favour.

1783   Braidwood moved his Academy from Edinburgh to Hackney.

Francis Green's *Vox oculis subjecta* published.

1790	Death of Samuel Heinecke.
1792	The first public school for the Deaf in Britain, the London Asylum for the Deaf and Dumb was opened in November. The headmaster was a kinsman of Thomas Braidwood, Joseph Watson (1765-1829).
1795	Deaf artist Walter Geikie born. He went on to become a member of the Scottish Academy. John Creasy known to be teaching at both Braidwood's Academy and with Joseph Watson's private pupils at the London Asylum.
1796	James Mitchell born deaf and blind. His name is linked with medical history, and attempts to restore his sight failed. Mitchell went on to become a most colourful and renowned character in his native Nairn in Scotland.
1798	Matthew Robert Burns born. Burns went on to become a celebrated figure in Deaf history, becoming headmaster of three schools for the deaf before turning to missionary work. John Braidwood (b.1756) died. His wife Isabella (b.1758) broke away from her father Thomas Braidwood's Academy and established her own school in Mare Street, Hackney, effectively running the oralist side to Thomas' combined system side.
1801	Henry Brothers Bingham born.
1802	Harriet Martineau born. She was one of the most famous authoresses of her time, writing books on religion and political matters. She was a champion of the poor and contributed books and articles to that effect and fought against slavery in the USA, an action that led to threats of personal injury against her.
1803	John Carmichael born. Educated under Robert Kinniburgh at the Edinburgh Institution for the Deaf and Dumb, Carmichael later emigrated to Australia where he became an artist and designer of renown, credited with the design of the first Australian postage stamp.
1804	William Hunter (1785-1861) became the first Deaf teacher of the deaf in a public school for the deaf. He went on to teach for 57 years. John William Lowe born. Lowe became Britain's first Deaf barrister when he was called to the Bar of the Society of Middle Temple on 28 November 1829. John Kitto born. Kitto later became a great biblical scholar.
1805	Thomas Pattison born. Another pupil under Kinniburgh at the Edinburgh Institution for the Deaf and Dumb, he emigrated to Australia and went on to found the first school for the deaf in Sydney in October 1860. Alexander Blackwood born. He established the Congregational Church for the Deaf and Dumb in Edinburgh in 1830.
1806	Death of Thomas Braidwood, the founder of education for the deaf in Britain.
1809	One of the first known moves to promote awareness of the Deaf in the form of a book for children, *The Invited Alphabet, Or Address of A to B: Containing His Friendly Proposal for the Amusement and Instruction of Good Children,* by R. Ransom. Birth of James Burke, a Deaf man who went on to become a bare-knuckle boxer. Joseph Watson wrote his famous *Instruction of the Deaf and Dumb.*

1811	John Braidwood departed abruptly for America in July, leaving the Edinburgh Institution without a head teacher. The school was suspended while another teacher, Robert Kinniburgh, was sent to the Braidwood Academy in Hackney to be trained in the art of teaching the deaf. The school was reopened in December.
1812	George Banton born. After education at the London Asylum, he went on to become a teacher of the deaf at that school until 1875, a year before his death.
1814	The Edgbaston Institution for the Deaf and Dumb opened with Thomas Braidwood (1782 -1825) as head teacher.
1815	Death of Francis Humberstone Mackenzie, Lord Seaforth.
1817	Eliza Cockerill born in London. After education at the London Asylum, she gained employment as a teacher at that school in 1836, becoming Britain's first ever Deaf female teacher. *The Crown vs. Jean Campbell, alias Bruce*, case took place in Glasgow in July 1817. This is the first recorded instance anywhere in the world where a court appointed a sign language interpreter.
1818	The first known mission was formed – The Edinburgh Deaf and Dumb Meeting.
1819	Glasgow Institution for the Deaf and Dumb opened with John Anderson as head teacher. Aberdeen School for the Deaf and Dumb opened with Robert Taylor as head teacher. Death of Isabella Braidwood, daughter of Thomas Braidwood.
1822	The Glasgow Adult Deaf and Dumb Mission formed under John Anderson, headmaster of the Glasgow Institution for the Deaf and Dumb.
1825	Death of Thomas Braidwood – and the Braidwood dynasty in the education of the deaf ended. The Edgbaston Classroom Revolt. Manchester School for the Deaf and Dumb opened with William Vaughn as head teacher. Liverpool School for the Deaf opened with John Anderson as head teacher. Anderson was transferred from the Glasgow Institution.
1826	George Tait born. Educated at Edinburgh under Kinniburgh, Tait emigrated to Canada where he met a former Edinburgh Institution pupil, William Gray (1806-1881), and persuaded him to join him in setting up a school for the deaf in Nova Scotia.
1827	Exeter Institution for the Deaf and Dumb opened with Henry Brothers Bingham as headmaster.
1829	Yorkshire Institution for the Deaf and Dumb (Doncaster) opened with Charles Baker (1803-1874) as headmaster. Death of Joseph Watson. Arthur Henry Bather born. Bather went on to become assistant Accountant General of the British Navy despite being deaf and severely speech-impaired.
1830	The first Congregational Church for the Deaf and Dumb established in Lady Stairs Close, Edinburgh, by Matthew Robert Burns, Alexander Blackwood and Walter Geikie.

1831   Belfast School for the Deaf opened with George Gordon as headmaster.
Frederick John Rose born. Rose later went to live in Australia where he founded a school for the deaf in Melbourne on 20 November 1860.
Death of Charles Shireff at Bath.

1833   James Burke became World Boxing Champion.

1837   Death of Walter Geikie.

1838   Death of John Philp Wood.

1839   Northern Counties School for the Deaf, Newcastle-upon-Tyne, opened with Andrew Patterson as headmaster.
First Deaf magazine, published by deaf pupils of the Edinburgh Institution for the Deaf and Dumb.

1841   Bristol Institution for the Deaf and Dumb opened with Matthew Robert Burns as headmaster.
The Refuge for the Destitute Deaf and Dumb established on 29 January. This organisation later became the Royal Association in aid of Deaf People (RAD).

1842   Brighton Institution for the Deaf and Dumb opened with William Sleight as headmaster.
Bath Institution for the Deaf and Dumb opened with Jane Elwes as headmistress.

1844   Joseph Hague born. He was Deafblind and attended the Manchester Schools under Andrew Patterson. Despite his handicap, Hague achieved independence and good educational skills. However, he was a workhouse inmate in his later years.

1846   Dundee Institution for the Deaf and Dumb opened with Alexander Drysdale as headmaster.
William Agnew, a Deaf Awareness pioneer, born.
Deaths of Charlotte Elizabeth Tonna and James Burke.

1847   Aberystwyth (Swansea) Institution for the Deaf and Dumb opened with Charles Rhind as headmaster.

1848   James Paul born. He founded the National Deaf and Dumb Society in 1877. Paul had a hand in the founding of the British Deaf and Dumb Association in 1890.

1850   Donaldson's Hospital (Edinburgh) opened with Angus McDiarmid as headmaster.

1854   Richard Aslatt Pearce born. Pearce was the first born-deaf person to be ordained as a priest by the Church of England on 21 May 1885.
Death of John Kitto.

1855   Edward Alfred Kirk born. After education under Charles Baker at the Yorkshire Institution for the Deaf and Dumb, Kirk later found fame in 1883 as headmaster of the deaf class that later grew into Leeds School for the Deaf. Kirk held the post until his death in 1924.
Death of John Creasy.
George Hutton attempted to create a dictionary of signs: the *Specimen Dictionary of Signs*.

1856   Britain's worst school for the deaf tragedy took place in Strabane (Ireland) when a boarding school caught fire and was destroyed, killing six children.

1858   Arthur James Wilson, the great Deaf entrepreneur, born.

1860   Death of Jane Poole.

1861   Francis Maginn born in Johnsgrove, County Cork. Along with James Paul, Maginn was instrumental in the founding of the British Deaf and Dumb Association in 1890.
Charles Gorham born. He went to become the first Secretary of the British Deaf and Dumb Association (BDDA) in 1890.

1863   Harry Ash, a Deaf Awareness pioneer, born.

1864   Glasgow Deaf Mutual Improvement Society formed. In the mid-19th century there was a serious problem with drunkenness. Many Deaf men spent their time drinking and being drunk, so groups of religious men formed clubs and societies to try to stop this.

1865   Mary Hare born. She grew to become a dominant oralist educator of the deaf, establishing her own school and method.
Joseph Hepworth born. He went on to become the editor of *Deaf Chronicle* and then *The British Deaf Mute.*
William McDougall born. He became the Secretary of the BDDA in 1906 and held the position for 29 years.

1868   Thomas Arnold (1816-1897) established the Oral School for the deaf in Northampton with Abraham Farrar (1861-1944) as his first and only pupil, and also established the Spring Hill School.

1869   Death of James Mitchell.

1871   Glasgow Deaf and Dumb Football Club formed. This was the first adult Deaf sports club in Britain.
George Annand Mackenzie born. He became the first Deaf person in Britain to attend Cambridge University in 1906.

1873   St. Saviour's Church opened in Oxford Street, London, its opening ceremony attended by members of the Royal Family.

1875   Queen Victoria became patron of the Royal Association in Aid of the Deaf and Dumb (RAD).
Death of Henry Brothers Bingham.

1876   Death of Harriet Martineau and John William Lowe.

1877   National Deaf and Dumb Society established in Manchester on 13 July.

1878   The first International Congress on the Education of the Deaf in Paris, France. Oralist collaborators plot their takeover of the education of the deaf.
The Manchester Adult Institute for the Deaf and Dumb, Britain's first building specifically erected as a social meeting place, opened.
Liverpool Deaf and Dumb Cricket and Football Club formed.

1879   Death of Joseph Hague.

1880 The second International Congress on the Education of the Deaf in Milan, Italy. The oralists turned out in large numbers to enforce their plot to monopolise the education of the deaf and triumphed. The beginning of the end for Deaf teachers and sign language in the education of the deaf.
Death of Matthew Robert Burns.

1882 First organised inter-club sports match – a cricket match between Derby and Sheffield. Derby won by one run.

1883 Clarendon Street School for the Deaf, Nottingham, founded.
Irene Rosetta Goldsack, the inspiration behind Ewingism, born.

1884 Collapse of the National Deaf and Dumb Society.

1885 Bradford School for the Deaf (Odsal House) founded.
Leslie Edwards born. He became the Secretary of the BDDA in 1935, a position he held for 16 years.

1886 The Deaf and Dumb Correspondence Association founded.

1887 Harry Ward born deaf in Cardiff. He was the first known deaf person to pass the army medical to become a soldier.

1888 The Deaf and Dumb Correspondence Association became The Deaf-Mute Association (DMA) with Francis Maginn as Chairman and John Thomson Maclean as Secretary/Treasurer.

1889 Collapse of the Deaf-Mute Association.

1890 The British Deaf and Dumb Association founded with Charles Gorham as the Secretary and James Paul as the Treasurer.
Gower Street Council School for the Deaf, Oldham, opened.

1891 First international football match between England and Scotland resulting in a 3-3 draw.

1892 Death of Arthur Henry Bather.

1893 Elementary Education (Blind and Deaf Children) Act 1893 made education compulsory for all deaf children over the age of seven years and also made oral education compulsory.

1894 Birmingham School for the Deaf, Gem Street, founded.
Birth of Alfred Reginald Thomson. Thomson went on to become an artist of renown, and became a Member of the Royal Academy.

1895 Cardiff School for the Deaf founded.

1896 Alexander Ewing born.

1897 Burnley School for the Deaf founded.

1898 Ackmar Road School in London founded.

1899 Ethel Constance Goldsack born. She went on to become the second Lady Ewing.

1900	Homerton College for the Deaf established with Frank Barnes as headmaster.
1901	Bernard Pitcher born. Pitcher went on to become Britain's first Deaf person to gain a Ph.D.
1902	Scottish Deaf Chess and Draughts Association formed.
1910	The first Deaf scout troop was formed at Preston.
1911	National Institute for the Deaf (NID) founded – initially known as the National Bureau for Promoting the General Welfare of the Deaf until 1924. Cadzow Street School for the Deaf, Aberdeen, founded.
1912	Birth of Clifford Bastin, who went on to become a professional footballer with Arsenal.
1921	Closure of Homerton College; the school moved to Rayners in Penn, Berkshire. Death of Joseph Hepworth.
1922	Death of Charles Gorham.
1924	Birth of John Denmark, who went on to become a renowned psychiatrist with the Deaf. Death of Edward Alfred Kirk, Deaf headmaster of Leeds School for the Deaf.
1926	A. J. Wilson became the first Deaf man in Britain's history to be fined for speeding in his car.
1928	Death of the Rev. Richard Aslatt Pearce.
1931	Dorothy Miles (nee Squire) born. She went on to become Britain's foremost poetess in sign language and was much involved in the training of sign language interpreters and the development of sign language qualifications.
1932	Deaf Council School, Stockton-on-Tees, opened.
1933	Dr A. Eichholz's *The Report of the Board of Education* published.
1934	Death of Harry Ash.
1935	London hosted the World Games for the Deaf.
1939	Royal School for Deaf Children, Margate, was the first school for the deaf to be bombed at the beginning of World War II.
1944	Education Act 1944 approved the formation of special schools, leading to the founding of Mary Hare Grammar School. Disabled Persons (Employment) Act 1944 required employers with 20 or more staff to employ disabled people up to 3% of their staff. Death of Abraham Farrar. Spring Hill School, Northampton, closed.
1945	Deaths of A. J. Wilson and Miss Mary Hare.
1948	Hearing Aids available on the NHS – Medresco aids.

1951	Deaths of William McDougall and Leslie Edwards.
1952	The film, "Mandy", was made at the Royal Deaf Schools, Manchester. This film was the flagship of the Ewingist propaganda.
1955	The BBC broadcasted a full-length church service from St. Saviour's in Acton, London. This was the first-ever church service broadcast on a national scale. Burwood Park Technical Secondary School for the Deaf opened in Walton-on-Thames, Surrey, with W. E. Wood as headmaster. *British Deaf News* started under the BDDA.
1959	Death of Irene Rosetta Ewing (nee Goldsack).
1961	The National Institute for the Deaf (NID) became the RNID. Formation of the RNID Mime Group.
1966	Behind the Ear (BTE) aids on the NHS.
1968	Lewis Report published. This report considered the place of fingerspelling in the education of the deaf and was inconclusive. Professor M. Lewis was the husband of Hilda Lewis, the authoress of the book, "The Day Shall Come", filmed as "Mandy" in 1952. The first psychiatric service for the Deaf established by Dr. John Denmark at Whittingham Hospital, Preston.
1969	The RNID Mime Group became the British Theatre of the Deaf.
1971	The British Deaf and Dumb Association (BDDA) dropped the word "Dumb" from its title and became the British Deaf Association (BDA). Allan B. Hayhurst, Secretary-Treasurer of the BDA, began moves to start work on the *BSL Dictionary*.
1972	English Deaf Chess Association formed.
1973	Burwood Park College (Norfolk House) established as a 6th form for deaf students.
1974	Warnock Report published. This report recommended greater integration of "special needs" children into mainstream schools.
1976	Education Act 1976 embodied the recommendations in the Warnock Report that deaf children should preferably be educated in mainstream education, not special schools. National Union of the Deaf (NUD) formed in Wimbledon. Scottish Workshop with the Deaf (SWD) formed.
1978	Sign Language Learning and Use was established at Bristol University under Jim Kyle. This led to the formation of the Centre for Deaf Studies. Closure of the British Theatre of the Deaf.
1979	The NUD and the BBC produced the first TV programme scripted, produced and presented by the Deaf, *Signs of Life*. The Edinburgh BSL Research Project began under Mary Brennan. Sign Language Linguistic Research Group established at the University of Newcastle. Death of Alfred Reginald Thomson, RA.

1980	Deaf Broadcasting Campaign founded to campaign for both TV programmes for the Deaf and subtitled programmes.
1981	Education Act 1981: provided the legal framework for the integration of deaf children into mainstream schools. BDA launched its first Deaf Awareness week. Death of Alexander Ewing.
1982	Deaf Studies Research Unit formed at Durham University. *BSL Dictionary* completed. Publication of *Charter of Rights of the Deaf* by the NUD. NUD declared and recognised Deaf people as members of a linguistic minority group using BSL as their first and preferred language.
1984	Cochlea implant first approved for clinical use for persons 18 years and older. Christine Reeves became the first Deaf person to give a speech in sign language at the Liberal Party Assembly. Lilian Lawson gave a signed speech at a fringe meeting of the Liberal Party Assembly.
1985	BSLTA began at Durham University with Clark Denmark. NUD-BDA (NWRC) joint demonstration and Alternative Congress during the International Congress on the Education of the Deaf in Manchester. Deaf Comedians formed and gave its first performance at the Alternative Congress.
1986	Common Ground Dance Theatre founded.
1987	First deaf child in the UK given a cochlea implant. NUD fired the first shots to begin the battle for BSL recognition with a demonstration outside the Department of Education and Science. Following the BDA's active part in the campaign, the European Parliament voted to recognise the sign languages of its member states.
1988	In June the European Parliament officially recognised sign language; the British Government remained silent.
1989	Irene Hall appointed editor of *British Deaf News*, becoming the first female editor of any major British Deaf journal. British Telecom and RNID joined together to create a national relay service for the deaf – now known as Typetalk.
1991	Death of Clifford Bastin
1993	Dorothy Miles committed suicide. British Deaf History Society co-founded by Raymond Lee and John A. Hay.
1995	The Disability Discrimination Act gave disabled people rights in areas of employment and access to goods and services. Jeff McWhinney appointed as Chief Executive Officer of the BDA.
1996	Closure of Burwood Park Technical Secondary School and Burwood Park College (Norfolk House).
1998	Death of Dr. John C. Denmark.

2000	Signaway formed to provide interpreters for theatres and shows.
2001	First digital hearing aids available on the NHS. BT TextDirect launched.
2002	Death of Bernard Pitcher. Deafinitely Theatre established in January.
2003	The British Government, through the Department for Work and Pensions (DWP) finally recognised BSL as a language on 18 March.
2004	Signaway changed its name to Theatresign. Final part of the DDA came into force on 1 October.

Sources and References

The main history of the British Deaf is derived from various sources such as magazines for the Deaf, that have been preserved by the organisations associated with the magazines, books and interviews.

1. The RNID Library
2. The British Deaf Association
3. Royal Association for Deaf People
4. SENSE

Sources are also taken from books that are held in both the RNID Library and the British Library. Certain books are in both these libraries, but they have been found in private ownership.

Compared with the record of the history of the hearing people of Britain, records of the history of the Deaf are almost non-existent in many public archives and libraries. The BDHS had to take to interviewing elder Deaf people for their reminiscences and experiences of life in days long gone. The names of those interviewed are listed in this section.

Primary Printed Sources

The following are the main sources from which information in this book has been obtained. The British Library also has the following books:

Philocophus; Or the Deafe and Dumbe Mans Friend
John Bulwer   1648 (London)   RNID Library

The History of the Life and Adventures of Mr Duncan Campbell, Deaf and Dumb
Daniel Defoe (William Bond)   1720 (London)   BDHS Library

The Secret Memoirs of the Late Duncan Campbell
(William Bond/Eliza Heywood?) 1730 (London)   BDHS Library

Vox Oculis Subjecta
Francis Green   1783 (London)   Raymond Lee Collection

The Instruction of the Deaf and Dumb
Joseph Watson   1809 (London)   RNID Library

Memoirs
John Townsend   1831 (Boston, USA)   Raymond Lee Collection

Specimen Dictionary of Signs for the Deaf and Dumb
George Hutton   1855 (Halifax, Canada)   Raymond Lee Collection

The Deaf and Dumb
Rev. Samuel Smith   1864 (London)   Raymond Lee Collection

The Education of the Deaf Thomas Arnold	1888 (London)	Raymond Lee Collection
Deaf Mutism J. Kerr-Love & W. H. Addison	1896 (Glasgow)	Raymond Lee Collection
Arnold's Education of the Deaf Abraham Farrar	1923 (Derby)	RNID Library
Surdus in Search of His Hearing Evan Yellon	1906 (London)	RNID Library
Snapshots of the Deaf W. R. Roe	1917 (Derby/London)	Raymond Lee Collection
Peeps into the Deaf World W. R. Roe	1917 (Derby/London)	Raymond Lee Collection
The Deaf and Their Problems Kenneth W. Hodgson	1953 (London)	RNID Library
The Integration and Disintegration of the Deaf in Society G.W.G. Montgomery (ed.)	1981 (Edinburgh)	Raymond Lee Collection
British Sign Language Margaret Deuchar	1984 (London)	BDHS Library
When The Mind Hears Harlan Lane	1984 (N.Y., USA)	RNID Library
Monastic Sign Languages Jean Umiker-Sebastian and Thomas A. Sebeok (editors)	1987 (Berlin)	Raymond Lee Collection
A History of the Education of the Deaf in England G.M. McLoughlin	1987 (Liverpool)	RNID Library
Britain's Deaf Heritage Peter W. Jackson	1990 (Edinburgh)	RNID Library
The Deaf Advance Brian Grant	1990 (Edinburgh)	RNID Library
Monasteriales Indica Debby Banham (ed.)	1991 (Pinner, Middlesex)	Raymond Lee Collection
Deaf Liberation Raymond Lee (ed.)	1992 (Feltham, Middlesex)	Raymond Lee Collection

A Pictorial History of Deaf Britain
Peter Jackson   2001 (Winsford, Cheshire)   RNID Library

Deaf Lives
Peter Jackson & Raymond Lee   2001 (Feltham, Middlesex)   BDHS Library

<u>Secondary Printed Sources</u>

All the BDHS books listed in Appendix 4 were consulted along with the entire volumes of
the following sources:

1. Deaf and Dumb Times   (RNID Library)
2. Deaf Chronicle   (RNID Library)
3. British Deaf Mute   (RNID Library)
4. British Deaf Monthly   (RNID Library)
5. British Deaf Times   (RNID Library)
6. British Deaf News   (RNID Library)
7. Deaf Quarterly News   (RNID Library)
8. Edinburgh Messenger   (RNID Library)
9. The Silent Messenger   (RNID Library)
10. The Deaf Mute   (RNID Library)
11. A Magazine chiefly Intended for the Deaf and Dumb / Deaf and Dumb Magazine
                                 (RNID Library)
12. Minutes of the London Asylum for the Deaf and Dumb
                                 (Royal School for the Deaf, Margate)
13. Deaf History Journal   (Raymond Lee Collection)

Also consulted were the annual reports of various schools for the Deaf and these are stored
in the RNID Library.

<u>Human Sources</u>

1. The following Deaf persons were interviewed by Elaine Lavery. Their reminiscences and
experiences were recorded on videotape; and these tapes are now stored in the BDHS
Archives in Doncaster.

<u>Name</u>	<u>Residence</u>
Stanley Evans, b.1918	Dagenham
Joan Evans, b.1919	Dagenham
Syd Gibbs, b.1920	Beckenham
Fred Cuddeford, b.1909	Feltham
James Mountcastle, b.1921	Leicester
Jane Stryker, b.1915	Manor House, London
Joyce Francis, b.1924	Thornton Heath
Arthur Dimmock, b.1918	Portsmouth
Leon Hasseck, b.1914	Barnet
Winnie Gilbert, b.1914	Leicester
Mary Cording, b.1913	Epsom, Surrey

The following were interviewed, but not filmed:

Betty Shrine, b.1918   Pinner, Middlesex
Phillip Gibbons, b.1913   Welling, Kent
Bob Paull, b.1916   Sutton, Surrey

2. The following Scottish Deaf persons were interviewed on tape by John A. Hay; and these tapes are now stored in the BDHS Archives in Doncaster.

Name	Residence
Reggie MacRoberts, b.1924	Glasgow
Edith MacRoberts, b.1922	Glasgow
Bob Baillie, b.1921	Edinburgh
Maisie Baillie, b.1925	Edinburgh
Margaret Cochrane, b.1918	Glasgow
Mary Ellen McEwan, b.1912	Glasgow
Catherine Kerr, b.1923	Glasgow
Alice Thomline, b.1906	Edinburgh
Peter Tullis, b.1928	Glasgow
Jack Griffen, b.1934	Glasgow
Margaret Lawrie, b.1924	Edinburgh

3. The following were interviewed on tape in connection with the histories of some Deaf clubs. This was in line with the aims of the BDHS's European Year of Disabled People (EYDP) project, but the interviews had to be edited out of this book simply for the sake of keeping the project brief and simple for students of Deaf history. Their contributions were nevertheless valuable and parts of what they said were used in this book.

St. Vincent's Deaf Club

Desmond Lavery   Mary Davies   Anthony Padden   Lena McMahon
Loretta Stratton   Annie Lanigan   Charlie Rodgers

66 Club

Richard Goulden

Green Star Club

Desmond Lavery   Jean Smith   Robert Smith   Jean Epps
Leon Hasseck   Elaine Lavery

National Deaf Club

Melinda Napier

4. The following are individuals who have been either consulted or approached over the past years and whose knowledge and research have contributed to fill the vital gaps in the history of the Deaf in Britain:

Peter R. Brown of Frant, Sussex, for his research into the early development of sign languages and his expert advice on the history of Royal School for the Deaf, Margate.

Peter W. Jackson of Winsford, Cheshire, for his valuable information on issues in Deaf history, as well as his expert advice in recommending the structure of this book suited to the needs of students in Deaf history. Thanks are also given to Peter for allowing his collection of photographs to be used in this book.

John A. Hay for his expertise on Scottish Deaf history and valuable information on various episodes in British Deaf history. He was the first to trace the history of Thomas Braidwood (1715-1806) and to list his pupils. His researches has led the editor to undertake further research in that area.

Gordon Hay for his contribution on modern Deaf sports and photographs.

Scott Rosser for the photograph of the bombed Southampton Deaf Club.

Elaine Lavery for her research into the saga of "Sonny" Blake and the notorious Blackshirts connection. Elaine is also credited with imparting valuable information on the histories of both St. Vincent's Deaf Club and Green Star Deaf Club.

Anthony J. Boyce, a retired teacher of the deaf and former head of Further Education Department at Yorkshire Residential School for the Deaf in Doncaster, for his wealth of information on modern day teaching and the schools for the deaf situation.

Geoffrey J. Eagling of Addlestone, Surrey, for his assistance on the wartime evacuations and facts pertaining to a number of London schools for the deaf. The editor also wishes to thank Geoffrey's daughter, Caroline, who typed the list of Deaf journals and magazines in Appendix 3.

Doreen E. Woodford of Much Wenlock, Shropshire, for her wealth of knowledge on schools for the deaf and teacher training programmes throughout the 20th century. The editor is also grateful for her valuable contribution to the *Ewingism* section of this book.

Bencie Woll of City University, London, whose assistance contributed to the correction of errors and clarified numerous issues in the *History of British Sign Language Research* section of this book.

G. W. G. Montgomery of Edinburgh who supplied information on the Scottish Workshop With the Deaf (SWD) publications besides comments on the present day situation of the education of deaf children.

Mary Plackett, retired librarian of the RNID Library, for her eagerness in seeking out requested sources and information stored in the RNID Library. Her assistance over the past year is immeasurable since approximately sixty to sixty-five per cent of information in this book came from the RNID Library.

5. The BDHS also wishes to thank the following for their support, contribution and encouragement that went a long way to make this work possible:

The Department for Works and Pensions, European Year of Disabled People Fund for the award of a grant that made this project possible.

The Deaf Internet Bookstore (DIB) for the time and assistance given in undertaking research and work in association with the experimental CD Questions and Answers Project, as well as supplying valuable articles for the coursework book. The DIB also designed a Timeline of British Deaf History chart, an entirely separate project linked with this book, and it is anticipated that completion of this Timeline chart will be around the end of 2004.

The Council for the Advancement of Communication with Deaf People (CACDP) for its encouragement and funding that helped to create a sample Deaf History and Culture Stage 2 course. The BDHS also acknowledges the CACDP's continuing support for this book.

City College, Manchester, for the help and contributions of their professional Deaf tutors on the subject of BSL courses and sign language issues that are vital to this book.

The British Deaf Association (BDA) for its kind assistance in the supply of copyright photographs from its magazines as well as its support for the project.

The Federation of Deaf People (FDP) for photographs and information on its foundation and activities.

The Deafinitely Theatre and The Royal Association for Deaf People (RAD) for their contributions to this book.

Richard Goulden for his assistance not only for proofreading, but also for his valuable advice and suggestions needed to clarify certain passages in this book that were not easily understood.

The editor wishes to finally thank the members of the Board of Trustees of the BDHS for their support and additional funding to publish this book on completion.

There were many others who contributed through personal communication with the editor over the years before work commenced on this book. Many of them are long departed. The editor however wishes to thank all those who contributed as the list of names is too long to be included in this limited space.